MW00592253

SHARK, THE BAKER'S SON

Based on a true story of a mercenary drug informant.

*Judy
Enjoy the Story

Anthony Aliberti*

ANTHONY T. ALIBERTI

PublishAmerica
Baltimore

© 2004 by Anthony T. Aliberti.
All rights reserved. No part of this book may be reproduced, stored in a retrieval system or transmitted in any form or by any means without the prior written permission of the publishers, except by a reviewer who may quote brief passages in a review to be printed in a newspaper, magazine or journal.

First printing

ISBN: 1-4137-3187-2
PUBLISHED BY PUBLISHAMERICA, LLLP
www.publishamerica.com
Baltimore

Printed in the United States of America

I dedicate this book to my parents because without their unconditional love and support throughout my whole life I would not have been able to write this story.

Special acknowledgments and a great deal of thanks go to Rick Shannon, who was my instructor, editor and proofreader; in addition, Rick Shannon helped me from the beginning of the first rough draft until the end of the writing and marketing process of this novel. Without Rick, this novel would not have been written.

Special thanks go to my wife, for she stuck with me throughout the entire time it took me to write this book; moreover, for her love, support and encouragement to continue writing when I felt like giving up.

Special thanks go to Frank Monteleone, for his help and knowledge of publications, protecting the copyrights of manuscripts, and his knowledge of computer abilities, which are professional and businesslike, when I felt as if I was going to throw my computer out of the window.

In Pittsburgh, Pennsylvania in 1975, I was only five years old, yet I can vividly remember everything about my life: what I did, what my father did and what my grandfather did. More acutely, I can see now the ways in which alcohol, gambling and the fast life got into my system, my head, my blood, my life and almost my death.

FAMILY

My father and mother were hard working people, my dad drove a bread truck for a bakery, and my mother worked at a Giant Eagle supermarket in East Liberty, so I spent a lot of time with my grandparents. Luigi, my grandfather, was happily retired from the post office. He used to work there in the day and at the V.F.W. at night. He'd been a Veteran of Foreign Wars. He was a paratrooper, adventurously jumping out of planes behind enemy lines. He was with 101st Airbourne Screaming Eagles, under the command of General McCaulif, honorably serving his country fighting in WWII.

My father, my grandfather and I used to go to Waterford Park horse race track regularly and watch the thoroughbreds race around the track. There, I learned about horses, odds, the parlays, and win, place and show. I usually looked at the racing forms, but I looked at the numbers too on the large, brightly lit board, which sat outside in the middle of the racetrack. Soon, I learned how to tell how many people bet on the horses and their odds of winning.

Pap Pap took me to see the horses in their stables and explained how much faster thoroughbreds were compared to the other horses. Superstitiously, my father made me pick the horses, and he'd bet because he thought I was his smart son of good fortune.

When I stayed with my grandparents, my grandfather usually brought me with him to the V.F.W. After we walked in through the main door, we would go through the bar, down a small set of stairs, passed the game room and then through a door that led into a darkened storage room, and finally, Pap Pap unlocked another door, which led us into a well-lit quiet room on the left side of the building. Here, I would silently help him count money on a big brown desk while we listened to the horse races on the radio. He counted the large bills and quarters very quickly and cheerfully, always with a broad smile on his face and a cigar in his mouth. I never knew exactly where this money came from. Why would I? I was only five years old. I never thought to ask because he would give me money to play games; plus, I didn't care. I would slowly

9

and quietly count the small change, pennies and nickels, never uttering a mere word unless Pap Pap spoke first. There was a tightly locked black safe that sat adjacent to the desk, and I would see him put most of the money in the safe and some money in his pocket. I remember him saying, "Go out, play some games and get a Coke." And, I did.

I played pinball machines and shot pool, and I really enjoyed drinking the old time Coca-Cola bottles of soda. As I look back now, those little bottles of Coke were very addictive; as a result, I never drank just one. I probably drank four or five Cokes in a row and would ask my grandfather for more money. As he was still counting money, he handed me more quarters and asked, "Are you alright out there?"

I said, "Yeah, I want to shoot some more pool and get another coke."

We never saw Pap Pap without his racing form. My grandfather firmly carried it with him, tucked under his arm. He knew how to bet because he always won big. He systematically based his bets on the statistics of the horses, and their odds of winning; moreover, he knew exactly how many races each horse won and how fast each horse ran in each race. He read his race form as he sat back in his recliner with his feet up and constantly talked on the phone making bets while he chewed on his cigar or smoked his pipe. One time at Waterford Park my grandfather won thousands, and he took our whole family out to an elegant restaurant for a classy dinner.

My grandmother, Angelina, was a terribly heavy smoker, but a very loving grandmother. She always had a cigarette in her mouth, and she constantly baked bread and made Italian food. My grandparents lived in an apartment above Stagno's bakery on Chislet Street in Morningside, so my grandmother just walked downstairs to get the ingredients for the food. I remember the aromatic smell of pungent onions and garlic she put in the tomato sauce as I walked up the stairs. Sunday was always pasta day at their house, and there always sat a big jug of red wine on the table. My grandmother started to smoke at the age of twelve and quit at the age of seventy. She was the strongest hearted woman I've ever known because of the downfalls she'd had in her life, like when my grandfather went off to War, and she was left alone to raise my father, who was newly born, and she worked downtown in a department store called *Gimble's*.

She also told stories about when she and my grandfather were young and made gin in the bathtub. She called it bathtub-gin. My grandmother told me the reason they made it in the bathtub was if the police came, they simply pulled the plug out of the tub, and all the gin went down the drain. She also told me that all of our paved roads used to be dirt roads, and they traveled by horses and buggies. When I stayed with my grandmother, she taught me how to play cards, poker and do crossword puzzles.

My grandparents were always willing to help our family anyway they could. My grandmother cooked every day, and our whole family would come to eat. When it was time to eat, my grandfather would get up from his recliner and set some wine on the table. They usually told me while laughing, "Take a sip of wine, Anth." And, I did.

After we ate, my grandfather loudly played his Frank Sinatra or Dean Martin or especially, the Opera *Carmine's* albums and sat back in his recliner as he lit his pipe. Sometimes, I put my feet on his, and he would dance me around laughing. Quite often, he took me with him to the Out of Town Papers and Tobacco store on Butler Street in Lawrenceville to get his cigars, pipe tobacco, a horse racing form and a newspaper. There were always a box of parodies by his side, and pipes in the cupboard. He would also take different medications all the time, for he was badly injured in World War II. One of his eyes went blind when a bomb blew up near him. A piece of burning hot scrap metal flew through the air and hit him in that eye; as a result, he needed to wear special eye glasses with the left lens blackened out.

I remember him saying, "Can't forget the blue pills. They're the good ones."

He also suffered from diabetes and heart problems. But, he was a very strong man and dealt with his many heart attacks by always surviving them. Except for the last one! He dangerously drove himself to the hospital while actually having a heart attack. Strangely, he didn't forget his racing form. He loved the horses. In fact, the only time I ever saw him without his racing form was around Christmas.

The V.F.W. held Christmas parties, mainly for the kids, in another larger backroom with an entrance in the back of the building, in addition to the bar's front entrance. My grandmother made food for everybody in the kitchen, and my grandfather put on the big, red Santa Clause suit, wore a long bushy fake white beard, played Santa Clause for all the children in the neighborhood and gave out gifts, after us kids sat on his lap and told him what we wanted for Christmas.

My grandfather was a huge fan of *The Godfather* movies and the musical soundtrack; he even purchased the albums and would play them all the time. My father still has my grandfather's *Godfather* albums today. They're a memento. Eventually, the albums will be mine, forever lasting memories.

On the other hand my father, Carlo, was really a boozer. He would come to the V.F.W. to pick me up after he worked all day at the bakery. We never left until he drank a few drinks. We used to live on Larimer Avenue in the early seventies. That's where my father, his friends and crew hung out. Sure I got involved with intramural sports, and I went to school, but I spent mostly all my time with my dad at bars or other social clubs. Sometimes, I even got up at three o'clock in the morning to go work with him at the bakery, and after work to the bar. So, I guess you could have called me a bar rat.

A New Beginning

Our family moved out to the eastern suburbs of Pittsburgh. Funny, we moved into a very nice house, precisely right next door to another V.F.W. My father eagerly got a job bartending there at night, in addition to his daytime job. He already had friends in this area and made new friends as time went by. This is where we lived throughout my entire childhood and into my young adulthood.

It seemed I was constantly in bars intensely watching my father and his friends drink, bullshit and watch football games. This is when the Pittsburgh Steelers football team won the Super Bowl four times. Therefore, it was really a crazy time to be hanging out with my father because he, his friends, and all the other members of the V.F.W. had Super Bowl parties in the back room of this other V.F.W. They put a big piece of plywood over the pool table, covered the plywood with a big tablecloth and laid out a spread of food; in addition, three tables were set up along the wall with more food and drinks on them. My dad and his friends all drank heavily, and they spoke loudly using fowl mannerisms while they watched the Super Bowl on the projection TV. They even got me to sell gambling blocks on a big white piece of cardboard at five dollars a block and let me collect the money. I wasn't even ten years old yet. I sold the blocks exactly to the dollar amount that was set. However, the guys who ran the gambling kept a very close eye on me.

Once, after my dad closed down the bar and locked the doors, he took me up a long set of stairs, which was restricted from the public, to a locked door that led into a little, poorly-lit room where three white canvas bags sat right in front of an old dusty desk. They were filled entirely to the top with money. He tried tightly stuffing even more money into these white canvas bags, and what money didn't fit in the bags went into his pocket. I asked, "What's all that money for, Dad?"

He abruptly replied, with an adamant leer, "Don't worry about it son! It's not my money. It's the V.F.W.'s money."

However, the V.F.W. was a nonprofit organization, and all the money that came in from the alcohol and food sales would supposedly go back into the V.F.W. for improvements. In addition, I saw people in the V.F.W., and other people from around the neighborhood, constantly hand my father money.

One time, we all went to a Pirates baseball game. There we were, my father, my good friend, who was my father's friend's son, and the rest of my father's crew. We all got on an old school bus and drove downtown to the Three Rivers Stadium. There was an ice-cold barrel of beer in the back of the bus, which was placed in a little, but wide, garbage can, and I can remember I smelled something funny as smoke filled the inside of the school bus. I didn't know then, but I later figured out that that was the first time I smelled marijuana. I honestly can't recall my father ever smoking pot or doing any other kind of drug. Instead, he primarily drank an enormous amount of alcohol, but still he worked vigorously at his two jobs.

My mother worked a full-time job; thus, my sister and I were alone a lot, for both of us were older and were able to stay by ourselves. We were teenagers now. My sister's a few years older than I am and spent most of her time down the street at her friend's house. Meanwhile, I would gladly stay home alone and play the guitar. That was one of my favorite things to do. Sometimes, I'd lose track of time while playing and oddly realized that ten hours quickly went by. A friend across the street, Jay, played the drums, and one day we got together and lamely tried to play some music.

THE CIRCUS BAND

Jay knew a good friend, Joe, who found an old beat up bass guitar his father put in the basement. The three of us started a trio and practiced constantly. Jay had four older brothers, Mickey, Gino, Danny Jr. and Bruce, and three older sisters, Lea, Carmela and Rose Maria. His was a very big Italian family. Jay's father, Danny Sr., made very good homemade wine with the red and green grapes he grew in his backyard.

He told us, "Try a little glass of wine, guys. It's homemade."

I was about to turn fifteen years old and growing up fast. I was used to taking sips of wine, so I never refused when somebody offered. In their backyards, the family had very big picnics on holidays like Memorial Day, the 4th of July and Labor Day. Their backyards connected Dan Sr. and Gino's houses, so it appeared to be one big yard. A bunch of people gathered and drank Rolling Rock beer out of a keg, which sat in the middle of the two backyards just up a set of wooden stairs from the Bocci ball court, we ate food, played Bocci ball, and all the Italian food they made was delicious. They even had a volleyball net set up on the side of Dan Sr.'s house. The older Italians brought mostly all of the food, and it was spread out on tables that sat on a deck. Tables and chairs filled the rest of the deck, and picnic tables were scattered around the backyards. Gino used the huge redbrick charcoal grill in his backyard, which sat down from the Bocci court, to cook the burgers, hotdogs, corn on the cob, a variety of peppers and just about anything else that could be grilled.

Children from babies, to infants and teenagers ran all around and played together with toys and big bouncy balls, the older women sat around on the deck talking, and usually the older and younger men took turns and played Bocci ball. Jay, Joe and I got to play bocci ball with the older guys quite often. A majority of the people smoked pot up on the hill towards the green grassy field, nearly right next to a garden where Dan Sr.'s vegetables grew, especially red ripe tomatoes and all different kinds of peppers. There would be a really big circle made out of people, normally all Jay's brothers' and sisters' friends standing there with beers in their hands and a cloud of smoke atop their heads. Of course, Jay, Joe and I were in the circle.

Our band usually practiced at Jay's house, and his father sat in at times with his trumpet. His mother would make food and tell us, "Muncha, muncha" as she spoke Italian. One of Jay's older brothers played in a band professionally. His name is also Dan, but we called him Dante Cat. That's the name he put on his CD covers, along with a picture of a black cat's eyes. He would happily let our band open up for his band in different bars around town. He'd always sing for our band. "That's the deal," he said cunningly. "I get to sing for your band since I let you guys open up for our band. I've always wanted to sing in the front for a band whose members were younger than I am."

Backstage, there were always people crazily getting high. Everybody drank, smoked joints, popped pills and did other things. I curiously watched the band members, the soundman and a couple of women as they sniffed white lines up their noses. All Jay, Joe and I did was take a hit or two of marijuana. That was common. That was the life for us boys.

Our band played school talent shows and would always be the last act to perform; furthermore, we'd play at people's birthday parties, other events around the community and in bars at times, but we were teenagers and not allowed in bars; because our friends and other younger people came into the bar, the bar didn't serve alcohol. Dan Sr. was also a professional jazz trumpeter and played for the Pittsburgh Jazz Society or any other gig he could get. He was highly known in Pittsburgh and played with the very best and most unique musicians in town. He even played trumpet with the likes of Frank Sinatra, The Who, Steely Dan and any other musicians who came to Pittsburgh to perform. Today, he is unfortunately retired because he suffers helplessly from throat cancer. He's been through a couple of operations, and his doctor's sorrowfully told him, "You definitely can't blow that horn anymore."

Dan Sr. was really disappointed because he played the trumpet his whole life. He loved to play in front of an audience. Dan Sr. actually introduced me to Joe Negrey. Mr. Negrey is a very good jazz guitarist in the Pittsburgh area. I even started nervously taking guitar lessons from him. But, he looked to be a very busy man and sent me to another guitar player who he had recently taught. I took guitar lessons from this guy, Sam, for years.

When our band played out in bars, Sam would nicely let me use his high tech guitar equipment, although he clearly told me, "Please don't touch anything. Everything is already set up properly. If something goes wrong, I'll hear it and come fix it, but nothing should go wrong as long as you don't touch anything."

The bass player in our band, Joe, was the son of the marvelous trombonist, Joe Sr., who played with Jay's father. They both were also the bandleaders of the Shrine Circus Jazz Band. Therefore, our band started traveling with the Shrine Circus as an intermission band. We played at the Civic Arena, went to Norfolk, Virginia, Providence, Rhode Island, and anywhere else the *Shrine Circus* would travel. At the Civic Arena, we played in front of sixteen thousand people, a packed house. The few security guards could barely hold teenage girls back from jumping over the hockey boards, trying to admirably get our autographs. After we performed, we did get to sign some autographs and briefly talk to these teenage girls. This was an unbelievable feeling, to play in front of all those people and then get to sign autographs for all the little, vivacious, young girls.

Those foreign circus performers were definitely crazy, and practically all of them were from different countries. They would habitually snort cocaine, smoke weed, smoke hashish or opium and drink alcohol before performing. Our band would coolly get high with them. A brother and sister were from France. John Paul and Mia were extremely dangerous, for they would insanely do drugs, and perfectly perform on a bar approximately forty to fifty feet in the air. John Paul would tightly hold his younger sister, while he hung upside down from his knees, and she would acrobatically do amazing spins and turns stunning everybody.

Mia was a teenage blonde girl with deep blue eyes, and her thin body was physically fit. She was three years older than me, and I had a deeply willed desire to be with her, for she would always flirt and teasingly talk to me. Jay, Joe and I always hung outside the ladies' locker room cracking jokes and ogling at the women, and Jay and Joe constantly dared me to go in the locker room, so one night after Mia's long performance I went in and found her all wet and soapy in the shower. She saw me come in and immediately and passionately asked me, "Hi, how you doing? Would you like to join me?"

I uttered nervously only one mere word, "Yeah."

How could I resist? I stripped my clothes off in a flash, stepped in behind her, and the cool water felt so good against my now hot burning skin. I slid my hands down her back as we kissed in the front and caressed her firm ass. I proceeded around the front over her silky thighs and flat stomach, and then to her soapy full breasts. As I ran my hands over her hard nipples, she turned to face me. I tried to continually touch her, but she pushed my hands away. She touched me with her fingers. Everywhere she touched me felt so good. Then, she ran her tongue down my chest to my stomach and stopped at my cock. I thought I was about to pass out. With a feathery touch, she flicked her tongue over the tip and slid my cock into her mouth. I fell back and enjoyed the sensations as my heart pounded rapidly. Then, as I had watched in the movies, I lifted her up around my waist with her back against the cold shower tiles, and with her legs squeezing tightly around me she said, "Here, slip it in!"

This was the first time I ever had sex, and it felt so good. Afterwards, I couldn't stop thinking about Mia. I wanted more and got it.

One thing led to another, and the entire time that the Shrine Circus entertained the Pittsburgh audience, Mia and I started a relationship strictly based on sex. We either had sex in a secluded place somewhere inside the Civic Arena or in Mia's trailer, which she and her brother traveled in. We'd sneak off at times, and she would blow me underneath the seats of the arena, where the audience watched the show.

The circus performers all traveled to different cities in their own vehicles. Mostly, all the performers towed or drove big trailers, which they lived in when they were on the road working with the circus.

Jay, Joe and I rode in Jay's father's car to the cities where the circus put on shows; indeed, Jay's father even towed a littler trailer that we lived out of. However, instead of staying in Jay's father's trailer, I stayed romantically with Mia in her trailer. Mia's trailer came equipped with a kitchen, a shower, a bathroom and two large and comfortable beds, which were on separate sides of the trailer, a heater and air-conditioner and a little living space with bench seats that surrounded a small table across from the television set and VCR. These people were filthy rich, and they all had nice trailers. But, they would always be on the road, and that's why some of them who had children considered the circus a family business. They would raise their children on the road, home schooling them, and teaching them the family business. Also, they worked for other circuses besides the Shrine Circus. But, the only time I got to see Mia was when they were with the Shrine Circus because Jay's and Joe's dads were the bandleaders.

My father wasn't like Jay's and Joe's fathers. Even though my family and Jay's family both came from Larimer Avenue, our fathers worked different professions and knew different people. Larimer Avenue in East Liberty used to be all Italian people in the 1960s and 1970s.

GAMBLING

My father was into booking numbers, booze, women and, sometimes, he stayed out all night playing cards. If he ever got arrested, the cops would release him and expunge his record. Gambling's the best business to be into because it's controlled easily, and there were police figures that gambled too.

Every Sunday my father always kept the paper in front of him opened to the sports section as he sat on the couch. I watched him impassively as he talked on the telephone about point spreads and wrote in the paper while he smoked cigarettes and drank coffee. I heard him say, "How much do you want to bet?"

The phone rang all morning until the football games started, and then my dad went next door to the V.F.W. We still ate pasta every Sunday as a tradition, and my job was to stir the sauce and secretly nip on the wine.

It seemed my dad knew everybody, and everybody knew him. He was known around town as "The Baker."

Although my father was either with his friends all the time or at work, he evidently found time to proudly coach my little league team. I really enjoyed playing baseball on the little league and pony league teams. Two years in a row, my pony league team was undefeated. I was very athletically fit, and my dad would encourage me to play my best. "Keep your eye on the ball," or "Eye of the tiger, Ant," he would yell while I was at bat. In the field playing second base, he would say to me, "Stay in front of the ball, so if you don't catch it, it'll hit you, and you can still throw the guy out."

Sports were one of the things I really learned from my dad.

SCHOOL DAYS

When I got into middle school, things started to change. I slowly quit going to baseball practice; instead, I made numerous amounts of friends, and we all had experimented with different things like drugs, alcohol and theft. Only now, the drugs were more plentiful, and using drugs became habitual for my friends and me.

Smoking marijuana made me feel like I was in a quiet, zoned-out state of mind, and everything looked and sounded a little different. The marijuana was expensive, but easily gotten, so my friends and I pitched in a few dollars apiece, and between all of us we were able to buy a nicely sized bag of weed, which we smoked up in a weekend. About ten of my friends and I hung out regularly, and we went into the woods to smoke marijuana, trip-out on acid and drink out of a keg of beer.

Two of my friends and I used to steal food and candy from the local grocery store up the street. We'd walk up to the store together, but when we arrived at the store, we each walked in alone and went in different directions. Afterwards, we met in the same woods that we partied in, which was right behind the supermarket. I'd take the bags of candy to school with me, and I separately sold each piece of candy to the other kids in school; thus, I ate free candy and made my few dollars to pitch in on the bags of weed. One time, when we were in this store stealing stuff, I noticed an older man with black hair following us, so I threw the stuff I had taken back on the shelf. This man was the manager of the store. I went and tried to find my friend and warn them, but they were nowhere to be found. And, when I turned around to leave the store, the manager was standing right behind me and grabbed me, took me in a back room and there I saw my two friends. He caught all three of us and took us to a back room. He called the police, and the officer who came to the store was one of my father's friends. Since I didn't have any of the candy on me and knew the cop, the cop immediately let me go and kept my two friends because they still had the stolen merchandise on them.

At this age, I didn't spend much time with my father anymore. My father worked constantly and would spend his leisure time at the V.F.W. But, one day while riding in the car with him, he boldly told me, "Don't ever get married and have kids, son. And, don't ever let me catch you doin' drugs or stealing!"

"I won't, Dad," I quietly replied and asked, "Why shouldn't I get married?"

He shrugged his shoulders and irritably said, "Just don't do it. Do what I say not what I do."

I'm sure my dad had talked with his cop friend about me shoplifting.

Evidently, my father was probably fighting with my mom at the time. They'd been a very loving couple for almost forty years, and I never saw them fight a lot; however, there were times when they did fight. It usually never lasted too long. My mother bitched mostly about my dad drinking constantly. I think that made him mad. My mother and father never seemed to talk too much. They were usually at work, and sometimes worked different hours. Therefore, they often didn't see one another.

My father was a very quiet person, also a really funny and happy guy when he got drunk; indeed, he would usually always crack a lot of jokes and have an unquestionably good time while he drank with his friends. But, he hardly ever said anything to me, and when I asked him a question, he'd only answer with a word or two speaking very confidently. He rarely told me about life and what lay ahead for me.

PAP PAP DIED

The year was 1986. I was only sixteen years old when my grandfather died from his last heart attack. As young as I was, I didn't know how to deal with the loss, although I sadly knew that I would never see him again. But, one night in bed, the night of the funeral, I cried with an emotional outpouring of tears. At the funeral, I first heard the song "Taps" played by a solo trumpeter and learned that they played that song for every American soldier's passing.

My dad took it really hard. He helplessly started drinking even more heavily than normal. My grandmother took it the hardest. I remember her sitting on a kitchen chair with her head down on the table while she sadly cried out, "Why did he leave me? Why?"

Not knowing how to comfort her, I called my father next door at the V.F.W., and he came right over, for my mom was at work, and I was home alone with my grandmother.

My mother didn't seem to care that much, but she did show feelings of sadness as tears ran down from her eyes smearing her makeup. My mother really wanted to see her real father, Carmine Trafficanti. Therefore, he came up to Pittsburgh from Florida, where he lived, to see us, and I finally found out whom my real blood grandfather was. Carmine Trafficanti was a little, but powerful, man from Sicily; also, he was a talented musician, who wanted to hear me play the guitar, so I played a few songs for him on my guitar, and he said to my mom, "He has some talent to be playing that good at only sixteen years old," and he urged me to play the guitar even more.

Experimenting Teenager

As Jay, Joe, and I kept playing music in a band, Jay's other older brother, Gino, would accommodatingly give us marijuana to smoke. Joe and I merely asked Jay, "Can you go get some weed off of your brother before we start rehearsal?"

Jay regularly replied while sighing, "I'll see if he's home," and he ran across the backyard to his brother's house and always came back with some weed. We sat on the back porch of Jay's house and smoked a joint and then went in and rehearsed the songs we played.

Jay's brother, Gino, was a very big marijuana dealer. I'm talking a million dollars worth of weed that came in from New Mexico or Arizona in a rental box truck, like a Ryder or U-haul. It wasn't just Gino. Jay and Gino had another brother who lived in Las Vegas, and Gino was with a crew of about six or seven guys in Pittsburgh. Between all of them, they came up with the million dollars to buy a truckload of marijuana. Therefore, we had very easy access to free weed. Smoking weed and playing music seemed to go together pretty well. The weed made the music sound better because we played the music with more feeling; therefore, the better we played rhythmically, the better it sounded.

Even though they bought weed for years, Gino's crew eventually got busted, but Gino wasn't at that particular deal the night the bust went down, and marijuana wasn't as plentiful as it once was, but Gino knew other people he got marijuana off of, so we still smoked free weed but just not as much. Gino always kept a huge stash of marijuana hidden and grew it as well.

As time went by, I slowly started to sell some weed to make money. I was only about sixteen or seventeen years old. Even though I smoked a lot of it, I still made some money. With the connections I made, I would trade the weed for L.S.D. or cocaine.

My first L.S.D. trip was absolutely crazy because I really didn't know what to expect. I never experienced anything like it before. At first, the trip slowly crept up on me, and I got a weird sensation up my back. My stomach churned as if I had the butterflies, and any moving object I looked at left trails behind. We walked to a party over at a girl's house we knew from school while the trip got more intense. By the time we got to her house, I was fully tripping out. Everything trailed, and the psychedelic music of Pink Floyd and The Grateful Dead that we listened to seemingly made the trip better. The girl's mother actually gave us pot to smoke. She came outside and dumped a big bag of marijuana on a table that sat on the patio with four chairs around it and an umbrella above. I barely uttered a word, and when I did, it didn't make any sense. I laughed at anything and everything as my heart pounded. I couldn't stop thinking how strange it was for the girl's mother to give us marijuana; we were minors; it was illegal, and the weed wasn't even the good stuff. This was the best part of tripping: the peak. I enjoyed the warped hallucinations, and how in depth my thoughts were. As we looked into each other's eyes, we laughed at the sight of our completely blackened pupils. Finally, after about eight hours, the acid started to wear off, and at one particular moment, I felt it just go away.

My first line of cocaine was also great. It was a quickly felt sensation of happiness and cheerfulness, and I couldn't stop talking. The feeling didn't last too long, but I sure felt like I was on a cloud floating high in the sky. I was at a party and walked in the bathroom to take a piss. My friend Bobby was in there snorting coke, and he offered me a line, and I asked him, "What's this shit going to do to me?"

"Just do it. It won't hurt you," he said.

I replied daringly, "Okay. Why not? I'll try a line."

I'll never forget how good I felt when I did my first line of cocaine; thus, I got more interested and used the cocaine by snorting it.

After I tried L.S.D. for the first time, my friends and I would insanely have acid parties in the woods on weekends. We would get a barrel of beer and many bags of ice. I was in charge of getting the weed, and another guy got the acid. Everybody from school used to show up there. These parties would usually last all night long, depending on the weather; however, there were an elite few of us that would stay out tripping wildly on acid, whether rain, snow or brutally cold conditions.

During these parties, Wayne would always want to fight somebody and normally did. People would fight each other just to see who was the stronger and better fighter. Nobody could ever beat Wayne. He was known to be crazy because he seemingly was.

A guy named Hassuan, who sold cocaine in high school, would come to these parties with cocaine. It was hard to snort coke outside, especially if the wind blew, but we managed to snort up a couple of lines. Hassuan and Mike always brought cocaine to high school parties that people would throw when their parents were out of town. Hassuan got caught with cocaine possession in school and got kicked out of school permanently, although he really didn't care because he made so much money selling the coke. He went into the Air Force, got sent to a Utah base, made many friends (connections), but the Air Force caught him mailing cocaine back to his older brother in Pittsburgh and filed charges and kicked him out.

My parents knew I was into drugs, but didn't know to what extent. As a junior in high school, I saw friends of mine who started to work. Since my parents were working people, my father gave me an ultimatum. He said alternatively, "Go to college or get a job. If you go to school, I'll buy you a car."

They knew I really hated school, and it was time to decide whether I wanted to go to college or get a job, so I immediately said, "I'll get a job."

I went to work at a grocery store stocking shelves, and I bagged groceries also. Plus, I still sold weed, so I made pretty good money. As soon as I got my driver's license, I quickly bought myself an old beater car. This way I could drive to school.

HIGH SCHOOL

After the merger in 1988, when all the other schools came to Churchill High School, it was renamed to Woodland Hills High School and there were an abundance of students, in contrast to teachers. Hence, we were able to skip school quite easily. If we did go to school, we always smoked a couple of joints before we went. Jay, Pat and I drove my old beater 1984 Buick Skylark to school every day. Every now and then, I would even drop a hit of L.S.D. with my other friends, and then go to school. In Algebra class, Cookie and I would snort lines of cocaine when the teacher turned her back. At this time, I was used to the euphoric feelings I got when I used drugs, and gained quite a tolerance to them. Some of the drugs I'd tried I didn't like; but on the other hand, some of the drugs I did like.

There was a group of us who would blow off school, go get high and still get credit for the day of school. We could do this because we were keen, and knew the attendance lady. She was Pat's mother.

Patrick was a very close friend of my family. His father was also named Pat, and he was a police chief who hung out with my father. Another friend of mind, Remi, his father was the local Magistrate, and I was sexually involved with Remi's sister. Carla was a little older than me; thus, she had already graduated and had a good job. Normally, Carla came to my house after she got done working. She had a boyfriend, so she slyly stopped at my house before she went home from work and we'd screw for hours in my finished basement and bedroom. She loved it, and we always kept in close contact. Therefore, I practically knew the local judge. Anyway, we signed in with the attendance lady, Pat's mom, went to homeroom and then left school, still getting credit for the classes. Our senior class was the first to graduate from Woodland Hills High School.

Pat's father always kept a cupboard full of old confiscated dried out marijuana and, sometimes, freshly new buds. One bag was labeled Acapulco Gold, 1972. Pat Jr. was a little wary about stealing it, his dad being a cop and all, but my friends and I persuaded him to take it. We silently went into the cupboard and discreetly took the Acapulco Gold bag. We smoked it, but it was so old and dry it really didn't get us high. In fact, we smoked three or four joints just to get a buzz. We never got caught because Patrick had four sisters, and his father didn't know who actually took it. They were about the same age as we were and went to the same schools throughout our childhoods.

I never went to get my diploma on commencement day. Instead, a couple of us stayed out smoking cocaine all night. Jerome, an older main man in the cocaine business around town, knew of a guy who sold quantities of coke and was out of town for the weekend. So, Jerome, Glenn and I broke into this guy's house at about nine o'clock at night. I slipped in through the window that held the air-conditioner and wasn't closed all the way. Then, when I got in I went and opened the door for Jerome who knew where to find the coke. We actually just sat right in this guy's house and smoked his cocaine for free.

Morning came quickly, and Glenn and I walked to Glenn's house. Glenn didn't have a car, so after I chilled out for awhile and came down from the wired-out cocaine buzz, I then called my mother for a ride home, and she came and picked me up. That was my very first time I smoked cocaine in mass quantities and man was it a rush! It felt like my head was separated from my body and a euphoric feeling of floating encased my mind. Jerome hung out with and dealt cocaine with Hassuan's older brother, but he got arrested a couple times real early in life and went to jail for a long time; in fact, I never saw that man again.

My parents were unhappy and disappointed that I didn't go get my diploma, but they knew how I was. I did get my diploma, but I just didn't go to the commencements. Mostly, all my friends didn't care about a piece of paper saying, "High School Graduate."

For example, Glenn was a deadhead who sold marijuana and the best L.S.D. in town that he got from The Grateful Dead concerts. He was another one who didn't care about a diploma. Nico H. went off to the Army and got sent to Germany. While he was there, he went to the hashish and marijuana bars in Amsterdam. He got caught when he tried to send two sheets of L.S.D. home. Nico put the sheets of acid between two post cards and mailed it to himself back in the United States. When he got home, the Army immediately put him in the brig because they found the L.S.D. He was dishonorably discharged from the United States Army. Wayne, who was always in fights, went off to the Marine Corp in the tenth grade and wound up in Iraq, fighting in "Desert Storm." When Wayne came home after the war, he acted as if he was brainwashed saying, "I'm the property of the United States Government and trained to kill. If I hurt anybody, I will seriously get in trouble."

Wayne and I were real tight, and the closest of friends. He told unbelievably scary stories about being in Iraq. He said, "Our guns shot a longer range than their guns did, so we would be back far and able to shoot them while their guns couldn't reach us!"

He quickly continued, "There were rattle snakes everywhere, and we made sure our sleeping bags were zipped up tight or else they would get inside. We even caught the snakes and ate them."

I was in awe and listened to him say, "I've seen the biggest scorpions you could ever imagine."

I asked, "You didn't eat the scorpions did you?"

He replied, "No, I didn't eat them, but there were those who did. I was the ammunition driver, and we all wore headphones because the guns and bombs were so loud. I never got out of the truck. I drove the ammo to the guys who fired weapons. They would unload the ammo, and I drove back to get more ammo where other guys loaded it onto the truck. The night sky was lit up from all the bombs that the planes dropped."

"What about all the oil?" I asked him curiously.

"The daytime looked like night time! There was so much oil burned up it just lingered in the sky above us, totally black."

"Wow! I heard about that on television," I replied.

Wayne didn't shut up. "We only had nine tanks where I was, and they had fifteen, but our tanks didn't get hit once because of the maneuverable abilities they had. We also had precision-guided weapons with nighttime sights, and the Iraqi tanks didn't have these kinds of weapons. The tank battle only lasted for ten to fifteen minutes."

Wayne and I continued to be friends, and I'd listen to what he said. I've been his friend a long time before the War, and I thought to myself, if that was me, I would want somebody to talk to also. He got a job and worked right after he came home, and he held that same job for many years; in fact, he stayed at that job the whole time I knew him.

WORK ON THE ROAD

Eventually, I got into landscaping. The money was a lot better, and it was more fun doing that than working in the grocery store. A friend of mine, Erik, whose older brother sold cocaine, got me that job. We could smoke pot and snort coke while working. The boss usually would trustingly let us go out and cut the grass ourselves saying, "You guys know how to get to the houses, right?"

We assured him by saying, "Don't worry about it. We know what we're doing, and we know where we're going."

As we drove down the boss's driveway, I chopped up lines of cocaine that we snorted up in a matter of minutes, and then we smoked a joint that was pre-rolled.

After high school, Erik knew some of his older brother's friends who worked heavy construction, and Erik and I both suddenly started to work heavy construction. This was a constantly traveling job and paid very well. I can remember coming home one day with my mother serenely floating on a raft in the in ground swimming pool, and I was thrilled when I told her, "Mom, I'm getting a job making sixteen to twenty dollars an hour!"

She lazily said, "You're full of shit. Nobody's going to pay you that much money." I was only eighteen. She hardly believed someone as young as I was could make as much as twenty dollars an hour in 1988.

I said happily, "You'll see. I'm leaving next week. It's a traveling job, and I can't pass up the opportunity." After she saw a couple of my paychecks, she became very proud of me.

Usually, we worked long hours, from sun up to sun down. We'd rather be hard at work than sitting in a lonely hotel room. We took long rides around the country, drove on many different highways and back roads and worked in different states. We got to see the whole country on someone else's dollar. We would have an unbelievably good time, as we stayed in really nice hotels and made a lot of money. However, some jobs were out in the middle of nowhere. Everybody who worked on a crew would eagerly go to nude bars in every single state we traveled to.

There was a chain of totally nude bars all over the country called, "De'Ja' Vu." The guys on the work crew and I stayed out all night drinking, shooting pool, throwing darts and getting lap dances at these bars or any other nude bars we found. Some states had only a few nude bars, whereas other states had an increasingly growing number and variety of nude bars. We'd normally come home every other weekend.

One weekend I came home, Pat and I went downtown to an all-nude bar. Since Pat was a very heavy drinker, he passed out with his head lying on the stage where the girls danced above. I took all kinds of pills, drank and got stoned, but stayed wide-awake and enjoyed the nude women dancing. While Pat lay there passed out with his head on the edge of the dance floor, I got one of the girls to place her breasts on Pat's head and got a picture taken. The girl who was the main attraction came out and started to strip as she danced around the stage exotically. I kept sticking money down her panties until she took them off. Then, she took the microphone and said, "I want to hear some noise." She tantalizingly said, "Whoever's the loudest gets their picture taken with me."

I sat right next to Pat by the stage and because I took so many pills and drank a lot, I screamed and yelled, "Ay Yo! Over here. Show me your tits."

She danced back and fourth on the stage, and I kept yelling at the top of my voice, "Come back down this end!" When she did, I said, "Here's a twenty. Pick it up with your snatch."

She squatted down, and she picked up the twenty with her snatch.

I determinately continued to scream louder and louder until she said, "I got a winner."

She strutted back over to me and said, "You're the winner. Come over here, and we'll take a picture."

"How do you want your picture taken with me?"

"Let me sit in front of you and put my head in between your tits," I told her. And, some guy who was with her took the picture.

The next day I showed Pat the pictures, and he said with a bummed out grin on his face, "No way dude. You did this? Wow! I can't believe I passed out."

I said, "Well, at least you got the picture to look at. And you were so drunk, I carried you out to the car."

I had a girlfriend before I started this traveling construction job, but I came home one weekend unannounced and found her in bed with my friend. I really didn't care because he was my friend, and I slept with women on the road. It was nearly impossible to hold a meaningful relationship with a woman because I traveled constantly. So, we would get lucky sometimes on the road, as we dressed exquisitely and went to the regular nightclubs to meet ladies. Women seemingly liked guys who weren't ordinarily going to be around too long, especially the married women. I've safely engaged in a lot of one-night stands in that particular period of my life. Sometimes, I'd keep a girlfriend until we finished the job.

On our way to Mississippi once, we drove in a big red passenger van with windows all around it. While traveling a long distance with a crew-full of guys, we entertained ourselves in the strangest ways. This particular trip we wrote in really big letters on a long piece of white paper with a black magic marker, "Show us your tits," and we hung it up on the inside of the van's windows as we passed up girls in cars hoping they would see the sign and show us their tits. As we passed one girl, we slowed down because she was young and looked like she would do it. One guy in the van mooned her, and I showed her a very big bag of marijuana. She liked the marijuana and pointed to us to pull over at the next rest stop, and we did. I got out of the van, went into her car, and smoked a joint with her, and then I asked, "Let me see your tits... Please?"

She asked, "Where are you from, and where you going?"

I told her, "We're on our way to Mississippi to work. Are you going to show me them titties?" I continued, "The guys in the van really want to see them. You'll make their day."

She showed me as she sensuously and slowly lifted up her shirt, and after I took a long glance at her big tits with her hardened nipples, I gave her a nice little bud of very good weed and got back in the van, and we headed on our way. She still drove right beside us as we continued to hold up the sign. Eventually, she lifted up her shirt and showed the whole van full of guys her gorgeous big tits right before she exited the highway. And, we went south on our way to work in Mississippi with the sign still hanging on the window.

We traveled from Miami, to Chicago, to San Francisco, to Los Angeles, to all over New York, the Carolinas, Mississippi, Colorado and everywhere in between. Once in a while, we had had some jobs close to home in Pennsylvania. However, we still worked very long hours. One job we did in York, Pennsylvania, was a federally funded job, and we needed to get drug tested. Our boss knew we all constantly smoked weed; therefore, he hired five older guys who were clean and didn't regularly use drugs. They were in the

31

hotel room right across the hall, and when the boss, Keith, came to get us for the drug test, he knocked on the door, and when we opened it, a cloud of marijuana smoke hovered all over the hallway.

Keith laughed, "You fucking guys are supposed to take a fucking a drug test, and you're in here smoking pot. Man, that smoke's going to get in your drug test bottles."

We walked across the hall to the other room, and the older guys they'd hired were in there. When it was time for us to piss in the bottle for the drug test, the older guys took our bottles, went into the bathroom and pissed for us as we stood there stoned and didn't do a thing except sign a piece of paper. When the guy who pissed for me was done, Keith brilliantly said, "Here, Anth, sign this. You're done."

When my drug test came back, they told me I had high blood sugar and some other liver problems. I was only nineteen, they diagnosed me with high blood sugar and high liver enzymes, and it was never even a question. The piss test worked perfectly, and I continued to do my job. There wasn't a lot of people who could work the way we did. Therefore, they needed to keep us working. The job was very physically demanding, and we traveled long distances.

Another time, we restlessly took an extremely long plane ride to Guam, stopping at L.A.X. international airport in Los Angeles to refuel before we flew over the vast Pacific Ocean. This was a federally funded job also paying twenty-five dollars an hour, but there wasn't a drug test. The job there was on a naval base, and Guam, a lonely island sitting in the middle of the Pacific Ocean, was a beautiful place to see. Palm trees, sunshine, little green poisonous snakes, very large lizards and all different types of colorful birds were everyday sights. This was probably the most exotic place I've ever been.

I used to take my acoustic guitar with me everywhere we went; it gave me something to do and I sat in at times at different bars if the band that played let me. Other times we sat around the hotel, drank beer, smoked pot and I played guitar for the guys. Anyway, we were on a job up state in New York by a town called Montgomery, and we went out to a bar after work one night and I asked to sit in with the band that played in the local bars, and they said, "Sure only for one or two songs."

I needed to get primed and ready to play, so I pounded Jack and Cokes and took too many Valium; however, I was so fucked up I saw double and couldn't walk straight. When I got up on stage to play, I strapped my guitar around my neck and fell backwards knocking over a couple of amplifiers. I never played that night; in fact, my friends threw me in the van and carried me back to the hotel room.

In Portsmouth, Ohio, I had the union steward on my ass because there was a strike going on and our work crew was the scabs. I got boldly disgusted with a couple of people who constantly nagged me about their union and told them, "Go fuck off, and leave me alone. I'm already in a union out of Boston."

I just told them I was in a union to get them off my back. They called my bosses back in Pittsburgh and complained about me. So, my company pulled me off the Ohio job and sent me to Colorado Springs, Colorado. This major construction company has been around for a long time and did jobs all over the world, and they also worked on the Alaskan Pipe Line, so they could have sent me anywhere. And, I would have gone. I stayed in Colorado Springs through late October and into November until the Thanksgiving holiday came up. It snowed so much the snow came half way up my hotel window.

I stayed on the first floor, and when I awoke the next morning, it was still snowing. It was my first time to Colorado, and I didn't expect all the snow.

I asked the guy in charge, "Can we work in this weather?"

"Yeah. I got a four wheel drive truck, and they normally keep the roads clear," he replied calmly with a grin on his face. "They use bulldozers to clear the heavily snow covered roads here."

As he walked in my room, he said, "You got some bugs in your ashtray."

"What? Bugs," I said, for I had no idea what he meant.

He referred to the roaches from the joints I smoked the night before, so on the way to work he fired up a packed bowl-full of marijuana. He was an older, heavy guy I'd just met, my superior and we were already smoking weed together. His name was JR., and he had long hair and a mustache and beard, similarly to a hippie of the '60s. I liked it in Colorado. We drove up to different parts of the mountains and smoked a joint or two as we pierced at the scenery. The Rocky Mountains were a beautiful sight, and I got to see Pikes Peak. Then, at night, we'd go to different types of bars and nightclubs to hang out, drink, shoot pool and meet women. It got cold on the mountains, and personally, I preferred warmer weather.

MEXICAN MARIJUANA

My favorite place was Corpus Christi, Texas. The weed was cheap, but the work surface and general area was viciously hot; nevertheless, when we got time off, we'd go directly to the beach. We filled a cooler full with beer and ice and went to the beach. I usually drove and whoever was with me at the time rolled joints, so they'd be ready to smoke whenever we wanted to smoke one. South Padre Island is the beach down there and would get overwhelmingly packed with people. We were allowed to drive our cars right up to the water and have ice-cold cans of beer. We weren't allowed to bring glass on the beach, but canned beer worked just as well. On holidays, as far as the eye could see both ways there were three rows of cars lined up that started at the water and went back towards the shore, and we actually couldn't see the end of the line of cars. Everywhere we looked there were people and cars. People swarmed liked bees everywhere. There were people selling food and drinks, people playing volleyball, catching Frisbee and football. Good-looking women were everywhere in thong bikinis, and all the guys held beers, everybody socialized. It was like one gigantic party.

There were strip clubs everywhere in Corpus, but we had two usual ones we hung out in. One was called "Lipsticks." This was a place where college girls stripped. Corpus was a college town, and the girls stripped to pay for school or to make extra money, so I gladly patronized them. For twenty dollars, I'd get a long hot lap dance. On the other hand, the other club we hung in was called, "The Zoo." And, it was a zoo. Both men and women were at this place because it was like a regular bar with a pool table, dartboards and gambling machines. This was a bar of more experienced and older strippers, and they'd do anything we asked if the money was right. I got a three girl lap dance for sixty bucks, and they practically gave me a hard on.

So, I asked, "How much for a blow job?"

One girl replied, "That's illegal. We can't do that here."

I slurred my words when I replied, "Nobody will even see us. We're way back in this dark corner, and there's nobody around."

34

The oldest and most experienced of the three said, "Give us sixty more dollars, and we'll blow you."

I agreed, and one of the girls went to talk to a man before I gave them the money, and when she returned the three naked girls surrounded me after the oldest girl took the money. One of them unbuckled my pants, unzipped my zipper and pulled my cock out, and they took turns blowing me while the other two tried to hide it because it was illegal. I had one girl's tits in my face, the other girl's legs were spread wide open, and I watched her play with her wet pink pussy while the other girl blew me. I was really drunk and took a lot of pain pills, so it was taking me awhile to get off. They switched positions again; moreover, the two girls who weren't blowing me played with each other's Pussys. That made me blow a load right on one of the girl's tits. Right after that, I went back to the poolroom and told the guys. Eric and Mark asked me to get the girls to come back to the hotel. Then, I went back and tried to get the three girls to come back to our hotel by asking them if they wanted to make some real money, but they looked to be too nervous and untrusting because they saw the rest of the guys I was with. There were five of us and three of them. I told them which hotel we stayed in, and they knew exactly where it was. I gave them the room number just in case they wanted to come, but they never showed.

The hotel we stayed in had an indoor-outdoor swimming pool, tennis courts, racquetball courts, a mini kitchen and a delicious breakfast buffet in the lobby every single day. This place was like a vacation, even though the job wasn't federally funded.

There was every fruit you could imagine, all different kinds of cereal, pancakes, waffles, eggs, bacon, toast, juices, sausage and different kinds of coffee. An omelet bar with a chef to make the omelets the way we ordered it. If we didn't go to work, we got into serious tennis matches at the tennis court, which sat directly in the middle of the hotel surrounded by the windows of the hotel rooms, and then we went to the beach and stopped for six-packs on the way.

We cheaply hired some Mexicans to do the heavy laboring part of the job. They certainly worked for their money, and they gladly showed us the town after the workday was over and told us everywhere to go to have a good time. In addition, the Mexicans told us that San Antonio was a happening town with many festivals on the weekends. Mark, Erik and I went up and checked out one of the festivals, and the river walk on a Saturday when we had the day off work. People gathered from everywhere: different parts of the country.

We even met people from Pittsburgh because a bowling convention was in town, and they were bowlers.

Mexican, or Tex-Mex, people sold beer, wine and different styles of Mexican food from huts and canopies that were built and sat on the side of the road in between and out front of the restaurants, bars and other fashion shops. We stayed in San Antonio for a couple of hours, but the South Padre Island was way more fun. Since we had Saturday off of work, we worked on Sunday, but only a half day. Then, we went to the beach. But, when it was time to work, we worked.

The material we worked with was extremely heavy, weighing in at two tons a roll. We would need twenty or thirty rolls at times, maybe more depending on the job. I was a technician, who carefully welded the materials together, along with the other technicians. Our welding tools were heavy. There were two of them, one weighed about one hundred pounds, and the other about seventy-five pounds. So, every place we went we hired laborers, who would do any work for the little bit of money we paid them. Five or six dollars an hour was a lot to people down south.

Anyway, marijuana didn't cost a fortune down in Corpus Christi as it did up north, and we got to know these Mexicans pretty well. There was Juan, Lionel and Havarti. These were the guys that labored for us. Evidently, they started to trust us; therefore, they casually sold us some weed. They sold us little bits to begin with like ounces and quarter-pounds, and when we got to know them better, they sold us larger quantities. Between all the guys on the work crew, we'd smoke up over a quarter pound a week, but that's with many men and women we met. Before I left to go north, I wanted to buy more to take home and sell.

The marijuana was so cheap I could hardly pass it up, for I knew I would profit greatly. So, Lionel brought me to his dealer's house. We took my red Chevy pickup work truck and went off into the desolate and dry lands of Southern Texas. After a twenty-minute drive, we arrived. The dealer's house looked to be a run-down place, but inside was nice, and there was a mediocre sized brown wooden shack out back that was well covered with waterproof tarps. Ceiling fans circled above as a Spanish television station played and everyone spoke Spanish. This guy was older and spoke broken English. He invited us into his house, so we went in. After the initial meeting over a beer, the three of us walked out the back door, which was through a clean kitchen with one sturdy wood table and a marble like surface and three chairs with high backs. The table sat below a rusty-screened window with sheer curtains that draped down over. We walked out the back door of his house, down the steps and across the yard and up five little steps into this little wooden shack. I seriously thought they were going to kill me and take all my money. Even though I trusted Lionel, it still seemed too shaky, like too good of a deal to be true. There in this little shack were brown cardboard boxes stacked to the ceiling and all of them filled with marijuana. Lionel said to his dealer, "This guy gave me a job, and I've known him for quite a while now. He's cool."

The dealer told me with his Mexican accent, "Go ahead, man, take how much you want and pay me." As if he could just get more instantly and at no charge.

I coolly replied, "How much for a pound?"

He laughed, "The more you buy, the cheaper it is going to be."

I said, "I want as much as I can get, but I only got one thousand dollars on me to spend."

He happily replied, " I give you four pounds for one thousand dollars."

I told him, "That works for me. Here you go," and I handed him the money and took my weed. That's two hundred and fifty dollars a pound, and the cheapest weed I've ever bought. Lionel and I left in my pickup truck. I sighed, and the paranoid feeling of dying I had slowly turned to joy and excitement as I figured the profit I'd make back home in Pittsburgh. When I got back to the hotel, I stashed the weed in a compartment in my suitcase and put my old dirty work clothes on top of it.

After I got the weed, I wanted to go into Mexico to get some pills. Juan and Lionel calmly took my friend and me over the border into a small, slightly deserted, dried-out town in Mexico. Lionel and I drove down in his dark blue El Camino. Erik and Juan drove in Juan's old beat-up truck. After driving through what seemed to be the desert, for it was so arid and desolate as I glanced all around, we went into a little town and pulled up to a pharmacy that looked like a run down, roach infested building and bought some Valium. In Mexico they sold Valium directly over the counter. I distinctly remember the whole bottle was entirely written in Spanish, except for the word Valium. That's all I needed to see, and I bought a couple bottles; however, I gave Lionel American money in exchange for him buying the pills with Mexican money. When we left the pharmacy, I saw women and boys in the streets and a couple of older guys outside a saloon, as we left the town and went back to Corpus. We never drove through any custom stops; in fact, we drove on dirt and dusty roads the entire trip.

Shortly after that, I started heading north. I gratefully told Lionel and

Juan, "Thanks for everything, guys. I couldn't have done this without your help. Can I get your phone number? Maybe I'll come back down."

I handed them a hundred dollar bill apiece and got their phone numbers. I worked in Corpus for seven months and made a Mexican marijuana connection.

I could have sold this weed outright for one thousand dollars a pound at home, but I was greedy. So, I broke it down into ounces, charged $175.00 for most clientele, but gave good deals at $135.00 an once to close friends and made a tremendous amount of money and a huge stash for myself. I was already known to sell marijuana; therefore, I easily got rid of it. Nevertheless, Gino helped to get rid of some of the weed because I went right back on the road to work again. People told me I looked like a Mexican when I got home from Corpus Christi. I was unbelievably tan. I had the Mexican marijuana and I even had the Tex-Mex accent. I also had the bottles of Valium written in Spanish, but only a few people got a couple of pills out of me; indeed, I took mostly all the Valium during the rest of the summer in New Jersey.

NEW JERSEY

Our work crew did a job in Cape May, New Jersey, approximately twenty minutes away from Atlantic City. It was a federally funded job paying twenty-three dollars an hour. Moreover, it was a union job, so the hours weren't that long and we didn't do seven-day work runs, but still made good money. We set it up so we could get our paychecks cashed right in one of the casinos in Atlantic City called Caesar's Palace. And, every time we got paid, we went straight to the casino and gambled after they cashed our paychecks. Since the alcohol was free in the casino, we usually stayed in Atlantic City all night long drinking and gambling. We never worked on Sunday; thus, on Saturday nights we stayed in Atlantic City and gambled all night long until Sunday evening. We'd go from Caesar's, to The Sands, to The Trump Taj Mahal and whichever other casino that looked interesting.

Sometimes, we went outside to the beach and boardwalk where the neon lights shined brightly from all the casinos and smoked a joint or two on the beach, under the boardwalk or just walking up the boardwalk itself, and then went back into the casinos to gamble. The bright neon lights and all the clanging noise of money falling from the slot machines got to be very alluring. Chips were down on the card tables, and the roulette wheel spun all night as people gathered around these and other gambling games that were set up in the casinos. One Friday night, we went into the pitch-black ocean to go night swimming, and when we came out of the water, police chased us on quads while shining spotlights yelling through a bullhorn, "You're not allowed on the beach at night."

So, we ran and hid underneath the boardwalk as the police drove by us on their quads. After they went by us, we hurried and got dressed and went back into the casino where we mixed in with all the people and drank and gambled until five o'clock in the morning. We went straight to work right from the casino plastered from all the alcohol and other drugs we'd done.

After another weekend of wildness and as we headed towards the door to leave for work one morning, I saw a blackjack table that just opened, and I went over and placed a hundred dollar bill on the table. It was only the lady card dealer and me. She dealt one hand, and I won a quick hundred with a pair of tens.

She told me with a smile, "Take the money and go."

This job lasted for over two months, and I met a woman. Her name was Gina, and she was a petite Italian girl with brown eyes and straight jet-black hair and exquisitely dressed all the time. She lived in New Jersey. We were together most of the two months I was there, but she knew I traveled and had to leave soon, but that didn't seem to bother her.

We had a relationship based strictly on sex. Although we hung out too, and she showed me a famous hoagie place, with pictures of celebrities who had come by the hoagie shop for a hoagie when they performed in Atlantic City. And, the hoagies were great. If we didn't go to the casinos, we usually got a half-keg of beer and partied in one or two of our hotel rooms. Gina would bring her girlfriends over with her, and the other guys got to know them. Sometimes, Gina and I stayed up all night and took long strolls on the beach and boardwalk after we gambled. The police on the beach were nowhere to be found at dawn. We usually lay on the beach and had sex. Then, we just watched the sun rise. And, I'd normally go to work and Gina would do the same.

I worked with this one guy we called Whacko, and he really was wacky. He was always drunk and took Xanax like they were candy. He used to be a truck driver and drove the eighteen-wheeler semis. Whacko talked about his old truck driving days, and how the drivers kept a box of money underneath the front seat in a little compartment until they got back to the dispatch. He told us that some drivers kept thousands of dollars in the box because they got sent from one state to the other, and they had to hold onto the money. So, we concocted a plan on how we could get the money. We needed other guys, so we asked Spudzee and Mario if they wanted in on the deal. They jumped at the opportunity.

On the drive to Atlantic City, there was a dark back road that ran along the side of the highway, and some of the truck drivers pulled into this small dirt area off the side of the road, down the street from a tavern/restaurant to sleep in their trucks or eat and drink at the tavern. The next couple of nights we went to this tavern and checked it out. It was a really small place and had very few people inside. We were estranged to the people in this little bar, but we let them think we were working in Jersey and needed a cheap place to drink. So, we drank, played darts, listened to music and shot pool, so it seemed we were just there to drink and have a good time. Plus, the owner saw how much money we spent on booze, food, games and slipping quarters into the jukebox. Therefore, he became quite friendly. I asked him, "Do you get a lot of truck drivers in here? I noticed a truck parked in your side lot."

"This is a usual stop over for truck drivers. They'll come in and grab a sandwich and some drinks, but they only stay for a night to rest."

Each night there was only one semi truck in the lot down the street. But, they were different trucks on different nights. So, we didn't know if another truck would be there the next night; on the other hand, from what the owner told me, we took our chances because we wanted the money. This night, we drove the little red cargo work van and stayed out of the tavern, and we parked further on up the road as we watched another semi truck pull into the lot. As we sat in the van, we watched the driver go into the tavern. Then, Whacko, Mario and I got out of the side door of the van and walked over to the truck.

Spudzee was supposed to sit in the van and watch for a signal from me to quickly come pick us up after we got the money. Whacko, Mario and I carried short heavy pipes we took from our job site, and we hid on the other side of the truck and waited for the guy to come back. It was dark and desolate, except for the cars we saw drive by quickly on the highway up across the street. After we sat with our backs against the big wheels of the semi for a while, we saw from underneath the truck a pair of legs walking our way: the guy coming back to his truck. And, just when he opened the door to get in, Mario and I grabbed him, and Mario, a very strong husky guy, tried to throw a few punches and knock the guy out, but the truck driver put up a fight, so Mario started to beat the driver with the pipe. But, the driver adamantly kept putting up a fight. So, I took a few swings with the pipe at the guy's legs to keep him down on the ground, and then I kept an eye out and watched if anyone was coming; moreover, I also watched Whacko because I really didn't trust him. Whacko knew exactly where the moneybox was, and he snatched it real quickly while Mario and I threw the truck driver in the back of the truck and locked the doors. Whacko yelled, "I got the box."

I ran out to the road and gave Spudzee the signal to come get us. When I took my hat off and raised both of my hands, he immediately drove to the truck and picked us up. With the side door of the van still open, we hopped right in and took off. We went straight back to the hotel and into Mario's room. After I broke the lock open with a hammer and chisel I grabbed from the toolbox in the van, I dumped all the cash and some checks on the bed. The checks got thrown away, yet we each nearly made close to two thousand dollars. Whacko was right. There was a lot of money in the box. So, we took the swag and went up to the casinos.

Another guy, Lou, or "Lucky Lou" we called him because he won all the time in the casinos thought out a plan on how we could rip off this small local liquor store in Wildwood, New Jersey. He told us his plan over drinks in the hotel bar while we listened to AC DC's song "Have a Drink on Me" play on the jukebox.

"We're only going to take the liquor," Lou told us. "We need a lot of people for this to work."

"What's the deal, Lou?" I asked.

"If we can get about eight or nine guys, we can go in two at a time, and a couple of us can distract the employee while the rest of us steal the booze."

"What about the other employees?"

"That's the beauty of it. There's only one guy who works there at night."

"I know Matt will definitely want in on this," I said. "We're going to need long coats with a lot of pockets. Booze is too expensive anyway."

So, we got the other guys to come down from their rooms to the hotel bar and told them what we preliminarily planned. It was Whacko, Lou, Matt, Erik, Rock and I. We were the only ones willing to do it. We got tired of spending money on liquor. There was no money to be made, just booze, but we all spent tons of money on drinking. We planned it for a Friday night, so we'd be at the job site the next day, which was out in an unpopulated area of New Jersey, by the waste plants and chemical plants, and nobody ever went near those places. A few of us got our coats that would hide the liquor, and the rest wore the coveralls we wore to work when it was cold. Then, we waited until the liquor store was almost closed, and we took the larger passenger company van and headed to the store.

We got to the store and went in two at a time in three minute intervals. Lou, Rock and I distracted the employee; thus, the other guys shoved bottles of booze in their jackets, pants, down their coveralls and anywhere else they could fit the bottles. As Lou and Rock tied up the employee by distracting him with questions, I then went and took a couple bottles of Captain Morgan's rum and put them in my coat pocket because that was my favorite drink. I needed to make sure I got my Captain Morgan's spiced rum. When we got back to the hotel room, we unloaded our coats and pants and placed the booze on the table. There was probably over four hundred dollars worth of booze. Of course, we took the good stuff.

Therefore, I called Gina and told her we were having a party and to bring her friends with her because the job was almost completed, and I had to go down to Texas. We spent what would be our last blissful night together, and we engaged in the wildest sex ever. With all the booze that was there, I simply grabbed a bottle of Champagne that somebody stole from the liquor store, and we went to our own room, got naked and enjoyed the night like we were never going to see each other again, and we never did.

BACK TO CORPUS

Erik and I got called to go back to Corpus Christi, Texas, to repair a hole in the material. We simply patched a couple holes our company knew of; in addition, we found two more holes when we did a quick check of all the material before we told our supervisors everything looked all right, and that was it. We drove all that way while we snorted cocaine and only worked three days, but we did get paid for driving time. Eight bucks an hour to drive there, and I got an extra quarter for every mile I put on my car. I made close to a thousand dollars just for the drive down there. Therefore, I made a little extra than Erik did. We were on the Corpus job from day one; therefore, we knew every inch of the job site; plus we were a great team, and that's why they sent us back.

While there, I contacted Lionel, asked how he was and told him that Erik and I were back in town. I never talked over the phone about drugs, so I just asked him if we could do what we did last time. He happily agreed because he knew I would hook him up with money, but instead of just money, I gave him the rest of the coke Erik and I snorted on the way down. This time I'd bought ten pounds for two grand. Erik wanted in on the deal, and he bought one grand's worth. We also went back over the border into Mexico for some more Valium. Erik and I took care of Lionel and Juan very nicely because what was a little bit of money to us was a lot to them. Then, we left for the long ride home to Pittsburgh.

I aggressively sped through Missouri on my way home from Texas; the state police pulled me over. I nervously sat there until the police officer approached my car. Erik kept his mouth shut, and they didn't ask him anything. I had all that marijuana and the Valium I'd gotten from Mexico. The officer asked authoritatively, with a southern accent, "License and registration please?"

I asked, "Was I speeding, sir?" as I handed him my license and registration.

He quickly replied, "Wait here. I'll be right back."

As he checked my license in his police car, his partner curiously looked at all the stuff in my hatchback. Erik sat quietly in the passenger's seat with his window rolled up because we had the air-conditioning on. All I thought about was the police finding the drugs in my car. When the other officer came back, he loudly said, "Did you know you were speeding?"

I answered respectfully, "I'm from Pittsburgh, Pennsylvania, sir, and I am not really sure what the speed limit is down here. I know I was doing about sixty-five or seventy."

He sternly told me, "The speed limit is fifty-five miles per hour down here."

He walked back to talk to his partner. I could see the two officers in my rear view mirror. I nervously sat there and waited. The officer came to my window and gave me my license and registration back.

He frowned darkly and suspiciously asked, "What's all the garbage in the trunk?"

I calmly told him, "I've been working in Corpus Christi for a while now, and I bought some things down there, plus the stuff I brought from home. I threw everything in the hatchback because I just want to get home to my family."

Luckily, the hatchback in my car was full of junk. Because of this, the cops didn't search my car. They wanted to, but as they looked at all the stuff I had acquired in Corpus Christi, they seemingly did not want to go through it all. The weed was at the bottom, along with the bottles of Valium.

They merely handed me a ticket and angrily told me, "You better slow down through Missouri."

I said, "I apologize, sir. Thank you. Have a nice day," and I went on my way with a pounding heart and a relieved smile on my face while Erik wiped the sweat that poured from his brows and said, "Man, that was close. I can't believe it."

I never did pay the ticket I got, and I've never been back to Missouri either.

CALIFORNIA FRIEND

Before I left Pittsburgh to go to San Francisco for the next job, I got a couple ounces of coke from my one friend Jimmy; he was one of the local cocaine dealers in town, and I asked him, "I'm going to San Francisco to work. I'll be back in a month or two. Can I pay you when I get back?"

"Yeah. Anth. No problem. Hey, you know what, man? Tim's going to see The Grateful Dead on New Years Eve. You might see him there."

Tim and Jimmy were very close friends. Years ago, they traveled around the country together watching The Grateful Dead shows. Tim also grew very good weed.

I went on this job with 'Rock' and a two other guys from Texas who met us on a connecting flight in St. Louis. Rock and I snorted most of the coke on the TWA commercial 747 airplane. We'd pull the flat tables down that were on the seats in front of us so we could lay out lines to snort. The flight only had a few people on it, and we sat alone in the back of the plane snorting lines. As I gazed out the small window of the airplane, all I saw was a red blinking light at the end of one of the wings, everything else appeared pitch black. We soared high in the sky over top the Rocky Mountains. When we arrived near San Francisco, the plane needed to keep circling around because the airport was all fogged in. Finally, we landed.

I tried to hold the rest of the coke for the weekends, but when we got to San Francisco, the crew of guys who worked with us bought the rest of the coke and snorted it up in no time. Luckily, someone else on that job knew somebody in San Jose, Ca., and he bought another ounce of cocaine.

I can remember Jimmy telling me about the Dead show. The Grateful Dead played at the Oakland Coliseum every New Years Eve. Since we were out west in December and January, and I knew The Grateful Dead played in the Coliseum, my work buddy 'Rock' and I took the company pickup truck and went to the show listening to The Grateful Dead on the radio. We had absolutely no idea where we were going; however, we saw a bunch of people with sandals on and tide-dyed t-shirts who looked like deadheads and hippies, and they all walked in the same direction. So, we figured we were driving in the right direction, but we stopped and asked one guy who walked alone if we were headed towards the Oakland Coliseum. He said yeah and asked for a ride. We told him to get in the back of the pickup truck because we didn't know this guy. I opened the sliding window in the back and asked the guy, "Do you got any weed to smoke?"

"Yeah. But, you gotta let me in the truck."

I stopped and let him get in the cab of the truck, and he fired up a really big joint and showed us how to get to the Oakland Coliseum while we smoked it. The Coliseum was crazily packed with people when we got there. It was like a party outside in the parking lot. Everybody tailgated, did and sold drugs. We got offered any and every kind of drug imaginable. Some, I'd never even heard of, so I took precautions about what I bought and who I bought it from.

I told Rock, "Don't buy any paper acid. You'll get ripped off."

"Why do you think I'll get ripped off?" he asked.

"People will sell you a piece of paper with no acid on it, and there's no way to tell," I replied. "We just got here. Let's wait. We'll find other people selling acid."

Rock was an acidhead. He loved to trip out and couldn't wait. So, he took the paper acid anyway, and he got ripped off. We walked all over the parking lot, or as I called it, "A flea market of drugs." We bought some really good marijuana they called Christmas-tree buds, some psychedelic mushrooms and ecstasy capsules. They also sold tie-dyed t-shirts, whippets (nitrous oxide, which gave a very short lasting, but very strong and intense head-rush) and a lot of other strange things were for sale, from beaded necklaces and bongs, to sandals and hemp made clothes. People sat on the ground with their legs crossed and appeared to be meditating. Everybody looked like they were tripped out on acid or highed up on some drug. The show was booked solid, and we couldn't get any tickets, but we started to feel the mushrooms and ecstasy kick in. I worried about driving the company truck. Therefore, I said to Rock, "Let's get out of here before we really start tripping out and I can't drive."

We started driving down a very dark road as my trip gradually grew more intense, and we drove right passed a police car that sat on the side of the darkened road. I knew we went the wrong way because this road was pitch-black, and there wasn't a street sign in sight, no street lights were visible nor were there any cars on this road, so I turned around and headed very nervously back passed the police car. I was tripped out pretty good at this

ANTHONY T. ALIBERTI

point, but I kept my cool and slowly drove passed the cop car. I had experienced tripping while I drove before, and I managed to get us back on the highway. I don't know how I did it; nevertheless, I got us back to the hotel safely, enjoyed the rest of my psychedelic hallucinations, and smoked the 'Christmas tree' marijuana with the rest of the work crew, who were all pissed off because we didn't take them with us.

I called Jimmy when we returned to the hotel and told him about the Dead show. It was one or two o'clock in the morning in San Fran. So, it must have been four or five o'clock in Pittsburgh, and Jimmy, Tony and Mike were still up, probably snorting cocaine.

I had a friend who lived in Los Angeles, so I called him up and asked, "What's up, Tex? I'm workin' up in San Francisco." I called him Tex because he was from Texas.

Surprisingly, he talked slowly with a deep baritone voice and said, "Hey! What's up? You're in California? Why don't you come down to Los Angeles on the weekends?"

Tex used to work with us when he lived in Pittsburgh, and he knew what the job was like. Tex and I also played guitar together on the road. Tex played guitar excellently, he was in a band in L.A. and we were good friends. So, I rented a car every weekend and drove down to L.A. He was in a country band, and I'd go to whichever bar his band played in and listen to them play while I chewed on some whiskey or drank a few beers. He showed me mostly all of Southern California. It was absolutely gorgeous in California, both in the north and the south; moreover, beautiful women roamed everywhere on the beaches in thong bikinis. Standing at the beginning of a pier, we saw models and film crews with cameras below that took pictures of the models who were in string bikinis. We watched them for a while and then went on to other beaches as we smoked joint after joint and drank beer after beer. Tex knew of all the cheapest nice places to go to. While it is true, California is a very large and widespread region of America, and it was totally impossible to see all of it in the short time I was out west.

Tex took me to one of the nicest music stores in L.A. He really liked to smoke pot, so I asked him if he could get me some weed because we didn't have too much up in San Francisco. I bought a pound of marijuana off of him and snorted a line of Crystal meth before I left to go back to San Francisco at midnight. As I sped up Interstate-5 smoking joints and listening to music, like The Door's song "L.A. Woman," Led-Zeppelin's song "Goin' to San Francisco," and Eric Clapton's acoustical song "San Francisco Bay." I got pulled over again. This time, the weed was in my little suitcase in the back seat, but I hadn't smoked one in a couple hours and the windows were open, for the ocean breeze kept me awake while I drove up to San Fran. In fact, no evident smell of marijuana existed either.

At first, I got really nervous. But as the cop approached me, I kept very cool because it was early in the morning, he seemed really nice and didn't appear to have a care in the world. The officer never even bothered to search my car. He just did his job.

He asked the usual, "License and registration please?"

I sincerely told him, "I'm working in San Francisco, sir, and I'm going to be late for work. I thought I could make it, but that fog down below Fresno held me up. I left L.A. at midnight, and I start work at seven."

At the time, it was six-thirty in the morning, and we started work at seven thirty or eight o'clock, yet I still had a two-hour ride to get back to work.

He told me, "You've been doing eighty-five for a long time," and he laughingly asked, " What's your hurry son?"

I replied again nicely and asked, "How did you know I was going that fast for so long? I just don't want to be late for work, sir."

"We got eyes in the skies." He replied, and he wrote me a ticket and sent me on my way. I ended up being late for work, but when I showed my boss the ticket and the weed I got in L.A., he forgot all about the time and fixed my time card. Shortly after that day, we finished the job in San Fran and got ready to go home.

When it was time to get on the plane, I broke the entire pound of weed down into littler bags, put the little bags in my socks, in the hidden pockets in my coat and all around my waist. I even taped some bags to my stomach. It was a late midnight flight, so there was hardly anyone on the plane. A couple up front sat together, a few business people were scattered in seats and half of our crew went to the back of the plane, for there was nobody back there.

My co-worker nervously said to me, "Man, I can smell that stuff way over here."

I just told him, "Be quiet and chill out. It smells good."

We arrived in Pittsburgh about nine or ten o'clock in the morning, Eastern Standard Time. I got off the plane and calmly stood there nonchalantly and waited for my luggage. I grabbed my suitcase off the conveyer belt and coolly walked out of the airport into a waiting black Corvette, which Jimmy drove because I'd called him previously and asked him to pick me up. I wanted Jimmy to pick me up, for he could get rid of the weed I brought back; plus, I wanted to pay the money I owed him.

Almost everybody who worked in this business got high on some kind of drug. The bosses who ran the jobs got high, the people in the other parts of the country who worked for our company got high or drank. The supervisors usually just drank, but that's the supervisors at the very top not the foreman who ran jobs; granted, the foreman liked to party too. Everywhere we went, no matter what state, we always found cocaine and marijuana. Usually the laborers we hired got the stuff for us, or one of us would know somebody like Tex in California. In Kentucky, the laborers got us this weed called 'Spider Bud.' If we didn't know anyone, we would dangerously hunt the drugs down from people we didn't know. We used our gut instinct and street smarts never traveling with less than a few. We constantly consumed cases of beer after work also. Sometimes, we'd drive to the next town to get alcohol because we worked in dry towns that didn't sell alcohol.

JIMMY

I came home one weekend and went to a party. The guy I bought cocaine from, Jimmy, was there and was looking for a job. I said to him, "You can come work with me. This company's always hiring."

Jimmy was used to traveling because he used to be a Deadhead. He traveled around to different cities in a van, which he lived out of, watching and listening to The Grateful Dead. Since he was the coke man, I figured if I got him a job, he'd take care of me when I wanted some cocaine, and that was primarily all the time. So, he hopped on board and started to work with us. When Jimmy and I worked on the same job, we usually roomed together in the hotel we stayed in, and we always drank at the hotel bars along with the rest of the work crew. Jimmy and I started to sell premium-crystallized marijuana to the crewmembers.

One job we did was in Kalamazoo, Michigan, and we met these two women in a bar one night. Throughout the entire job in Kalamazoo, Jimmy and I both kept girlfriends. These ladies were hot, rough and tough. The four of us went out, drank in tough, rugged bars, which these two girls took us to, with other rough and tough looking people, and we partied all night long. The two girls lived together in a two-story redbrick house. Jimmy and I lived out of their house, which was small, but kept nice, neat, it looked lived in, and had two bathrooms and three bedrooms, in addition to our hotel room. Christi, a long blonde haired girl in her early thirties with a slender but lustful body was the girl I was with, and she always knew where to get Crystal meth and Xanax. Moreover, Jimmy always brought weed, and he partied with Christi's friend Debby. We'd stay up all night screwing in the bathroom on the sink, on the floor, on the couch or on the beds. At times, Christi and I stayed in my hotel room while Debby and Jimmy stayed at Debby's house. That gave us more privacy

Once, I asked Christi for a couple Xanax, for I was strung out on Crystal meth and wanted to come down, so she threw me a bottle across the brightly lit hotel room. And, there were ninety one milligram Xanax in the bottle. She

51

gave me the whole bottle. Jimmy and I got laid all night and then went to work in the morning after the girls left or we left, if we stayed at their house. Jimmy and I even took days of off work to hangout with Christi and Debby. One time, we blew off work because the Blue Angels' airplanes were in town to put on a show. So, the four of us went out to a green grassy lea, lied down on blankets we'd thrown down and watched the planes do different tricks and acrobatic stunts, and they maneuvered quickly but precisely while smoking a joint and drinking some beers we'd put into a cooler full of ice. After the Kalamazoo job, Jimmy seemed slowed down a bit. It seemed that Jimmy didn't want to work those long sun up to sun down hours doing heavy construction work.

Jimmy didn't work with us too long, only a couple of months after that. All of a sudden he quit. I really couldn't understand that. We were making an extraordinary amount of money, and he just quit. I thought that maybe the job was too physical for him, but he was a strong man. This was a very demanding job and took a toll on one's body, and we needed to be physically fit to work this type of job, but Jimmy didn't need that much more money because he made money by selling drugs. This job just let him get out of town for awhile.

At this time, I was making thirty to forty thousand dollars annually and legally, and I was only twenty years old. I really didn't have any bills, and I didn't pay any rent when I was in Pittsburgh because I'd stay at my parent's house or shack up with a girlfriend for the few days I got to stay home. I spent most of the money on cars, quads and a monster truck, in addition to all the drugs I bought. I saved the rest of the money in a local bank down the street from my house. I put the quads in the bed of the truck, went out to the country with Erik to a guy who lived out of a trailer, went four wheeling and rode the quads. We were so far out in the country, we saw five or six people on horses up on the hill, and other people rode their own quads. My favorite thing to do was go four wheelin'. I had a big black monster truck that was put together with parts of different years and makes of ford trucks, with a 390 engine under the hood and a manual four speed, in addition to the three-inch lift-kit, which heightened the sight of the truck. This truck would go straight up a hill, running over trees, making its own path; moreover, the monster truck could lay tire half way down a street. It needed to be cared for and got to be expensive, so I would buy all the parts, some very expensive, and right them off at tax time. The universal joint that was connected to the back differential always broke because of how high the truck sat off the ground. I needed to keep extra universal joints and a toolbox in the truck just in case it broke. I'd go four wheeling and ride my quads mostly when the wintry weather stopped us from work or when I needed a break from work.

I'd save all the receipts for any part or gas needed for the truck; in addition to the receipts from my car, so when the taxman came every year, I was able to write off work clothes, gasoline, different parts for vehicles and mileage when I used my own car, plane tickets and turnpike tolls. I wrote off all the parts for the truck, and its gas, and mileage. I was actually in a higher tax bracket than my mother. I was twenty years old, and I made more money than my own mother. Since I was hardly ever home, I didn't really see the need to spend money on an apartment. When I did come home, I was usually at a bar, a party or at somebody's house snorting and smoking cocaine all night while getting laid by beautiful women who wanted cocaine and cock. I never got to spend more than three days at home because there was always another job to go do in another state. We were needed to do a job because there were not too many people who worked as well as we did. We knew the business, and we got paid generously for our work.

Mostly all the jobs were federally funded, paying a very high wage. That's how we made a lot of money. We got on federally funded jobs and worked tons of overtime, except in places like San Francisco where we were making twenty-eight dollars an hour. Therefore, they only let us work forty hours a week. In my business, that was like a half of a week of work. Since I had the free time and was in California, I figured why not see California and my old buddy, Tex. So, I rented a car and drove down and got to go see my friend, Tex, in L.A.

The only way to get on high paying jobs was to work all the time and know all the bosses or foremen who oversaw the jobs. This way we'd get inside information as to what jobs were coming up, and how much the jobs paid. Therefore, when we were asked to go on a job, we knew which ones to refuse and which ones to take.

Places like San Francisco or New York are genuinely high living communities with a lot of people and are more likely to pay better working wages, not just New York City, but anywhere in the state of New York. Our crews worked mostly up state when we worked in New York: Montgomery, Cortland, Monticello and down to Ithaca and north of Cornell College over to the east by Batavia, which sits by Niagara Falls. But, we did a few jobs that were close enough to New York City that we just took a fifteen minute drive, and we were in the city. There were times we went to places like Murfreesboro, Arkansas or Texarkana. Actually, all the towns down south didn't pay well, and the population was scarce. I supplemented my income by selling cocaine.

I got the cocaine from Jimmy very cheaply and sold it at a high price to the people at work. All the foremen wanted me to work on their jobs, and naturally I'd hook them up with some coke. One time, I was in the middle of working on something, and the foreman came to me and said, "Hey, don't you got to make a phone call, Anth?"

"No. I don't think so. Do I?"

"Yeah, you do. Lets go for a ride in the truck," he said.

We got in the truck, and he said to me, "Lets snort up a couple of lines. Lay them out, man."

I said, "Sure. I always like to get paid while I snort coke. Here's a nice big fat line for you, but don't forget about that extra overtime on my time card now, you hear?"

It didn't matter how much I made when I sold the cocaine because I got on all the high paying jobs, and that's where I made the real money. I sold cocaine to do mine free. Another guy that worked with us, Charlie Brown, knew a pharmacist in East Liver Pool, Ohio, where he lived, and he always brought different kinds of pills with him, mainly pain pills. He sold narcotics to do his narcotics free. In addition, we made money from the other workers. Charlie and I used to trade cocaine for narcotics. Work had become a drug haven. Especially when we worked in Corpus Christi. Nevertheless, up north, Charlie sold my cocaine in Ohio to his connections, and I sold Charlie's narcotics in Pittsburgh to my connections. When we were off work and back at home in the Pittsburgh area, Charlie Brown and I still traded cocaine for narcotics because Pittsburgh is only an hour to East Liverpool, Ohio. Charlie also knew people south of Cleveland, Ohio, who bought ounces of coke at a time paying with hundreds, fifties and twenties. Charlie and I could have become a huge drug empire with the connections he knew and with the connections I knew.

Back Injury

I was in Corpus once again with a guy called "L," and we had to leave Corpus Christi to stop in Dallas, Texas, to do a job. Before I left this time, I bought ten pounds of marijuana from the same old Mexican weed dealer before we left Corpus; only I told "L" nothing about buying the herb. We got done in Corpus; afterwards, we went up to Denton, Texas. Denton is just north of Dallas. I very much wanted to be in Corpus because South Padre Island Beach was down there, but the supervisor sent me to oversee the job in Denton. The job they wanted us to do was inside, and it was impossible to do the job inside. I called my supervisor back in Pennsylvania and told him, "This job has to be done outside on the job site. It'll be too hard to do inside, and it cannot be done to a level of professional standard."

He said, "My superiors want you to try to make it work."

It was just "L," another guy, Ron and me. Ron was a local laborer who lived in Denton, Texas. I noticed Ron kept cunningly sneaking off around the back of the little brick building and coming back smelling like marijuana. So, I told "L" to ask him if he knew where to get any drugs. "L" told me, "Ron said he got some weed, and his roommate got some pain pills and Xanax."

The three of us tried to do the job inside, but it just wasn't possible. We were in the proximity of a tiny building, trying to do a job that should have been done outside in the open on the job site, where we could have moved the heavy material around easily; instead, we struggled, the work wasn't getting done according to the specifications and we honestly tried, but I knew the workers out in the field would end up fixing what we were supposed to have prefabricated and ready to go into the water treatment tanks. As we tried to move this heavy material around, I accidentally lost my grip on the material and fell backwards painfully landing on my right side. I was in excruciating pain because when I fell, I heard something pop.

I remembered that Ron could get pain pills; thus, I asked him, "Do you mind if we chill out at your apartment for a little while before we head back to Pittsburgh." I didn't want to just ask him for pain pills.

He replied, "No. I don't mind, but my roommate might."

When we got to Ron's run down apartment, there were holes in the couches and a bong that sat next to the ripped up recliner, the coffee table cluttered with junk sat in front of the couch and there was a group of people sitting on four old chairs that were around the kitchen table, and they passed around the two joints that were lit.

I came right out and blatantly said, "Let me hit that joint."

They smoked the weed with us, and I asked Ron, "Who got the pain pills?"

"Let me ask my roommate."

"L" and I waited on the couches and recliner in the living room. My feet were on the dirty coffee table, and I was relaxed. He came back with his roommate, and his roommate sat on the couch and brought a big bottle filled with Percocets and Xanax that were sealed up in plastic, as if they came from the factory, and he asked me, "How many do you want?"

"All of them." As I stood up and said to him calmly and quietly, but in a monotone voice, which sounded as if I was taking all those pills whether he took the money or not.

He said, "I can't give you all of them."

"I want them all!" I said. As I pulled out a very large wad of fifties and twenties, he quickly changed his mind, so I gave him the amount of money he wanted, took the whole bottle of pain pills and all the Xanax, and headed back to Pittsburgh from Dallas.

It was a considerably long ride back home. We left after we stopped at a nice restaurant in Dallas and got some food in us. This restaurant made the best bread and severed it hot, a woman swung on a swing above a man who played a black grand piano. Afterwards, we started the long journey home, and I drove knowing "L" couldn't drive because his driver's license was suspended, and he didn't want to risk getting pulled over, and I wasn't taking a chance with all the drugs in the car. It was a two-day trip by car. I stopped at truck stops and bought pep pills, so I could keep driving through the night. I did 120 mph the whole way home, and the yellow and white lines on the road were a blur. I drove by the St. Louis Arch so fast I barely saw it and said to "L," "There went the St. Louis Arch."

But, he slept in the passenger's seat snoring, farting and burping, and I kept the car's gas pedal floored. I then sped very quickly past a police car that sat on the side of the road, and the policeman either didn't see me, he was asleep or just didn't want to come after me because I was driving so fast, and it was in the middle of the night. I drove from Dallas to Pittsburgh nonstop;

nevertheless, I finally made it home the next day, and I went straight to my house and fell asleep after I popped about five Xanax.

I was home for a week, sold off most off the weed and gave the rest to Gino and asked him to get rid of it and pay me when I got back home. Then, I got a phone call. I got sent back to Corpus Christi for another repair job. They told me Erik was to come with me. Something had gone wrong. "L" put another hole in the material we worked with. He was very inexperienced and didn't really seem to take pride in his work. I saw Jimmy to get some coke before we left. Then, I called my Mexican friend Lionel and told him that Erik and I were coming back down, and I asked, "Can we do the same thing as last time."

"Yeah, we can do it. Call when you get here."

I said, "I'll see you in two days."

I picked up Erik, and we drove to the airport while snorting lines of cocaine. We split an ounce of coke. Erik and I flew back down to Corpus Christi, got a rental car on the company's credit card and went to repair the hole. It was July, and we wanted to see exactly how hot the work surface was. So, we put a regular thermometer on the work surface, and it blew up; however, when we got a digital thermometer, the temperature went up to two hundred and thirty five degrees Fahrenheit. We quickly patched the hole in the material that "L" put in it, and we found another hole as we inspected and looked for other defaults as we normally did. One hole was flat on the ground, and the other was on a sloped hill. The hole on the sloped hill took two people to fix it. Erik held the rope that was tied around me for safety, and I climbed slowly down a rope ladder with my seventy-five pound extruding tool, patched that hole quite easily, and then we went to see Lionel and Juan.

We all met and just sat around a local bar filled with Mexicans and drank tequila while bullshitting and listening to Mexican music and some rock-n-roll. Erik and Juan stayed at the bar while Lionel took me to get more marijuana off of the same older man. Seemingly, we had gotten to know each other pretty well because I wasn't as anxious this time nor was the dealer, and I bought ten pounds for three grand and at least tripled my money when I got back home. As long as I kept working in Corpus, I could make a lot of extra money from the weed I sold, and I sold it very quickly.

After Lionel and I got back, Erik and I went straight to South Padre Island one last time. We hung out on the beach, smoked weed, talked to some women and drank beer until it was time to board our plane. Our stuff was already packed, so we got into the rental car and drove back to the airport. The weed was so compressed it fit right in my carry on suitcase, but I needed room, so I put some of my clothes in a plastic garbage bag. I was on an airplane with ten pounds of marijuana above me in the overhead compartment, and the thought never crossed my mind that I could get arrested. When we arrived in Pittsburgh, we got off the plane, and Erik and I separated because it looked less suspicious being alone. I walked straight out of the airport, and nobody even glanced at me. Erik was nervous and left the airport quickly, but waited for me outside, not far from where we left the car at Pittsburgh's airport.

Even though my back was screwed up, and the doctors told me not to work heavy construction anymore or else my back would get worse, I still continued to work. I loved the job; furthermore, I loved the money, traveling and the connections I made. I lived hard, worked hard, played hard, and didn't seem to have a care in the world.

THE COCAINE BUSINESS

I came home one weekend and went to see Jimmy to buy some coke. I normally would buy an ounce to snort, smoke and sell. By selling some of it, I got to snort and smoke mine for free. Meanwhile, I constantly kept a couple ounces of marijuana in the freezer because I couldn't go a day without smoking some weed.

Instead of going back to work, I hung out with Jimmy and other friends in town. He wasn't traveling to see The Grateful Dead play anymore. I asked him why, and he replied, "I'm making too much money with my friends selling coke; you know most of the guys."

There was Mike Jr., Tony Jr., Frankie and Hassuan. I went to high school with mostly all of them. Tony was always very quiet and the main guy in charge, for his father was in the business; therefore, Tony Jr. grew up around big time cocaine dealers, and he knew how the business ran. He was a short, but also a very husky man. Mike Jr. was a tall guy with black hair, a little more outgoing than Tony and was the second man down the cocaine pole. Equally important, Hassuan was always irritably paranoid because he was the only one who had been arrested before and done time, and he had his own family connections. Jimmy was involved with every one of those guys, and Frankie never really got involved too deeply in selling the coke. His father owned a bar in Swissvale, Amato's, and that's where the cocaine got shipped. Therefore, they kept Frankie out of the coke deals.

Tony, Mike and I graduated high school together, and most of us were never in school anyway. Tony and Mike's fathers used to sell cocaine years ago when they were younger. Their names were Tony and Mike. How ironic, two totally different generations of fathers and sons, with exactly the same names selling the exact same drugs. The fathers both had been incarcerated before; in fact, Tony's father and his partner Paul used to supply a New York mafia family with cocaine through a guy named Henry, who was in an organized crimes syndicate.

Henry had grown up among the Italian crime families; in addition, he'd gotten too deeply involved with criminal activities, grand theft from airplanes that carried untraceable cash money, which flew into New York City's airports from other countries, protection money, racketeering, furs, booze and then, the cocaine took over his life. Hollywood even made a movie about him called, *Goodfellas.* The movie was based on Nicholas Pileggi's novel, *Wise Guys.*

Henry had gone to Lewisburg Federal Penitentiary, which was near the old, dark, abandoned coal mines in the middle of Pennsylvania. He went because he roughed up a guy down in Florida, whose sister worked for the F.B.I. and ratted him out. While Henry was in prison, he got to know a guy, Paul, who got busted selling marijuana in Pittsburgh. Henry quickly started to book numbers, sell narcotics, marijuana, cocaine, hash, amphetamines, and quaaludes in jail. He had his wife sneak the stuff in and had become partners with Paul, but Paul got deeply into debt with Henry owing him $15,000. Henry always had moneymaking schemes worked out between the guys in the jail, the prison guards, and even people on the outside. Supposedly, all the inmates did their time on acid or some other drug that Henry or somebody else sneaked into the jail.

As soon as Henry got out of prison, he immediately flew to Pittsburgh to get the money Paul owed him from his share of the drug deals, but Paul didn't have the money. Instead, he gave him a big suitcase filled with premium Columbian marijuana.

On one of Henry's increasingly frequent trips to Pittsburgh, he met Tony Sr., a local bookmaker, cocaine dealer and a close friend of Paul. Tony Sr. told Henry, "I got a basketball player up in Boston College who'll shave points on some games."

Tony Sr. cultivated this basketball player, Rich, for over a year. He even got his big strong brother Bubba to bribe Rich. Tony Sr. needed Henry because of his Mafioso connections, so he could back Tony Sr. up with money. Tony Sr., Henry and Henry's mob guys placed bets with dozens of bookmakers, and they even let a few of the bookmakers know what was going on, so they could help spread the bets around.

When the game didn't go as planned, Henry, along with a lot of other people wanted to kill Rich because they lost money; instead, Tony Sr. got to Rich again and fixed another game. At this game, Henry and his Mafioso friends sat right behind Rich's parents, and when Rich saw this, he made sure to miss points, and everything worked out fine this time; moreover, everybody made money.

Meanwhile, back in Pittsburgh, Henry told Paul to send him more marijuana, quaaludes, uppers, heroin and cocaine. Eventually, Henry and Tony Sr. had some dealings of their own. A connection together with Henry meant 'you had back up,' and if someone wanted to unload quantities of drugs, it was done quite easily because Henry was a mafia figure. Henry found the cocaine to be very profitable, and he brought some other fellows in to help distribute the drugs.

Anyway, that all happened in the '70s and '80s and set the stage for the Tony Jr., Mike Jr., and Hassuan cocaine circle to profit a great deal of money from the cocaine they sold as young guys who just got out of high school, and they welcomed my friend Jimmy with open arms because Jimmy was a terrifically good seller. He made all of them generously wealthier than they already were, and Jimmy got me into the circle of dealers.

Jimmy took me with him to meet Tony one day. They took me to downtown Pittsburgh to see an attorney they knew and sold coke to. His name was Tom. Jimmy went down to sell Tom some coke and in large quantities, which meant large amounts of cash. Since Jimmy's cocaine business grew so fast, Jimmy wanted me to start supplying Tom with coke. Tom and I talked about my back injury that day, and he mentioned to me that I definitely had a workers' compensation case. As Tom watched how I moved, and even the way I sat down, he could tell that my back hurt me.

Tom selfishly told me, "I can tell your back hurts by the way you're sitting. You know you can have a workers' compensation claim."

Just like an attorney, always looking for a good case, I got in with Tom and filed a petition for workers' compensation. It wasn't long after that we started to go to court hearings. Tom knew I was in with Tony and Jimmy; thus, he asked me for coke or weed every time I went to see him. And, I'd usually give him a nice bag of whatever I had extra. We also smoked pot after the court hearings. Nevertheless, he did give the names of some doctor friends of his and advisably told me, "Go see these people and tell them I sent you."

I proceeded to see these doctors and found out I did have a seriously injured back. In fact, one doctor wanted to operate immediately on me, but I wouldn't dare let anyone cut me open because I could still walk; plus, I asked other people and doctors if an operation was one hundred percent curable, and the doctors said no; furthermore, all the people I knew who had back surgeries said it either made their back condition worsen, or the operation only helped for a short period of time before the pain came back and only a small percentage of the people I asked said their back didn't hurt anymore.

Therefore, I waited and decided to live in pain or until newer technology on back surgery was discovered. I did let them stick me with needles. I took all the medications they gave me, went to physical therapy all the time and a work hardening program. This is when I got hooked on pain pills and other narcotics to extremes. I used to take pills occasionally as I got them on the street, but I never had a doctor prescribe me pain pills in abundance. It wasn't like I hunted them down when I got them on the streets, but when I called my doctor, he called the pills into the pharmacy; indeed, I didn't even pay for them. The insurance company who insured the industry's construction company paid for them.

All I needed to ask was, "Can I get a refill on my prescriptions?" In a matter of hours the prescriptions were phoned into the pharmacy.

The workers' compensation checks started rolling in every other week. I was getting more money collecting workers' compensation than other people who worked regular jobs and all I did was party. I wasn't totally disabled, but disabled enough to stop me from working the heavy construction job I had.

THE CROPS

Meanwhile, Jimmy and I went to Athens, Ohio, where his friend, Tim, grew massive crops of marijuana, in which he used Kinetin to enhance the growth of the plants. We'd take weekend trips to see Tim every once in awhile, usually on acid, mushrooms, and everybody smoked marijuana. On the way to Athens once, Jimmy was driving my gold metallic painted car with red and black pinstripes on an old, dark dirt road that led into the country, and I fell deeply asleep in my hatchback and strangely dreamed we hit a very big deer. I quickly awoke and looked out the front window and yelled, "Watch out for the deer!" When Jimmy abruptly turned around and asked, "What?"

We hit a very old, dark brown ten-point buck. Jimmy apologetically said to me, "I'm sorry, man. I didn't see it. I turned around to see what you said."

As we got out of the car to look, we saw the dead deer lying on the side of the road. The buck's legs were still flopping around. My car was still drivable, so I told Jimmy, "Don't worry about it. It's only a car. I'll get it fixed. My insurance will cover it."

When we got to Jimmy's friend's house. We told Tim.

Tim asked, "Was it a big ten point buck?"

Jimmy asked, "How did you know that?"

He jealously said, "I've been trying to shoot that big old buck all year."

Tim's hair was long, and he was unshaven, just as a hippie from the sixties appeared. Tim lit up a joint, and we all started smoking it. The weed was so good, both Jimmy and I fell rapidly asleep on the old couches before the joint was half gone.

Tim's house or cottage was like an old wooden shack that sat desolate out in the countryside. The house had a big, black wood-burning heater in the middle of the room that heated the whole house and a couple of couches, which sat along the walls and were torn up with holes in them. The kitchen was dirty and barely had any food in it. The wooden stairs creaked as we walked up to the second floor. It was harvest season, and Tim already hung some of the plants upside down from the ceiling with sturdy ropes, which were hooked and tied taut from wall to wall. There were two rooms and five ropes per room. When hung upside down, all the T.H.C. in the plant flows down the long green stem, into the branches of the plant and finally into the green, red and even little white haired buds. We lined the floors of the two big rooms upstairs with old newspapers and that's where we cut up the plants.

The crops that Tim grew were plentiful and great to smoke, with crystallized buds that looked to be fury and the plants omitted such an aroma that the house reeked of a skink smell of marijuana. I thought I've seen it all, but it was the first time I ever really saw a marijuana crop field. This was an incredible sight to see.

The next morning, the three of us went out to the crop field to reap what Tim had sown, and we each took a wheelbarrow. As we walked through the marijuana field, most of the plants were taller than I was and wider than a Christmas tree. Plants were scattered everywhere, and the aroma of marijuana filled the air. We stuck right by Tim's side because he set out booby traps to protect the crops from animals, and any people who would want to steal the plants. Every year, we found tall plants that were broken in half because an animal nibbled at it so much it broke. Other plants were eaten from the bottom, like gophers or groundhogs would eat a plant. We either grabbed the plant by the root or used a shovel; if we couldn't pull the roots of the plants out by hand, we'd dig it out. When the wheelbarrows were full, we wheeled the plants back to the house, and the girls, Amy and Jennifer, helped unload the wheelbarrows, and then they started to hang the plants upside down after they took the plants down that already hung long enough. By hanging upside down, a process in the growth of marijuana takes place; all the T.H.C. flowed out of the plant's roots and into the plant's buds. We made about four or five trips out to the crops bringing back pounds of marijuana in one morning.

With the old newspapers already lying all over the old wooden floors, we threw the plants we took down off of the ropes onto the newspapers, and then we finished helping Amy and Jennifer hang the fresh plants upside down off of the rope. We started carefully trimming the leaves off of the plant's buds with the scissors, which were brand new and just taken out of the plastic wrap, the plants lied on the newspaper covered floor. We cut the leaves off all the buds while Tim's two other girlfriends put the fresh buds in big plastic freezer bags with the zippers. Jimmy and I stuck around for the weekend, helped cut up the weed and partied with friends at local bars and friends' houses. This was a college town and everybody smoked pot, tripped, snorted or smoked cocaine or drank.

Monday morning, after a weekend of partying and cutting up weed, we took the luggage out of the hatchback of my car, the spare tire, a few little grocery bags and a couple extra coolers, the big cooler was empty, but the smaller cooler was filled with some sodas, water and Gatorades covered with ice. We stuck all the weed in the spare tire compartment and some in a suitcase. We threw all the other junk over top and covered the weed up and then we started the drive home. Once again, my hatchback was full of marijuana, but this time I drove carefully home without getting pulled over.

Respect

Jimmy and I started to be known respectfully around town as the guys with the best drugs; indeed, nobody could beat the quality of the cocaine, acid and marijuana and sometimes, Hash-shish and Opium would suddenly pop up from one of us guys. I got a little taste of how easily it was to make money selling coke, so I started to buy quantities of cocaine from Jimmy, mainly ounces and quarter pounds at times. It all depended on if I had the buyers, or clientele, to sell the coke to. I liked to get rid of it right away before I started using the coke because if I started using it, I would lose money. It was hard for me to stop once I got started.

This cocaine sold itself because it was about 90% pure. I made more money dealing than I ever made when I worked heavy construction. In addition, I had money legally coming in from the insurance company of the workers' compensation claim. I got a little bit over five hundred dollars a week, tax-free. Of course, my attorney would take his twenty percent, but I made money off of him by selling him coke and marijuana.

The year was now 1992. Jimmy and I got an apartment together, and I started testing the cocaine for him because he knew if he started to snort the stuff, he wouldn't be able to quit. That's all this apartment was for, to keep and to test the purity of the cocaine. Plus, if we ever needed a place to stay, we stayed in the apartment. A small kitchen, with only a small living area, a bathroom was on the right, half way down the hallway to the bedroom, it was small, but the place was nicely furnished. I kept the test tubes in the back bedroom and the blowtorch too. I would always test it by snorting it and cooking it. Even though I could tell by experience and just the plain sight of quality cocaine was evident to me. I'd lay long lines out on the long black dresser in the bedroom and snort them, cooking the powdered form of a rock of powdered cocaine into a small smoke-able rock, crack cocaine, and I'd smoke the little white rocks in a glass pipe. The taste was like candy, it smelled so sweet, and alluringly tempting, or I'd use a little valve or test tube, which was already set up to use and test the coke in a way that told the exact percentage of pure cocaine. I'd put a little bit of powdered coke in a little breakable valve and break the valve. The bluer it was in the valve, the purer it was. I'm talking 85% to 90% pure. This allowed us to put a lot of cut on it.

We mainly used nisotol to cut coke. Although I rarely put any cut on my coke. Other dealers would use lithacaine, but we really didn't want to use too much lithacaine because it was differently colored than pure cocaine. Lithacaine was primarily a numbing agent to put on the coke, but the cocaine we sold was already numbingly powerful. So, nisotol was the best thing to cut our cocaine with because you couldn't taste it, smell it or tell by color. Triple beam scales, baggies and other necessities needed to break down, cut-up and sell the coke all sat on the dresser

Hassuan always used a re-rock machine to mix and cut- up his coke, so he could make as much money as possible. This machine looked like a big silver press, with round shaped configurations in the middle of it. That enabled him to cut the coke in mass quantities and put it back into its original powdered rock form, as if it appeared to be pure; thus, the people he sold to thought they were getting pure cocaine because it was one big rock. Little did they know it was all cut up. Hassuan was half white and half black with blue eyes. Therefore, he sold to the white people and the black people. Jimmy used to set me up with Hassuan when Jimmy went out of town, so I could keep my business going. I really hated that because I truly knew Hassuan cut his coke too much. But, it never seemed to matter. People bought the coke anyway. They were addicted to this cocaine and would buy it whether it was pure or cut up. Nobody could tell the difference.

Cocaine that is pure is sticky, pearl colored and has a glassy, sparkly look to it, along with an indescribable distinctive smell. I always used the pure coke.

Now, I was pretty much in good with Tony, Mike, Frank, Hassuan and Jimmy. So, I would get inside tips from Tony about college basketball games that his father fixed. And, a couple other guys we hung out with took numbers, so we'd be laying down bets all the time. A couple of times Tony's father was able to get some players to shave points off the Pitt Panthers' basketball games. I advantageously bet a lot of money and won a lot of money. Many bookmakers were around town at that time, and we all knew different people who took numbers, so all the money went to different bookies. Only the guys who were in direct contact with the main big cocaine dealers got in on this. I even told my father to bet on the games, but I don't know if he did.

Jimmy and Tony eventually got a condominium in Carnegie because it was very close to the airport. Fifteen hundred dollars a month rent, but this place was laid out with stretching high ceilings atop the loft. A fireplace glowed and snow fell onto the balcony, which was outside through the two huge glass doors that were in the middle of the glass wall; moreover, two bedrooms, a den, a kitchen, a dining room and bathrooms were behind and to the left of the living room. Upstairs was an enormous room, where a weight bench and weights were set up and then into a large bedroom and finally into a nice big bathroom that was next to a walk in closet. Because of this condo, they didn't have to drive far with a trunk full of cocaine. Tony used to fly to Los Angeles and put the coke on a cargo freight airplane addressed to Amato's bar in Swissvale. He tightly wrapped five to ten Kilos' separately in plastic wrap and then wrapped it in silvery duct tape. He put it in a crate filled with straw and coffee, and put the crate on the plane. This worked very successfully.

Hassuan got his cocaine from his uncle in Pittsburgh, although he never revealed too much information because he knew what the business was like. Hassuan told me once that he met some people who sold good cocaine in Utah, when he was in the Air Force. However, his uncle's stuff came in from New York. People would get busted and snitch on their dealers. Also, there were a few confidential informants who hung around the local bars, but they never got close to our group.

We always got information on which cops were watching us from Mike's dad, who was partners with Tony's dad. We knew who got busted and whom they got their coke from; therefore, the person who got busted was immediately out of the picture, never able to get in contact with any of us. Mike's father would take care of the cops for the information they gave him. Our cocaine business was booming and the demand for the cocaine from our customers grew stronger every month. The shipments started to get bigger and bigger.

It was a very fearfully exciting life to live. Everybody knew who we were, and what we were into; therefore, nobody ever fucked with us, because if they did, they'd get shut off from the cocaine and anything else for that matter. That's the vicious power that came along with the coke business. We had all the cocaine, and everybody wanted cocaine. People would do anything to get coke, especially once they started to snort or smoke the coke; it would take a tremendous amount of will power to stop; however, there's no will power when it came to cocaine addiction. Usually people stopped when they were totally broke and had nothing left to bargain with. Then, they would steal and trade stolen goods for cocaine. Except for the women; without a doubt, they would give their bodies for cocaine, and if we didn't want them, we'd tell them to go fuck or blow someone else whom we owed a favor to. We took care of people who criminally helped us out. We got people all over town to do things for us, give us things and helped us make more money. The money and power actually got to be addictive.

I had two girls who would regularly come over every now and then, Missy and Jill. We grew up together and were friends, but they liked to snort cocaine. So, they would come over to my place looking hot as can be and smelling of desirable fragrances, mini-skirts and real small and so tightly fit t-shirts that the curves of their bodies, breasts and hips showed with temptation, but the clothes never stayed on that long, and we'd casually talk and have sex, or they'd blow me. They normally hung around for a couple of hours and drank a couple beers while we talked, snorted lines, had sex again or sometimes smoked a joint, and then I'd give them a big pearly colored shiny rock of coke in a baggie. The coke was so strong that I smelled the coke while it was in the bag and held ten feet away from me; it smelled like candy. It was pretty much free for me. Missy tended to stop over during the week too; whereas, Jill only came by on Friday and Saturday nights. I never paid for coke because I got it so cheaply and sold it very expensively. Any extra left over was all profit. I could have snorted it, smoked it or sold it out right and made quick cash, or I could have broke it down into smaller weights, sold it slowly and made thousands of dollars. We regularly sold to older people who had money. I never liked to take money off the younger people I knew. But, I only took money off of people I knew that had the money to throw away.

Tony even knew some actors he sold to when they stopped in Pittsburgh. I remember seeing movie stars, a husband and wife, one evening at Donzi's bar on the boardwalk while the sun was setting and reflecting off of the rivers; a Calypso Band played on top of a floating stage on the dirty brown colored Allegheny River, and a beautiful actress sat across the bar from me in nice expensive and elegant evening gown. This was right after I'd seen Tony there. My buddy, Morgan and I saw Tony on our way into Donzi's and just said a quick, "What's up? How ya doing?" And, that was it. Normally, a big black limousine came and went. I saw the actor leave while the actress stayed at the bar and drank a couple drinks until the man who left in the limo quickly returned. He ran down the entrance ramp, grabbed his wife and then they both walked hurriedly towards the limo, hopped in and left.

I knew what was up but kept my mouth shut. One thing about Tony, he didn't like people who talked and asked a lot of questions. Tony would continually say, "Watch that Jimmy" or "You can't be doing that Ant." He was constantly barking orders at people very worrisome; indeed, his black hair was turning gray, and he was only in his twenties.

Tony really liked being in charge and had a lot of power. I hated that. I would think to myself, go fuck off man; who the hell do you think you are. But, I would never say that because Tony would have kicked me out of the business. Tony had the final say! I liked the money, women, coke and power too much. I never really dealt with Tony anyway. I strictly dealt with Jimmy, so I didn't have to listen to Tony that much, except in certain circumstances. Jimmy and I hung out with Tony once in awhile, and sometimes I saw Tony on my own, hanging out at Amato's bar; in addition, if Tony had an ounce or two of blow lying around, he knew I could turn it quickly for him, so I'd seldom take a couple ounces off Tony.

Tony and Mike brought in a couple more people to help get rid of the cocaine because the business grew so much. These were other people our age, and they already sold some kind of drug, usually cocaine, which was terrible in quality and quantity, compared to ours. I never got to know some of the people who were with us, and I really didn't want to know them. That's how it was. Sometimes, neither knowing certain things nor knowing certain people was better. Nevertheless, my certain other crew with the likes of Wayne, who fought in Desert Storm; Nico, who went to the Army; and Glenn, who followed *The Grateful Dead*, and they had their own connections to get good weed and liquid acid, in which no others compare to. However, they couldn't get any better coke than they got from me. Most of the time, I'd trade coke for nice red- and white-haired buds or the best acid in town that was dropped onto a sugar cube or some other kind of piece of candy.

Tony, Mike, Jimmy and the rest of our crew had easier access to cheaper and better quality cocaine than anybody else in Pittsburgh. We gave a better deal than the cocaine user's normal drug connection. Therefore, the users started to buy our cocaine from our dealers. Cocaine was a rich man's high, and the purity of the quality of the cocaine mattered, especially when large quantified deals went down. We ordered for more cocaine to come into Pittsburgh and a couple more guys to help distribute in different areas. Our supply couldn't keep up with the demand, and we all sold mass quantities of cocaine weekly and made tens of thousands of dollars. New, fresh money, it smelled so good.

Now, there was Cookie, Tony's little brother Carmine, Fagnucci, Howie and a friend of ours, Donny. Donny never sold the cocaine. He knew us from school and was Cookie's good friend. So, we used him for other special things that needed done; thus, just knowing Donny meant you knew or were going to find out something about someone, somewhere on the streets. Donny went around town and found out what all the coke dealers who bought coke from us were into, what they did with the coke and whom they sold the coke to. Donny could even tell us what the dealers used to cut their cocaine with. He was like an informant for the cocaine dealers; he kept tabs on people. Donny was really good at befriending people and getting them to talk. I never heard about or even saw Carmine. Because he was Tony's little brother, Carmine remained anonymous, similar to Tony. Most people didn't want to know too much about anything.

Cookie got his own cocaine business going in no time and bought himself a golden metallic 1979 Corvette. Cookie was a small, wiry looking man, but heavily connected. Cookie could get anything anybody wanted, and he did. Cookie's cousin, Vince, was a son of one of the Pittsburgh organized crime syndicate persons.

Cookie's mom and dad were cool. They let us smoke pot in their house while we played cards and listened to Cypress Hill or Sublime on the radio that played throughout the entire house. We'd listen to everything from the Stones rock-n-roll to Ice-T's rapping and even George Clinton and Parliament Funk. It was a usual thing for us to get together at Cookie's house.

We were a bunch of guys in our twenties with everything and anything we wanted and had nothing else to do but play poker with ones, fives and ten dollar bills, sit around, smoke pot, and drink, in between sniffing lines. In the summertime, we'd play cards outside on Cookie's covered and private patio in the backyard that was through the living room and out the sliding glass doors. The in-ground swimming pool, the yard and pool were dimly lit at night, and the distinct aroma of marijuana came from the patio where we sat around a circular table.

We'd invite five or ten women over to go swimming, so they'd come over in just their bathing suits with a robe, a cover-up or a towel and some girls were comfortable with just their g-string bikinis on; nevertheless, they all looked great with nice curvy and busty figures. Most of us played cards and the women swam naked in the pool and relaxed in the hot tub. Sometimes grabbing one of us from the game and into the arms of five or six naked wet women for a quick fuck or blowjob, when that happened it was considered a folded hand. Nobody ever complained.

Certain times, Cookie's dad came out and smoked the weed with us, but he didn't know anything about the cocaine. We also drank different rums, bourbons, tequila, different types of import and domestic beers and whiskey, imported Italian red and white wines, along with fine wines from Napa Valley Winery in California, or we drank practically any alcohol we felt like drinking at the time. Cookie's dad kept a wine collection in a little room in the basement. The room was small, but filled with great imported wines as well as domestic wines, so once in awhile cookies dad let us sample, smell and taste theses wines. The scent on a cork from a bottle of wine was overwhelmingly strong.

I particularly liked the imported Italian red. Cookie's dad showed us how to test the quality of the wine by swirling it in our glass first, then watching for the film to slide slowly down the inner-side of the glass. Secondly, we took a little drink of the wine; however, we didn't swallow the wine, we held our heads down and sucked air through our mouths with the wine up in front of our teeth by our lips. Third, if we got light headed, it was considered good wine. Lastly, we gurgled the wine and finally swallowed it or spit the wine out.

THE CIRCLE

Everybody came to us to get their cocaine, and to Jimmy and me for their marijuana and narcotics. If Jimmy needed narcotics, I hooked him up with as much as he wanted, at a reasonably low profit, but he'd usually just knock the money off of what I owed for the cocaine. Everybody I hung around with was generously giving when it came to drugs because they knew that if they didn't have any drugs one day or night, somebody else would be giving and take care of him or her. The drugs were multitudinous. We took care of the bar owners who never said anything when we sold coke in their bars because the people who did the coke would stay up all night and spend money in the bars that we supplied. Furthermore, if the people bought weed off of us instead of coke, they'd get the munchies after burning a joint in the parking lot and buy food from the bars. We took care of the bartenders also; in exchange, we ate and drank free.

Cookie, Paul, Fagnucci and I were like secondary men, and sometimes we didn't like going into bars all the time. We took the cocaine off the four main guys who dealt with kilos, snorted and smoked abundances of coke after we sold it to people under us, who in turn sold it to the people under them, usually the street junkies or the high class functional cokeheads, which we saw much more of because cocaine was very expensive and attracted the rich people more than the poor.

In addition to the couple of close contacts, who took quantity off of me, there were two local bars I supplied: first, Hoffimanto's Bar in Monroeville, through a guy we called "Bird" who lived right next door to the bar. Bird would keep the coke in a hole in the ground cut up and put into smaller weighed out Baggies, and he'd run back and forth, from the bar to the hole in the ground near to his house. Secondly, Tuggies the bar everybody called Druggies because of the high volume of drugs that were distributed in Druggies, a bar right down the street from my apartment. I knew one of the bartenders, Mickey and Gino were known in Tuggies, and even my dad, Carlo, knew the owner and everybody who worked there. Dealing with the cocaine and seeing the same faces, and some new ones every now and then got to be a business, with money coming in every week and money going out every week; it was a business.

Bobby was my buddy, through Mickey, and Bobby lived in the same apartment complex as I did, only on the top floor, so it was easy to transfer the coke to him, and I knew where he was to get the money when he sold the coke for me in the bar while he bartended. The bigger deals between Tony, Mike, Jimmy, Cookie, Hassuan, Paul and me would take place in parking lots, our unknown about apartments or any inconspicuous place where there weren't any people, valuables or property to lose.

At this point, the money was flowing in on a weekly basis. I really didn't care anymore about the little bit of money I made when I sold marijuana. The cocaine was the money. It was like having gold. The glassy look of the cocaine, the way it sparkled, yet felt slippery, but sticky, alluringly and with an appeal to people.

TRADES

People who owned businesses like automobile rental agencies or very small car dealerships and even service stations gave us deals on car repair, wrote up falsified evidence for insurance claims, and they'd do that because the cocaine addiction had gotten control over the particular person, and we took the money or detailed trades in exchange for cocaine. Jewelry stores gave us great deals on gold chains, bracelets and even some very expensive diamonds we'd get for our girlfriends or ourselves. I mean, two thousand dollar bracelets for women could be traded for a half-ounce or an ounce of cocaine. If I knew somebody who worked in a jewelry store and was hooked on cocaine, I could give the person a quarter or a half-ounce, something that cost me one or two hundred dollars, in exchange for a piece of jewelry that was worth one thousand dollars. The deals we got all depended on how addicted the store owners were to the cocaine.

My one friend, Nico the Army guy who got caught trying to send acid home from Germany, worked the night-shift at a mini-mart gas station, and I would go in at two or three o'clock in the morning. We'd go in the office and close the door over a bit, so when a patron came in Nico could fly out and wait on him or her. After I laid out about ten nice lines by chopping them up with a sharp razorblade, I snorted three or four of them and left the rest for Nico, and I'd get free gas; moreover, he'd give me shopping bags and told me to take whatever I wanted off the shelves; it was free food. I never even thought about working anymore. People, who use cocaine heavily and on a regular basis, offered us anything from fine jewelry to food stamps.

Hassuan and Mike opened up a car detail shop in North Braddock to launder the money. There was hardly ever a car in this place or any equipment, and when there was, it was one of our cars. On a busy day, we'd all have our cars vacuumed and washed. The wax was optional. There were two very large black rottweilers chained up outside, so if anyone came around, they got scared and left. I even hated to go there because of those dogs. Eventually, Mike got a dump truck and a pick up, along with tools for landscaping and opened a landscaping company. Mike got patrons quickly because he was well known and people just wanted to patronize him out of respect.

Jimmy and Tony also had another house down the street from the Penn Hills police station. They kept all the money and cocaine there sometimes. The coke was hidden in the dryer, and the money was upstairs stacked along the walls. I remember the first time I saw all the money stacked along the walls. It didn't even look like money at first, until I took a closer look. I couldn't believe my eyes. Twenties, fifties and hundred dollar bills were stacked along two walls half way up to the ceiling. There was even a safe up there filled with money and cocaine. It was an amazing sight to see. Things like this were usually kept secret, and only Tony, Mike, Jimmy and Hassuan knew about it. But, one day I went to pay Jimmy the money I owed him at this Penn Hills house. There was Jimmy, Tony and a man and woman who stayed in the house. I didn't know them. Jimmy nonchalantly brought me upstairs with him, and Tony said to Jimmy as we walked up the steps, "You better watch that Jimmy!"

He was paranoid Tony didn't like too many people to know about stuff like money, deals, where things were kept or who's involved. When we got upstairs, I told Jimmy when I handed him the money, "Wow! There's a lot of money up here."

He quietly, but blatantly replied, "Don't say anything, Shark. This money is from selling coke, and it buys the coke too. You never saw any of this. Got me?"

I cunningly said, "You don't need my money if you guys got all this money do you?"

Jimmy still took my money and gave me more cocaine. We got into a little argument over this. I didn't want to disrespect him, but I told him, "I got you a job and took care of you when you needed money. You started your coke business with the money I helped you get."

"What do you mean?" he said, as if he forgot our past.

"Remember the construction job I got you a long time ago?"

"Oh yeah. I forgot about that, but what's that got to do with anything?"

"You told me once that you were able to start your cocaine business with the money you made when you worked with me. Can't you give me a break once in a while?" I said.

Jimmy acted as if his mind was on too many things, and it probably was. He said, "Here, you can have this coke for the price I got it for. I won't make any money on you this time."

I said, "Thanks, man. I really appreciate it. I'll see you next week."

Jimmy, Tony, Mike and Hassuan changed the places where they kept the coke and money. The coke was once kept in a car storage facility along with the money in the back of an old Chevy pickup truck, which was covered with a tarp. Things like that had to be changed regularly.

Jimmy and I would see each other every week or two, so we could do our deals. That's how quickly people bought cocaine. It was getting to be a regular job.

I started to use even more cocaine; in fact, I started to get the coke fronted to me because I couldn't come up with the money to buy it outright. Jimmy trustingly gave me the coke. I would sell it, and then give Jimmy his money and get another batch of cocaine fronted to me.

My old friend Erik, who I worked with in the past, snorted and smoked all my coke with me as we went to different bars and shot pool, drank and played darts. We'd party and pick up women. Erik even sold some of the coke for me; in fact, he introduced me to Bird, but I told Erik, "We can't keep doing all this cocaine man 'cause I'm losing too much money."

Although Jimmy was the kind of guy who let me slide once in a while because I usually brought him lots of money which made his business bigger, I called him one time and hesitantly said, "Jimmy, can you stop over?"

"I'll be over around three or four. Okay?"

"Yeah. I'll see you then."

"Hey man, I fucked up and did all the coke."

He unpleasantly replied, "Shark, why did you do that, man?"

I told him, "I was with Erik, and we started to smoke it and couldn't quit."

He said, "Fuck, I needed that money Anth. This shit's not free."

"It'll never happen again. I'm sorry, man."

"All right this time, but if you do it again, don't even bother calling me."

So, I made certain that never happened again. Jimmy was pissed off.

Erik and I did Crystal Meth one time by eating it on bread because our sinuses were so full of coke that we couldn't fit anymore up our noses. We ate the Crystal Meth. Sometimes, I used to use Tavist-D decongestant pills to clear my sinuses; therefore, I would still be able to snort more coke or crank.

Crystal Meth is also called "Crank" on the streets because it cranks people up and wires them out for days. When I snorted it, the burning sensation felt like I was snorting glass. It burned my nose so badly, but just a little bit kept me up for days, and it was very cheap; thus, I only needed to do a line or two.

So, I started to snort crank with Erik, instead of using the coke I sold. Erik and I snorted crank and would stay up for days going from one bar to the next shooting pool and drinking while I got rid of some blow and made some cash. And, when the bars closed, we stayed up and built things like sound systems for our cars or other people's cars and charge them, or we painted our houses. Sometimes, we'd get women to come party with us and screw all night; we would then go to a bar that opened at seven o'clock in the morning.

I said to Erik, "This is crazy, man. It's seven o'clock in the morning and were still drinking."

Erik laughed and replied, "We're drinking orange juice with our vodka. That's a breakfast drink."

We'd shoot some pool and drink a few screwdrivers until people we knew who worked got up early at eight or nine, and then we'd go see them, either to collect money or to get some kind of narcotics or get rid of some. Wayne started to buy the crank too because he used to do it. He said to me, "In the Marines before we went to war, mostly all the marines snorted Crystal Meth. We would stay up all night drinking, and at five a.m. we went on our five mile run."

Wayne seemed to like the people I got involved with, I showed my brother-in-law what I was into, and he couldn't believe the quality of the cocaine. "Big John" we called him because his name was John, and he was six feet seven inches tall. He was an undefeated boxer in the Army and fought in the Vietnam War. He was ranked a sergeant. Big John was a man who radiated some dangerous force.

One time, I gave John some acid, and it was very good liquid acid that my friend Glenn and I dropped on the candy, "Wacky Wafers." In turn, John gave the wacky wafer to an old army buddy, Weasel. Weasel lived through the 1960s and took acid his whole life. He told John, "Man! That was the best fucking acid I've ever took."

Our crew had all the gilt-edged drugs. Not just the cocaine, but also all pills, weed and acid or magic mushrooms.

Big John was known fearfully around the whole east side of Pittsburgh. I saw a guy come after him with a very large baseball bat, and John took the bat off the guy and beat the shit out of him at a bar in Lawrenceville. He held the bat in his left hand and threw one punch at this guy's forehead, and the guy flew against the wall and didn't seem like he was able to get up, as he bounced off a wall and hit the floor. Then John threw the bat aside and stood the guy up straight and punched him once more; thus, the guy got lifted off his feet and slammed into the dirty wall behind him before he hit the floor again and never got up. John never fought dirty, but other people had to fight him dirty if they wanted a chance to beat him. John's a stand up guy; however, if someone would try to get over on John, he would turn fiercely mean. John could take on two or three guys at once, and if they pulled a weapon out, John took the weapon and threw it aside as he started throwing punches.

"L," the guy I drove home from Denton, Texas, with, asked me to front him an ounce of coke once. I never sold coke to "L" before; however, he seemed like he wouldn't rip me off and would pay me the money, but he did ripped me off. I did the guy a favor, and he took advantage of me. So, I did what I had to do to get Jimmy's and my money. I called Big John up and asked for a favor, "There's a guy right by you. Would you go get my money off this motherfucker? He ripped me off. He owes fourteen hundred dollars."

"What's his name, and where's he live or where do I find him?"

"They call him 'L,' and he lives right across route thirty from you and hangs in the bars out that way."

John asked, "How much do I get?"

"If you put that nervy bastard in the hospital and get my money, I'll split it with you," I told him. "That's $700."

John said, "I got to ask around and find him first. Give me a couple days."

"Make sure you say my name before you fuck him up. Make sure man! I want him to know I wasn't going to be ripped off. I got another guy out this way who sells for me."

It took John a few days to track him down; however, he knew a majority of the people out there where he lived, and he found "L" quite easily.

As soon as John found "L," he brutally beat the shit out of him. Within days, John collected my money and gave it to me. I never reneged on any deal, so I gave John half of the money. "Seven hundred for finding someone, beating them up and collecting money. You can't beat that," I said.

Big John quickly started to work for me selling cocaine; furthermore, he was my muscle. He lived in the country and was tied in with the Pagans motorcycle gang, and nobody ever fucked with them. John started supplying the Pagans with cocaine, and they loved it. I sold the pure coke to John, and he sold it to his Pagan friends pure. John never did cocaine. Once the Pagan's got a taste of the coke, my business got extremely larger. As a result, I started to get larger quantities of cocaine off Jimmy. When Tony, Mike, Hassuan and Jimmy found out I supplied the Pagans, they wanted me to get closer to them because I'd come up with thousands of dollars a week. This made me practically one of the top guys, and I got in their circle, but I really showed no interest. I didn't want Tony and Mike and Hassuan to know whom I dealt with, and, frankly, I didn't want to know anything about them. The less I knew the safer I was.

All the bigger dealers who I was in with were trustworthy and loyal to one another, but it was the small time dealers under us, and people who addictively used the cocaine who we watched out for because they got into using the cocaine themselves way too much, instead of selling it like they were supposed to. This screwed up the money flow.

Eventually, I got my cousin, Joey, to sell coke for me in Bloomfield where he lived. Bloomfield was just like the little Italy of Pittsburgh. Joey knew all the older Italians. The people in Bloomfield never did cocaine as pure as this. They were used to the bunk cut up coke. Therefore, I'd throw a little nisotol on the coke and broke the big rocks into littler rocks, and Joey sold it to his connections in Bloomfield. I'd get bundles of heroin and boxes of cigarettes from Joey's connections cheaply or by the trade way, and Joey got rid of the stuff that he or I didn't keep for us. Joey never asked, but I took care of him. This way I made more money. As long as Joey was happy and got his drugs, he sold the coke and heroin for me. Joey knew everybody around Bloomfield and Lawrenceville and what everybody did; therefore, he got rid of a lot of coke for me. I consolidated and enlarged my business through my family members like Joey, and his little brother Anthony, who I gave a piece of the action to as well, for Anthony knew all the younger people in that particular area. Nevertheless, they dealt with their customers; therefore, they needed to collect the money from their customers.

Once before, I had sat Joey and Anthony down and talked. I told them, "I can get great coke, and if you two want to make a little extra cash, because you're family, I'll give it to you on the front, but I want my money weekly, so think about it. I don't like to fuck with little weight, think big, but take a close guess as to how much you can get rid of and let me know in a few days, but if I don't get my money in one week, you're shut off! Give me the money, and I'll front you another bag."

Anthony cut in, "Man, if it's that bomb shit we did the other night, I could get rid of at least an ounce or two a week. "

Joey was always nervous and protective when he dealt with cocaine and told me, "Be careful, man. You got to watch yourself down here, Anth. People rip other people off, especially drug dealers."

I said, "You're the one who should be careful then. You make all the deals.

I just front you the blow because I know you won't jag me off and not pay the money."

Joey would make me cook-up the coke into the rock form, crack cocaine; thus, it sold very quickly and easily. He was a nagging pain at times, who wouldn't ever shut up, but nobody worked the streets the way Joey worked them. Moreover, he always got boxes of cigarettes cheaply and monthly, and I took the cigarettes out to the suburbs and sold them to people in bars for twenty bucks a carton; to be sure, the first one of my dealers who came to see me, I had told him I picked up some cartons of cigarettes if he wanted any, and he must have told somebody because I started to get phone calls for cigarettes. I usually took care of Joey by giving him three cartons, and he'd unload them for two bucks a pack or twenty bucks a carton. I just liked the deal on the cigarettes, for they were way less expensive than buying them in the store.

Between Joey and Anthony, I figured I now cover all of Bloomfield and all of Lawrenceville. However, now many people relied on me to supply them with cocaine. I even brought coke to Hilton Head when I went on vacations, and my friend Jeff sold it for me down there. Everywhere I went, even when I worked construction on the road; I tried to go on vacations and get away from the sales of drugs because it all started to drive me crazy and run my life, but I sold drugs and it was a job, and people are the same basically anywhere when it comes down to doing drugs; naturally, everybody who did drugs liked the best drugs, and that's what our little mob was known for, having the best quality of drugs; hence, that's what brought the customer back.

I had my own little regime; my life was becoming a world of drugs, money, attorneys, guns and women. My life was amuck and seemingly was too much to handle, so I turned to the narcotics, herb and drinking.

VACATION

It was 1993, and I'd gotten back in touch with my old band mate and close friend, Jay. As I still dealt marijuana with his older brother Gino, Gino told me, "Don't get Jay involved with any of that shit."

I agreed with Gino because we both knew that cocaine meant bad news; surely, Gino never even got involved. He looked out for his family and knew how dangerous the streets can be. Jay was a little younger than I was and involved with decent paying and locally famous rock bands, in addition to being a member of the Pittsburgh Jazz union. Jay wanted to somehow be successful in a music career. Moreover, he did it. I knew I was into bad news; therefore, I never would bring Jay into this business. He was my closest friend, just like a brother.

One time, out of the blue, I asked Jay, "Do you want to go on vacation?" He answered, "I can't afford to go on vacation."

I nicely replied, "Don't worry about it. I'm paying. We'll rent a car to drive down. I know a guy who'll give me a very good deal on a rental car.

"Pat and his sister live in Hilton Head, and we can stay with them."

Jay said happily with a broad smile, "My brother Dante Cat lives in Fort Lauderdale, and we can stay with him. And, Joe lives on Key Cujo, so everywhere we go we got a place to stay."

We got in the car and left for vacation only paying for weed, gas, food, alcohol and other luxuries. Vacationing became a usual thing for Jay and I to go on adventurous trips down the east coast. Everywhere we went people were getting stoned, drunk and using cocaine.

We'd go down there twice a year, once in May and once in September. This gave us a prolonged summer. We'd go down in the beginning of May when it was already hot in Florida, then, in late September, when it was colder in Pittsburgh. One of our trips was to Paradise Island in the Bahamas. We went there on a cruise ship.

Jay thought I still had money saved from when I worked construction; however, he didn't know I sold coke. My driver's license was suspended, but

I didn't care. I made this trip so many times I didn't even need a map. Jay and I rolled about forty joints before we left and put them in my cigarette packs. When I went on vacation, I never brought any cocaine with me for personal use because I wanted to get away from it, and I didn't want Jay to get into coke. When we got to Hilton Head, I dropped an ounce of blow off to Jeff, and then on the way back from the Keys, I'd pick up my money. After hanging with Jeff, we went to Pat's place usually unannounced, Patrick was always stunned to see us, and the first words out of his mouth were, "Anth, did you bring some of that good crystallized bud with you?"

"What do you think?" I affirmatively said. "When have you ever known me not to have weed?"

"Sit down and fire up a joint. Do you guys need a place to stay?"

We quickly replied, "Yeah. That'd be cool."

Patrick was a heavy drinker because his dad was a cop, and he didn't want to get involved with hard drugs. Jay and I told Pat our vacation plans for the Bahamas while we smoked a joint and drank some beers. We stayed in Hilton Head for a day or two, and then we left for Fort Lauderdale. Pat asked us, "Are you guys going to stop back here on your way home?"

I replied, "We'll be back."

We stayed in Hilton Head for a few days, and one day we got up real early in the morning and took off for Fort Lauderdale to see Jay's brother. Jay called and made sure his brother was there because Dante Cat still played in a band. His band played in Southern Florida and the Florida Keys. Dante regularly played in a bar/hotel on Key Islamorada, one of our regular stops on the way to the Key Cujo to see Joe. Jay and I stayed at his brother's house in Fort Lauderdale and got a good home cooked meal. We visited with Dante and M.J, Dante's wife, and hung out at the beach. We would normally smoke some weed and play music while at Dante's. M.J. was a stewardess, and she wasn't home much of the time.

I always brought my guitar with me because it was fun to play at Dante's and at Joe's, and sometimes we'd sit in with his band. But, at his house we sat around, smoked a couple joints and played acoustical music, or Dante showed us nice beaches to go to in Ft. Lauderdale; in addition, he showed us great strip clubs; one was a place where women or men would do anything asked for money. Also, Dante took us to a local bar in Pompano Beach that was a Pittsburgh bar. Everything in the bar was Pittsburgh Steelers, Pirates or Penguins, and everything was colored in all black and gold.

We briefly stayed with Dante, and he drove us to the cruise ship so I could leave my car at his house. He warned us to be very careful in the Bahamas just like an older brother would. "Don't talk to anyone you don't know and don't venture off too far from the hotel."

Jay and I boarded the massive cruise ship and instantly met two women from Chicago. We hung out with these women on the cruise over to the Bahamas. We talked, drank, danced and just had an alluringly good time. To cruise there took six or seven hours. We tried to get lucky with the girls, but it was extremely hard. It was clearly impossible, for there were people everywhere on the ship. We even got them separated and alone. Jay stayed with one girl, and I went with the other; nevertheless, every room on the ship was filled with people. Otherwise, we may have gotten lucky. So, I asked them, "Do you girls smoke weed."

They replied, "Sometimes we do."

I asked, "Is now sometimes?" They both looked at each other with a silly grin on their faces and said, "Sure, why not?"

We all went to the top of the ship, where lounge chairs were laid out for sunbathing and smoked a joint. At this point, Jay and I really didn't care about the few people up on the sun deck. We were already pretty drunk from the rumrunners we drank, and the one girl nervously said, "What about those people over there."

I gave a witty replied, "What about them? They're not getting any of my pot."

We laughed and finished the joint. We all admiringly watched dolphins racing along the ship as they kept bobbing in and out of the crystal clear blue waters of the Caribbean. They were right next to us keeping up with this huge cruise ship. We went to the all you can eat buffet on board the ship for dinner; indeed, the food was delicious and very plentiful. When the ship docked in Paradise Island, we nicely said to the girls, "This was fun, and it was very nice meeting you. It's always nice to meet and talk to friendly people."

Jay and I were staying in the Bahamas, but the women only went for the cruise and then went back to Florida. In fact, they never even got off the ship.

Jay and I got off the ship, and there was a car waiting to take us to our hotel. We got sent through a small building, showed our passports and preceded to the car that waited for us. I immediately noticed the steering wheel was on the right side of the car.

I drunkenly said to Jay, "Looks like we're in England, man. Where's the steering wheel?"

Jay and I laughed hysterically, for we'd just smoked a joint before we got off the ship, and we were really stoned and drunk.

We arrived at the hotel about six o'clock in the evening, and the first thing we did was jump in this gigantic swimming pool with a swim-up bar. So, I swam up to the bar and got a beer. They made their own beer in the Bahamas called Kalick, and it was potently stronger than any domestic beer I've ever drunk. Jay usually took it easy on the booze and drugs; on the other hand, I drank and used drugs to extremes. At the end of the night, Jay played volleyball in the pool with other people who stayed in the hotel, and I passed out on the edge of the pool. Consequently, Jay told a young kid, "You see that guy asleep over there? Go push him in the pool."

He did, and I agitatedly awoke when I hit the water, but it felt very refreshing. Shortly after that, I went up to our room and quickly fell fast asleep.

In the morning when we woke up, we ate the free continental breakfast, then we got on a boat to go snorkeling and headed out to sea as we drank dark spiced rum and danced to the reggae and Calypso music that played out of two large speakers that were on board. Jay got a little sea sick, but I remained calm and serene, for I took a couple of Valium before we left. When we got out to the snorkeling spot, we put on our fins, masks, and goggles. It wasn't even noon and I was already stoned and drunk and was the first one to jump in the water. Jay hesitantly took his time because he had never been out in the vast depths of the ocean before. He was used to the beaches. The snorkeling guides instructed people on how to snorkel. Meanwhile, it was seemingly self-explanatory to me.

Eventually, Jay finally came into the water along with everybody else on the boat, and we snorkeled most of the day. We saw a lot of stingray and a couple of little brightly colored fish. It wasn't very exciting; nevertheless, just to be in the deep crystal clear warm water was a thrill. The little boat took us to an island after we got done snorkeling where there was a lay out of food and alcohol. I continually drank, and I ate a little bit of food. After we took a walk along the beach and smoked a joint, we lounged back on the beach with a bunch of palm trees behind us, and we subtly looked at the blue and green-changing colors of the water and the horizon that was far beyond. It must have been over a hundred degrees as the sweat dripped like water off my forehead. It was the middle of August, and the sun was blazing hot. We'd jump in the water every so often, and one time Jay came out with a starfish. We admiringly looked and touched it and then got a lady to take a picture while Jay held it. Another guy came out with a little two or three foot baby shark.

As Jay and I lounged around, Jay said, "It's wonderful down here."
I replied brightly, "Yeah, it's beautiful. Do you know what's even nicer?"
"No, what could be nicer than this?"
"I'm getting paid right now for lying on a beach drinking margaritas and smoking marijuana in the Bahamas," I told him with a devilish grin.

I collected workers' compensation still, and the money went right to my parents' house. So, if I ever needed money while on vacation, I simply called my mother, and she Western Unioned me as much money as I told her to. Seemingly, life was great as we sat under a palm tree, a joint in one hand and a frozen margarita in the other.

When I saw that little shark the guy caught, it gave me an idea. I asked Jay, "Do you want to go swimming with the sharks?"

He said, "What! Are you serious?"

"Yeah, I'm serious. Let's do it."

Since Jay was an adventurous person, he dared to try new and different things and agreed to go. We got back to the hotel and made reservations to swim with sharks, but we couldn't go until the next day. You had to wear scuba gear and be certified, and we weren't certified. Hence, they gave classes on scuba diving, and Jay and I got certified. The classes were taught in one of the very deep swimming pools and lasted about two hours. After we got certified, we made the reservations for the next day.

There was a hotel bar and restaurant, and a calypso band played right in the lobby next to the bar of the hotel we stayed in with local Bahamian players. I started to drink Long Island iced teas at the bar. That was one of my favorite drinks, and I was used to drinking them; in fact, I asked the bartender, "If I can drink six of these, will you give them to me for free?"

He said, "There's no way you can drink six of these. If you can, you can have them on me."

The bartender agreed to my deal and kept the drinks coming. Jay and I sat and talked with the bartender for a little while, and Jay drank frozen rumrunners. Then, Jay went over to the band and asked if he could sit in for a song, and they let him. After my third Long Island iced tea, I felt the alcohol hit me when I stood up from the bar to watch Jay play with this calypso band. When he was done I walked up to the bartender and told him, "You won, man. I can't drink anymore."

I was stumbling and mumbling, as I paid for the drinks and left a nice tip. Jay and I hung around the hotel the rest of the day, and lay out by the pool, where I fell into a drug-induced sleep on a lounge chair. When I awoke a couple hours later, we drank, smoked pot, played tennis and lounged around ogling the gorgeous women in thong bikinis.

We got on another boat the next morning after I popped some Valium. This time I drank rumrunners on the boat, and Jay didn't drink anything because he didn't want to get sick again. I offered him a Valium, but he didn't want it. When we got to the scuba site, we were hesitant to jump in the water. There were sharks in there.

I said, "You go first."

"You wanted to do this, and you brought me out here. You're going first."

"Okay," I said and jumped into the shark-infested sea.

I was calmed from the Valium I took before we left the hotel, and the rumrunners I drank on the boat kicked the Valium in even stronger. There were also professionals in the water; therefore, I felt safe. The professional scuba divers put out some bait, and the sharks suddenly started to come around. Jay and I paired up because they told us it was safer to be with another person. They also told us the sharks were reef sharks, but I thought I'd saw a couple white tip sharks also. I looked all around me at the clear blue water filled with a frenzy of sharks. The sharks were so close I could have reached out and touched one. My heart was pounding rapidly as we got back on the boat, but I brought a lot of Valium with me. So, I popped a couple more of them and had some more drinks, and I became even more calmed on the way back to the hotel while I laid sprawled out on the bow of the boat. Back at the hotel we both decided to stay on land for a while. From that day on, everyone started to call me "Shark."

We also enjoyed the water slides that were at the hotel, and the declivity of the one slide was almost straight down. The swimming pools at the hotel were actually three very large pools in one as they were connected to one another, and there were beautifully tanned women everywhere we looked. The hotel also had hot tubs, spas and racquetball courts, and an underwater aquarium. We walked through a tube-like structure made out of very thick glass and saw all different kinds of fish, sharks and stingrays. Without a doubt, we saw more fish in the aquarium than we did when we went snorkeling.

I wasn't going to dare try to bring weed back through U.S. customs, so I left a little bag in my car at Dante's for the ride home to Pittsburgh. I carried legal prescription bottles for the pain pills and Valium I brought; therefore, I didn't worry about them when I went through customs. I took a lot of weed with me, and we needed to smoke it before we got back to the United States, so we smoked an incredible amount of marijuana. The cruise home was very relaxing as we smoked up the rest of the weed I had on me. And then, a few hours later, we caught sight of the Florida coastline as the sun had just started to set; that reddish glow from the sunset along the coastal land looked astonishing. Dante Cat picked us up and took us back to his house where my car was.

Jay needed to be back in Pittsburgh because he had a gig to play the next day. So, we got in the car at nine o'clock at night and headed home. I tried to drive through the night but pulled over to get some sleep when we hit Hilton Head. I tried to sleep for a little bit; nevertheless, I couldn't fall asleep, so I started to drive again. I needed to fly off of route 95 and go into Hilton Head to pick up my money from Jeff. He sold the whole ounce of coke in a week. Jay took a turn behind the wheel, but I was used to long quiet drives from the job I had when I traveled and worked construction; therefore, I continued to drive with my eyes half shut. I did veer off the road at times, but never actually fell asleep. Except one time, I must have dosed off for a second because the car was in the center of the dividing highways when I suddenly awoke and quickly swerved all the way across the one highway we were supposed to be on and veered off to the other grass area on the other side of the road before I got the car under control and started to drive straight again.

I made it all the way up to the high peaks of the Appalachian Mountains of West Virginia, and once again I got pulled over by a State Trooper. I thought for sure I was going to get busted, for my license was suspended, and I had a little marijuana left in a bag with some Valium in it also. The police officer came to the window and calmly asked, "License and registration please?"

I didn't utter a word. I just handed him my registration and insurance card and prayed he let me go. I could see him in my rear view mirror with an officer in training. She stood in back of the car and listened and learned, as the other officer said, "Can I have your permission to search your car? Do you know your license is suspended?"

"Yes, I know, sir. Do you have a warrant to search my car?" I replied.

"No, but I can take you in for driving with a suspended license and search the car there if you'd like."

In an instant I told him, "Sure, you can search my car."

I knew I didn't have enough drugs in there for him to arrest me. There was a little bit of marijuana in a bag with a couple of Valium in my counsel. There was more weed in my pocket, but I knew the law. They had to search my car before they could search me. So, he searched my car and found the little bit of weed and a couple of Valium, and asked me, "Do you always keep your Valium with your marijuana?"

I replied, "Yes, sir. Normally."

I pleaded with him and said, "Jay drove all night sir. I was just giving him a break because we need to be in Pittsburgh for work in a few hours."

He told Jay, "You're going to have to drive the rest of the way, son."

The cop took the little bag and never even searched me. Since I wasn't driving anymore until we made it to Pennsylvania, I rolled up the last couple of joints I stashed in my pants pocket and smoked them up. We made it home just in time for Jay's gig.

Back to Business

As soon as I got home and turned my pager on it went nuts with phone numbers of people trying to get in touch with me. Everyone was out of coke and needed more. I was only gone for ten days, and everybody sold all the coke I'd given them. I went to see Jimmy in a heartbeat because I ran out of money on the vacation; however, I paid him some of the money I owed him with what Jeff gave me, but I owed more than that; thus, all I needed to do was get the coke and sell it. Jimmy trusted me. Then, I took care of John and the people who worked in the bars for me. I only fronted cocaine to a couple of trusting people, for I knew they were good for the money. Some people were into the money, and others were into the cocaine high and usually did the coke themselves. Those were the people I knew not to front coke to.

I wasn't home for three or four hours and brought in over four thousand dollars. I then called Bird because he kept on paging me and told him I was on my way up. There were certain people I didn't let come to my place for personal reasons. If the person I sold to did the cocaine and didn't sell that much, they weren't coming to my place, and I didn't even want them to know where I lived.

Tony, Mike, Jimmy and Hassuan brought the coke in and broke it down into ounces. They only talked to each other when they needed to, for fear of being associated or connected to one another. Nobody wanted to be revealed. All four dealers dealt with each of the men under them privately and separately. All had to be alert.

Some of the time Jimmy and I met, we'd go out to eat at a classy restaurant, and we got the most expensive dishes on the menu. Sometimes, we even got a bottle of hundred-dollar Champagne. But, mostly all the deals went so smoothly and quickly we'd just pull up next to each other in our cars and I'd throw the wad of money into his window and he'd throw the cocaine in my window, and we both took off never having to check if the money was right or if the coke was all there because we trusted one another.

We always talked in code over the telephone. There were different names for the coke. We called it: white, milo, toot, more, flake and cane. We also used encoded numbers on our pagers: 911-meant emergency, 123 were my numbers and when people saw it on their pagers, they knew it was me. All of the main guys had their own numbers. We only saw and talked to each other when the money and cocaine switched hands. We strictly used cell phones, pagers and pay phones. Somebody could leave a series of numbers on my pager, and I'd know exactly who it was, and what they wanted, but Jimmy and I worked it differently.

I would tell Jimmy in person when we met, "I'm going to need a quarter pound next time we see each other."

Then, he told me, "Put your number in first, and all odd numbers up to nine when you page me, and I'll put the time in your pager, and we'll meet in the parking lot of the grocery store down the street from your house."

It constantly changed every time we met. There were different numbers, and different places. We didn't even need to talk to each other. The time and place was already set. We already discussed the quantity and price. This way, if anybody watched us, they wouldn't have a clue about what went down or where. Nobody could decipher our encoded messages.

Eventually, the insurance company watched me and took pictures of me. I collected workers' compensation for over five years. One day in court, I mentioned that I did a little bit of musical work for a band, but I didn't get paid; thus, they caught onto me and pictures were taken in Morgantown, West Virginia, and at Point State Park in Pittsburgh.

I started to get a little bit paranoid, no, a lot paranoid. Plus, I smoked and snorted a hell of a lot of cocaine, which brought the paranoia on greater.

None of us had regular jobs because we made so much money from dealing. I usually hung out with Donny and Cookie, and we'd go to see every movie the day the movies came out. We usually had a meal at a nice restaurant first. We never really did cocaine together because that looked bad. A cocaine dealer had a saying: "Don't get high on your own supply."

So, when I hung with other dealers in the circle, we'd go to movies, play tennis, play cards or monopoly at someone's house, hang out in bars shooting pool, drank a lot of alcohol and smoked a lot of pot. I learned how to play a little con on the poker machines. I'd get a ten dollar bill, put a piece of scotch tape on it, then slide it into the poker machine while holding onto the piece of tape. When the money registered, I'd pull the ten-dollar bill back out of the machine. I could sit and do this all night long.

I was a very early morning person and got up with the sun. I got up at six or seven o'clock in the morning and would be half drunk on alcohol and pain pills before noon. I would then walk up to one of the local taverns called The Plaza Bar, or I went right next door to my parents' house at the V.F.W. But, that place didn't open until two o'clock in the afternoon.

I took more and more pain pills and enjoyed the glorious endorphin rush I got from the opiates in the pain pills, and I started to get drunk more often also. My life started to get really tedious because I didn't work, and I dealt with the same people week after week and did the same things all the time. So, I looked up my old friend Jay again, and we planned another vacation.

THE ISLANDS OF AMERICA

Jay called up Joe, our old bass player who's now a music teacher at Key West elementary school in the Florida Keys, and Jay asked him, "Me and the Shark are heading down to Dante Cat's house in Fort Lauderdale, and we wanted to come see you."

Joe replied very happily, "Sure! When you coming?"

Joe was always in a good mood and seemed to be happy all the time. He never took any drugs, and when he drank, it was only socially.

Jay told him, "We'll call you when we get to Dante's house."

Within the next week we were gone on vacation again, only this time headed to the Florida Keys. I loved the tropical places, the 80 degrees, the wildlife, the palm trees and the ocean of the Florida Keys. We got to Jay's brother's house, called Joe, and said that we'd be down tomorrow because Dante Cat had a gig that night in Key Islamorada, and we wanted to go see his band play. There was a hotel right next to the nightclub Dante's band played at, and Jay and I stayed there on a regular basis; it was a very nice tropical getaway.

Every time we went to the Keys to see Joe, we'd stay in this hotel at least for a night or two. This place was the wildest nightclub in the Keys. At about ten or eleven at night, the nightclub hopped and crawled with good-looking broads. Most of the time we'd get two girls in our hotel room, one in Jay's bed and one in mine. This place had deep bluish-green lagoons, wind surfing, scuba diving, and volleyball and palm trees. The main drink they served down there was called "Pain in the Ass." It was a combination of frozen rumrunners and pina-coladas. We used to drink them so fast while lying on the lounge chairs like they were ice water. They also had a nice little hometown restaurant that was out front of the hotel by the road, and Jay and I usually grabbed breakfast before we went across the Keys to Joe's house.

This vacation we smoked many joints and listened to Bob Marley and the Wailers and other Reggae music on the way down to Joe's. As we drove across all the long, narrow bridges that carried us over the top of the ocean beneath us and connected all the little islands, we admiringly looked at all the water which totally surrounded us, and we were in awe of the sight of the seven mile bridge that spanned out and over the water and seemingly took forever to drive across. We actually couldn't see any land on either side of us, in front or in back of us; on the other hand, we saw only the miles and miles of deep ocean beneath us and the long bridge ahead that we needed to cross.

We got to Joe's a couple hours later, and since we all hadn't seen each other in a while, it was a joyous reunion for the three of us since we experienced so many wild times as younger kids who played in a band. Joe's house was beautiful, and it sat by a water inlet that led to his backyard, where the blue and white jet skis and green and pink kayaks were kept. The first thing we did before we even unpacked the car was Jay and I smoked a joint, and then we jumped into the dark warm water behind Joe's house.

Joe told us, "Watch out for the barracudas. They have really sharp teeth."

I asked nervously, "Are there barracudas in here?"

"There ain't any barracudas in here, are there?" Jay asked.

Joe said, "Yeah, there are barracudas around all the Keys." After we smoked another joint, we got his jet skis down from a winch that they were hooked to and grabbed the kneeboard he kept in his garage, along with the other water sport equipment he had in there. I drove one Jet Ski and pulled Joe on the kneeboard while Jay drove the other Jet Ski, and we rode quickly out to another little uninhabited island with white sand and palm trees all around that only the locals knew about in the Florida Keys.

Joe told me to follow the green signs that stuck up out of the water. Those will take us to the island.

I told Joe, "Hang on, man. I'm good at driving these things." And, he hung on with no problem, as he was very good at knee boarding.

When we got to this tiny island, Joe said, "That's how I get around down here. I drive the jet ski from island to island to see my friends."

Jay followed nearly behind. There weren't any people on the island. Everyone was probably home because it was kind of late on a week day, but it was a local hang out for the people that lived down there. We drove the jet skis right up to the sand, hopped off and checked out the island first. Then, we knee boarded for hours and rode Joe's very quick jet skis over the really warm crystal clear blue water that was so calm it looked like glass. We went back to Joe's house to a meal his wife cooked. She was also a music teacher in the same school as Joe.

The next morning I rented a big snorkeling boat, and we all went out to a very popular reef called Lou Key. It is known to be one of the nicest snorkeling locations in the United States. The waters were calm that particular day, and the weather was a balmy ninety degrees. The reef went from one foot deep at the top peak down to eight feet, and then twelve feet, then twenty feet, then, it quickly dropped off and went all the way down to two hundred feet deep. And, it sat only forty-eight miles from Cuba.

We weren't allowed to touch the reef because that's the law in Florida. The National Wildlife Association protects all the reefs in the Florida Keys. We were the only ones out there for about an hour until this scuba diving boat full of tourists with scuba gear arrived. I drove the boat because I knew how and had experience. When we got out there, Joe jumped in the two hundred feet deep water and hooked a strong, sturdy rope from our boat to another rope that was attached to a buoy that floated on top of the water. This kept the boat in tact so it couldn't float away because we couldn't drop anchor on the reef.

Joe got back on the boat to put his snorkeling gear on, and Jay already had his stuff on, so I put mine on very quickly, and we all jumped in the water. It was a feeling of weightlessness and wonder, yet thrillingly scary to float around in the two hundred feet deep ocean. The water took us where it wanted to take us, so it was better to just float with the life jackets and go with the flow of the water instead of trying to fight it and swim. We floated on the surface with our faces looking down into the water, held hands as the trio band we were and breathed out of our snorkels. We saw an abundance of several species of differently colored fish.

I said to Jay and Joe, "Let's dive down deeper and see what's down there." Without a word from either of them, we dove down and explored the oceans growth and different species of fish. But, we could only hold our breaths for so long.

Eventually, the three of us headed back to Joe's house, and we ate the dinner that his wife made us. When Joe and his wife worked in the day, Jay and I ate at a local restaurant right by Joe's house, this restaurant was a small place, and it wasn't expensive like the fancy tourist restaurants, but they served very good food. They usually served the catch of the day, and the breaded orange roughy tasted wonderfully delicious after we smoked a joint.

We decided to go scuba diving the next day. Joe called and rented the scuba gear using my credit card. It wasn't even that expensive because Joe ordered it, and he's a local. Businesses down there take care of the local, friendly people.

This time when we headed out to Lou Key, the ocean was very rough like something you'd see in a movie with swells nine or ten feet high. As we drove out, we hit really big swells of water, and the water came gushing over the bow of the boat and scared the shit out of us. So, we turned around and went back in closer to land. We sat and smoked a joint while rocking back and forth and waited for the swells to calm down, but they weren't going down that much. We decided to give it another try and went back out. The swells of the powerful water still came over the bow of the boat; however, this time we bravely decided to keep going because we had scuba gear with oxygen tanks, Joe drove the boat and we figured if anything happened, we could put the scuba gear on and remain safely alive in the water.

Joe said, "This boat will make it out there. I've seen it rougher."

One time, Joe even drove his jet ski out to the reef. At Lou Key, we saw schools of fish: stingrays, eel heads popped out of the reef further down in the deep water; also, dolphins were all around and jellyfish surrounded us from above. When we got done scuba diving we wanted to go check out Key West. On the way down to Key West, we smoked a couple joints between Jay and me and went to a nice big raw bar with a deck that spanned right out over the water. As I looked at the menu, I saw a shrimp dinner for nineteen dollars and ninety-five cents. I asked the waitress, "How many shrimp do I get for this nineteen dollar dinner?"

She replied kindly with a nice friendly smile on her face, "You get four shrimp with that, sir."

"What? Did you say four shrimp?" I hurriedly asked.

"They are very large shrimp," she said.

I hesitated, took a sip of my drink and told her, "I have to see these nineteen dollar shrimp."

These were the largest shrimp I've ever seen, and they even brought me a steak knife to cut the already butterflied shrimp. Jay had linguini with white clam sauce, and even the size of the clams was humongous. Joe just ate at the raw bar and drank a few beers from the pitcher we ordered.

We left the raw bar and restaurant and went over to Duvall Street; that was the main street everyone hung out on, and it was lined up with different bars, souvenir shops and the loud lively night clubs where the bands played. We got really drunk from the beer we drank and the frozen drinks we drank, and yet Joe showed us the sights, one being the southern most spot in the United States. Then, we headed over to a big brick wall where people gathered, in which everybody could stand on and watch a gorgeous sunset. There were many people here, mainly tourists.

As we walked back along Duvall Street, we came across an old black man down at the end of the street who stood on the corner and played the acoustic guitar while he sang songs, and people circled around him and listened. We watched admirably, for we ourselves all loved to play music and listen to music. We stood there for probably an hour, and the guy asked us to sing back up on a song for him, and we did. He told us what to sing, and we stood behind him and sang backup. We sang the lyrics, "Day'o, ~ Day'o, Daylight Come an' me wan' go home."

Key West was a very weird place with a lot of gay people, so we mainly kept to ourselves and walked the streets. As we walked by a nightclub, we heard a wild funk band playing that was from New York, so we went in to listen and bullshit about the old days over tropical drinks. I saw the back of a really big fat biker when I walked to the bar to get a couple more drinks, and when he turned around, he had make up all over his face. I hurried back to the table after I got us some drinks and told Jay and Joe, "Hey! Look at that big fat biker with the jean jacket on. He got make up on his face."

Joe told us, "That's mostly what you'll see down in Key West all the time. Everybody's gay there." I drink at a local bar by my house. It's really a cool little bar, a cheap place to drink and play darts or shoot pool."

I said, "We should go there tomorrow night after we play some music."

Jay agreed, and we left the nightclub we were in after about three drinks apiece. I really wanted to smoke a joint and so did Jay. So, I fired up a joint I had previously rolled as we drunkenly walked down a brightly lit street from all the shops and bars, and we smoked the joint while hiding it in our cupped hands. When we were finished with the joint, we ran right into these two girls. The one came running right up to us and said, "Hi, Jay. Do you remember who I am?"

Jay looked puzzled trying to figure out who she was and suddenly had an insight and said, "Julie."

"Yes. What are you doing down here?" she said.

Jay replied with a big smile on his face, "I'm here visiting Joe. What are you doing here?"

She answered, "I live down here now and have been for four years."

She asked if we wanted to come back to her apartment, and we said sure. The girl she was with was one of the prettiest girls I've ever seen. She was 5' 6" with blue eyes, blonde hair and a perfectly curved body. We hung out with them the rest of the night and partied. Jay got a phone number, and his old girlfriend told us to call her tomorrow while Joe was at work. She knew of a beach we could go to.

First thing in the morning Jay called her, and we picked her and her girlfriend up and went to a desolate beach where there weren't any other people anywhere. This beach sat next to a navy base, and nobody was allowed on it. They took off their clothes as soon as we walked on the beach, and Jay and I did the same. We laid out in the hot sun tanning naked for a majority of the day, and every once in a while we jumped into the water to cool off. Julie and Jay started to kiss and make out, and Tammy and I watched curiously. Watching them made us really horny, so we also started to make out right on the beach, in the middle of the day with the hot sun beating down on us and not a soul in sight.

I gazed into Tammy's azure eyes as I caressed the fullness of her breasts. She started to stroke me tenderly as she spread her legs open, so I could see her blonde triangular bush in between her legs. I rubbed and sucked on her hardening nipples while I worked my hands down in between her legs, I started to play with her wetting clit in a soft, but hard circular motion. I looked over at Jay and Julie to see Jay on top pounding away. As I was already rock hard, Tammy got up, spread her legs over me in a straddled position and started to ride me with her back arched as I gently played with her very large nipples. She started to moan; likewise, Julie also moaned in pleasure as Jay continually pounded away until I heard them both getting off. Tammy was like a wild woman on top of me as she rode away until she slowed down in pleasure, and then I flipped her over and stuck it in her grasping wet lips as she hung on with her legs and contracted her muscles around my cock as I got off with a loud moan, and then we all laid there on the secluded beach naked in a sexually relieved state.

About two thirty, we told the girls we were going scuba diving and had to leave. So, we dropped the girls off and started to go back to Joe's house. Joe nicely gave us a key to his house, so we could come and go as we pleased. On the way back, Jay and I hardly said a word to each other; however, we both had broad smiles on our faces and occasionally laughed outrageously in unbelief at our sexual exploits.

We got to Joe's house, went in and watched television until Joe got home from work about a half an hour later. The three of us stood in the garage as Jay and I burned a joint. We told Joe about our day, and Joe started to laugh uncontrollably as we laughed too, and then we went to get the scuba gear and proceeded out to the reef. We'd bought a case of beer the day before and loaded up a cooler with ice and beer. I popped a couple Valium and pain pills before we headed back out to Lou Key. The water had little swells about four or five feet high. Joe drove the boat, and I lit up another joint as I laid spread out on the front of the boat trying to get a very dark tan. Jay sat on the seats that were along the sides of the boat and admired the sights of the ocean. After I lit the joint, both Jay and I went back to the driver's area with Joe, and we continued to smoke the joint until we got to the reef.

Joe said, "Somebody has to go into the water and hook the boat to the buoy."

Jay and I looked at each other, and I knew he wasn't going to go in. So, I jumped boldly alone into the two hundred feet deep ocean with the rope that was hooked to the boat, and I tried to hook the rope that was attached to the boat to the buoy, but it didn't work and the rope got pulled out of my hand. I felt afraid of what lurked beneath me because I didn't have on my goggles. I even got more wary as I floated on the top of the water and watched the boat get further away. So, I stayed right by the buoy and waited. Joe drove the boat back towards me. When the boat got close to me, I grabbed the rope and quickly hooked it to the buoy and got back on the boat to put my scuba gear on, and we all jumped into the water and went down into the depths of the ocean. This time we saw the deeper part of the coral reef with all the sea life that grew on it, and we saw many different fish.

Later, we went back to Joe's place and decided to go to the local bar Joe told us about. It was an average little tavern that sat back on the tropical island. We drove down a dark, lonely dirt road to get there as we smoked a joint. When we pulled up to this little wooden shack of a bar, I said, "This is my kind of place. It seemed every place we went to was my kind of place."

There was a pool table, dartboard and a jukebox inside. Surprisingly, the bar was packed with people. We drank bottles of beer, played pool and threw darts. It felt like I was at home. We stayed with Joe on Key Cujo for a week and a half and then headed back up the long road with the miles and miles of bridges in the Florida Keys. I decided I wanted to stop in Miami for a couple nights, and Jay wanted to too. We got there sometime around midnight, and we went straight to South Beach. We tried to get a room, but everywhere we tried, we couldn't find a place to stay. All the hotels were booked solid. We saw that the nightclubs were all packed with people who seemed rich in their elegant and sexy clothes. So, I said to Jay, "Fuck it. You want to go check out some bars, and then we'll crash on the beach?"

"Lets go. Which bar do you want to hit first?"

"Mangos. Man, it looks wild in there."

All the bars hopped, and had long lines of waiting people. There were exquisitely good-looking people everywhere dressed in elegant and sexy clothes. Mangos had Latino women dancing on the bar and a live Latin band that played all night long. We saw Jamaicans, Puerto Ricans, Germans, Columbians and any other nationality we thought of. After standing in line for awhile, we got into Mangos and stayed in Mangos and partied all night. It was three-thirty in the morning, and the bar kept getting more crowded and crowded. I was beat and asked Jay if he was ready to go. Jay was ready, for we had an extremely long day, nevertheless, a wonderful day. When we got outside, there were people everywhere on the street still trying to get in all the nightclubs. Jay and I went on the beach, which was right across the street from all the bars and hotels. I lit up a joint that was already pre-rolled, and we smoked it while listening to the sounds of the waves that crashed onto the beach. We fell asleep right away.

The next morning the sun rose and awoke us. I was very hung over from all the drinks. We hardly got any sleep. Maybe two or three hours, so I said to Jay, "Man, I feel like shit."

"Me too. Lets just stay here on the beach for a while."

"That's a plan to me," I complacently replied.

It was beautiful to watch the sun rise over the extensively clear blue water. We just lay back serenely, and I said to Jay. "Look over there. That girl doesn't have her bikini top on, and her thong is going right up her ass crack. She's practically naked."

Jay ogled and said, "Lets stay here the rest of the day."

I said. "Lets smoke a joint first."

"All right," he said without hesitation.

We sat right in the same place where we woke up and smoked the joint. People started to come onto the beach early in the morning, but we continued to finish the joint. As we walked down the beach, Jay said stunningly, "Look, there's another girl without her top on, and she's laying on her back."

"You know what, man. I think women are allowed to sunbathe in Miami without tops on. This is like a free titty bar."

We stayed on the beach most of the day with our sunglasses on and discreetly checked out all the women. Beautiful looking women were everywhere: at the hotel pools, on the boardwalk and at the beach. All we saw were tanned tits and ass. Life couldn't have been better. I laid back on the beach and watched topless women walking by.

Later, we went to The Hard Rock Café and Planet Hollywood to get shirts and hats to bring back to our families as souvenirs. We ate lunch at the famous restaurant Joe's Stone Crab and then started the long ride back to Pittsburgh.

Ripped Off

Before I went on vacation, I hooked my sellers up with a sufficient amount of cocaine, but when I got home, there was a problem. One of my dealers, Bird, owed me fourteen hundred dollars, and he flew away as a bird would, and when I tried to get a hold of him, he was nowhere to be found. I knew he had ripped me off.

Bird sold a lot of coke for me, and I did give him some leeway at times when he didn't come up with all the money, but this time he could have jeopardized my business. Consequently, I didn't have enough money to pay Jimmy. I was short one thousand dollars because I spent so much money on vacation. This called for drastic measures, and I did what I needed to do. I called Big John.

I asked, "Can you meet me somewhere right now? I got a problem I need taken care of."

"Where and when?"

"The Giant Eagle parking lot down the street from the usual place as soon as you can get there."

We usually met in the daytime in the parking lot of a bar on route 30 that was closed, but this time things were different. I got to the Giant Eagle parking lot very early and anxiously waited. Finally, he showed up, and I told him, "Someone stiffed me for fourteen hundred dollars again."

"What? Come on, man. Someone owes you? Do you want me to get it or what?"

"Yeah, but you don't know him. His name is Rick, but he's known to be called Bird. Come over to my apartment early tomorrow morning, and we'll have coffee and try to concoct something."

John showed up expeditiously the next morning, and we planned out how we were going to get Bird.

"What if they call the cops?" he asked.

"They won't because his wife is wanted. There's a warrant out for her arrest. If they call the cops, his wife goes to jail."

"You can keep four hundred and give me the thousand if you do me a favor and go get the money," I said with a sardonic smile. "I want him roughed up too."

"When do you want to do this?"

"Now," I told him. "I owe my man and counted on this fuck head to have my money. Now I'm short a grand."

John and I went and sat off by the woods near Bird's house and waited to see him. Soon after, I saw Bird come out of the woods that led to another road right next to his house. It looked like he was being extremely cautious moving quickly but quietly. I told John, "There's that long haired prick."

John jumped out of the car and ran over to Bird and grabbed him by his throat as Bird tried to run away, picked him up and said, "You owe Shark money. You got two days to pay him, or I'll come back." He roughed him up a little bit and ran back to the car, and we got the hell out of there.

Bird called me up the very next day and told me to come get the money. And, I did, but I said to him, "I let you slide too many times, man, and I ain't giving you any more coke. Don't even bother to call. It's over between you and me."

Without saying another word I just turned around and walked out the door. I was really pissed because he used to bring me a lot of money.

He gave me fourteen hundred dollars, which was more than enough to pay Jimmy, and I gave John his four hundred, as I said I would. I lost a good customer, but that's how it had to be. There could be no question of treachery because if I came up short too many times, I'd lose my privileges with Jimmy.

When I told Jimmy what happened, he said, "You did the right thing by cutting Bird off. If you let one person get over on you, everybody will think they can get over on you. Let me know when shit like that happens. I'll help you out, Shark." We laughed because we really didn't lose that much money ever, even if we did get stiffed once in awhile.

I still sold cocaine to my cousin in Bloomfield, John still supplied the Pagans, the bartender, who worked in Tuggies, sold to the people who came into the bar, and my old friend who I worked with, Erik, was a regular customer. These guys were standup men who couldn't resist monetary profit. We weren't petty criminals. We were white collared criminals. We were "Drug dealers."

We never sold to school kids; instead, we sold to grown adults who had jobs and lots of extra money to spend. The cocaine business we were into was organized, controlled, and we made sure no trouble came out of it. But, that didn't mean trouble wasn't around.

A guy named Schretti and I had a beef with each other over a hundred dollars. He was a good friend with Jimmy who snorted coke all the time and took boxing lessons. He was about six feet tall with a slim build from doing too much cocaine. I owed him one hundred dollars because I accidentally spilled his coke on the floor at a party at Pat's house. A pile of coke sat right next to me, and when I snorted the line, my elbow hit the pile of coke, and it spilled all over the rug.

He told me, "That cost me a hundred dollars."

I apologize to him, but he was really mad.

"You're paying for that. That's a hundred bucks. Now, my night's ruined. You better leave a hundred dollars in my mailbox tomorrow. I won't be there when you come."

I should have known better, but I left the hundred in the mailbox; however, Schretti said the money was not there, and that I never put it there. He tried to pull a scheme over on me; thus, he kept grousing to me. I knew he got the money, but he was trying to get another hundred out of me. A hundred dollars wasn't much money; it was the principal of the matter. I even told him I'd give him the coke he lost. When I went to Jimmy and told him what happened, he wanted no part of it because Jimmy was a good friend with both Schretti and me, and he knew Schretti was out of control. Nevertheless, Schretti kept trying to get the money off me, but I avoided him constantly, until one day after a long college football game I pulled up right behind a car that Schretti was in. He sat in the back seat. When he looked back and recognized me, he jumped out of the car and got in the passenger's seat of my car before I had a chance to lock the doors. He told me at gunpoint to follow that car, and I did. I knew all the other people in the car, so I thought I would be all right, but when we got to Fagnucci's house, Schretti asked, "Do you got my money?"

"No! I told you. I put it in your mailbox like you asked me to do."

I could tell he wanted to beat the shit out of me; nevertheless, I played it really cool and tried to get out of the situation, but I couldn't manage to get away. Then, he sucker punched me. I didn't have much of a chance, so I picked up a big brick after I got back up from the sucker punch, and I slammed him in the head with it. But, he kept coming after me as blood trickled down his forehead. I took a really bad beating.

I figured I had people beaten up, so I took the beating like a man and gave Schretti a little bag of coke that kept him off my back. I knew that's what he wanted anyway. He played a con game on me. But, what I didn't know until weeks later, Tony and Jimmy set the whole thing up. They wanted to see what I would do, and how I would react.

I hurt from the fight, and I ran out of pain pills, so it was time to call the doctor again. He hesitantly gave me another prescription and told me, "I can't keep giving you all these narcotics. I don't want to risk losing my license nor my practice, but I'll give you one more month supply. And that's it."

PRESCRIPTION DRUGS

Once the doctor took me off the pain pills, I started to go to East Liverpool, Ohio, to see Charlie Brown more often and cheaply acquire pain pills from him mainly from trading cocaine, but I paid cash at times also. Big John and I drove over there every other week and picked up two or three hundred pills that were still in the long sealed pharmaceutical strips. I usually took all of my pills. I never sold them because I had so much money coming in from the coke deals. I found other doctors in Pittsburgh and pretty much conned them to prescribe me pain pills. I did have a legitimate reason for taking medications because my back was terribly injured. I even got established with two doctors down in Hilton Head, and one doctor in Fort Lauderdale. So, when I went down there on vacations, I already had doctors set up to treat me. I'd use my friend, and my Hilton Head cocaine dealer, Jeff's, address. This way the doctors thought I lived there.

The one doctor treated me for anxiety and depression, and he gave me Xanax to calm my nerves and referred me to a surgeon for my back problem. He was an older gentleman with white hair, and he seemed to have back problems of his own as he walked with a limp. A surgeon checked me out and ordered an M.R.I. because she saw my back was injured; thus, she gave me a prescription for pain pills because she saw the magnitude of my back injuries. She once told me I could become a paraplegic if I got into a bad accident or got hit the wrong way. She was a middle-aged woman who kindly and carefully took care of me. She could only prescribe me ninety extra strength vicodins a month by law. I paid twelve hundred dollars for the M.R.I., in addition to the seventy-five dollar office visits. But every month, I got my ninety pain pills.

Also, I got into fraudulent check cashing and eventually got caught at a store right down the street from my house. I got two years probation for that and a very large fine. Plus, I had to pay the lawyer's fee. Yet, with the money I had coming in at the time from dealing, I was able to pay the fine off. And, I paid my attorney with cocaine.

I noticed my father as he more attentively noticed me changing visibly in a way he never envisioned me to be. My father and I drank together, and I'd hang out over at the V.F.W. with him and his friends at times. It appeared I lived in three different states. I had two different apartments in Pittsburgh and still kept a room at my parents' house. Everything was getting so insanely out of control. I snorted more coke than I sold, and people constantly called or stopped over at my apartments.

My mother said to me, "You're so skinny. What have you been doing?"

"Nothing much, Ma. My back's been killing me."

Meanwhile I did crystal meth, tripped, and smoked marijuana from the time I got up until the time I went to sleep. People called me day and night, and if I weren't at one of my apartments, they'd call or stop at my parents' house. My father grew very suspicious. He may not have done drugs, but my father knew the street life, and he knew I was involved in something, but didn't know what. If I stayed with my parents, I got many phone calls usually late at night or even in the middle of the night. In the daytime, there were people who stopped by in Cadillacs, corvettes, nice trucks, and regular cars. There were just too many people hounding me for drugs, mainly cocaine. I now knew what the meaning of trafficking drugs was.

MONEY

So, I got out of my parents' house and went back to one of my apartments. Every one of us made so much money and the blow sold so quickly that Tony, Mike and Hassuan needed to get bigger quantities of coke, so that the demand was met.

Meanwhile, my attorney and I got ready for the final court hearing of my workers compensation claim. I made a lot of money from him when I sold him coke and weed. And, if I ever needed a couple hundred or so, I'd ask Tom, and he'd give it to me because he knew I was going to collect on the work comp claim, or I would pay him off with cocaine or marijuana.

I received seventy-five thousand dollars minus the twenty percent my attorney took. I was very grateful for what Tom did for me. However, within the next two years my money supply ran low, so I had Tom reopen the workers' comp claim. Once we went to court, the insurance checks started to come in the mail again.

I immediately bought a new car and went on another vacation. I was able to pay off Jimmy and buy outright a half of a kilo of cocaine, and I went to see Gino, Jay's older brother in which I still dealt marijuana with for all these years. I saw Mickey at Gino's place many times. I knew their family my whole life, and I usually owed Gino money because he treated me like family and just gave me weed; however, I'd brought him four thousand dollars in one hundred dollar bills. He lived right across the street from my parent's house, so my dad saw me over there at times and knew what I was doing because he knew what Gino did. Meanwhile, my father begun to notice the expensive guitars, the nice cars, the big trucks, the gold chains and jewelry I bought. He wasn't stupid. He'd see me coming in at five in the morning when he left for work. My dad also slyly saw me pull out big wads of cash when we sat in the V.F.W. and drank.

All my dad's friends knew me and watched me grow up. One smoked marijuana with me and bought pounds of marijuana off of me. I'm sure he told my father about the dealings. His name was Dominic, and he owned a big business and sold it for over a million dollars. He bought a place in Key West, in addition to his home in Pittsburgh. He also bought a Winnebago, and we met behind the V.F.W. to make the exchanges before he went on trips in his Winnebago. He always traveled to Alaska or Key West as he towed his new fishing boat with the Winnebago. Because of him, I made four hundred dollars in fifteen minutes. But, that didn't happen too many times because he had his own connections, but he liked the quality of the weed I sold him.

Mickey was another one of Jay's brothers, and he was three years older than I was. We dealt with marijuana on many occasions, and we knew a lot of the same people. Although Mickey never liked cocaine, he was into weed. I'd get two pounds of marijuana a week from Mickey and sold it to Aaron, who in-turn sold it to the people who went to Edinboro University as he went to school there too. That's five hundred dollars a week profit for me in one day of work. Meanwhile, I hung with Jay, Mickey and Wayne most of the time. We were all the best of friends, and we'd always go to rock concerts together.

All throughout my teenage years and my twenties, my friends and I would go to rock concerts. I saw every famously known band anyone could imagine. One time, Donny and I even went to Cleveland to see the Rolling Stones, and that was the third time I saw them play. They constantly put on a great show. Every concert I went to I usually took a couple hits of acid, a handful of differently colored pills and drank them down with a beer or some whiskey. The alcohol kicked in the pills, which kicked in the L.S.D.

Mickey once said to me, " Man, Shark, you take enough drugs to knock out or kill a normal person."

Mickey never got into cocaine or pills that often; he just liked to smoke pot and always kept a hidden stash, and Gino normally kept us supplied with weed. Eventually, Gino's crew got busted, but Gino wasn't at that particular deal the night the bust went down, but he lost the two hundred and fifty thousand dollars he put in to buy the weed; as a result, marijuana wasn't as plentiful as it once was; still, Gino knew tons of people and had many connections, so he hooked up with other dealers and just dealt on a smaller scale; moreover, he even grew some of his own buds, and they always turned out to be very good buds. We always rolled a bunch of joints up before we left for a concert so they were ready to smoke.

The Allman Brothers Band was my favorite. I can't even remember how many times I saw the Allman Brothers Band. At one of their shows, I either took too many pills or drank too many beers because I passed out right on the cold wet grassy field of the Star Lake Amphitheater. My friends woke me up at the end of the show to go home.

The best shows were Pink Floyd or The Grateful Dead. When I took acid and saw these bands, it was like I was in a totally different isolated state of mind, in a world of my own, unattached from the rest of the world.

Before one concert, everybody met at my parents' house because my parents weren't home, we swam in our in-ground pool and I bought a keg of beer, so we could all party before the show. About a dozen people showed up. Mike was there with a whole bunch of coke, and people smoked joint after joint while others snorted lines in the bathroom. I did a little bit of everything. We ordered a limo to drive us to the show because we had money to throw away. The whole way there in the back of the limo, which had a stocked bar, we snorted about a half ounce of blow between seven of us and drank the booze that was in the limo. When we got to the show, everybody had different seats, so we split up. But, it didn't matter to me because it was the sounds that fueled my brain and body.

Jay and I would go to rock concerts in some of the different cities we traveled to. After one of my vacations, I went to check on my cousin Joey in Bloomfield, who was a good man, but wasn't right in the head. Although he never liked to participate in the selling of drugs, he still had many different connections all throughout Bloomfield. He had gotten back in touch with the friend he knew who sold cigarettes that he'd stolen. Since Joey knew I had a lot of money all the time, he set up the deal for me. I didn't like him to set up deals with my money, but this one was okay. I bought these cigarettes extremely cheap, and with Joey's people in Bloomfield I nearly doubled my money, and Joey did all the work this time. I didn't feel like messing around with that little bits of money schemes; however, I did take about four or five cartons of Marlboros for myself, and I just backed Joey up with money and gave him a nice chunk of change, along with some pain pills.

One time, Wayne brought a guy from his work with him to my house, and the guy talked about large quantities of cocaine. This guy told me, "I can get rid of a lot of coke because the coke they sell where I live is not as pure as your coke."

I replied, "I don't know who you are, but if you want some of this stuff, you got to go through Wayne."

I told the guy to wait in the other room and asked Wayne, "Why are you bringing people here that I don't know?"

"He's cool. I've worked with him for awhile now," Wayne said with respect.

ANTHONY T. ALIBERTI

"Yeah. But I don't know him, and I ain't selling anything to him. If you want to make some money, you can sell it to him." So, Wayne started a little cocaine business with the people he knew from work.

Wayne pissed me off that day. He knew better than to bring someone to my house that I didn't know, but I didn't let Wayne know how mad I was because he was extra muscle and my friend. Days later, Wayne and I smoked a lot of coke. We must have been up for two or three days when Wayne decided to go home; meanwhile, I continually smoked and snorted cocaine until Wayne came back two weeks later. He rang the doorbell, and I let him in. He told me, "You look like shit, man."

"I've been up since you left two weeks ago," I said, wired out.

"Did you eat anything?" he asked.

"No. Nothing."

Wayne actually made me a sandwich and insisted I ate it. That's how bad things got for me.

Missy and Jill wanted to come over once, but I knew I probably wouldn't be able to get it up any way from doing so much coke, so I continued to smoke cocaine and told them I was busy. I passed up sex to sit and snort and smoke cocaine.

If I ever ran out of money or drugs, I simply went and got more coke to get more money. I had good credit on the streets, so many people would just hand me over drugs because they knew I'd get them back later with either money or drugs. This life got too insane for me. I even tried heroin, although I never liked heroin, but it was free for the taking, and I took it. A lot of people shot that shit in their veins, but I wouldn't think of putting a needle in my arm. I'd snort a couple of lines every once in a while to come down from all the coke I used.

HIGHLY ADDICTED

At this time, I was caught in the grips of addiction, money, power and everything else that came along with the business of cocaine and drugs. I was helplessly in the addiction cycle. I had to tell Jimmy I was doing most of the coke. I was one of Jimmy's best buyers and brought him the most money. Since I brought him a lot of money, he still didn't cut me off; in fact, he gave me an ounce of coke for free and told me, "Get back on your feet, and just don't start doing the coke. You know better than that! You know if you do the first line you'll do all the coke."

Usually the smaller time dealers would have gotten cut off from the coke immediately; however, I made too much money to be cut off. As I continued to deal, I still managed to get money together. As long as I didn't use the coke, I made money; on the other hand, the cocaine was more alluring than the money, and I continued to abuse the coke as well as other narcotics.

Because my back problems allowed me to get narcotics from doctors, I managed to slow down on the cocaine by substituting the high with pain pills, Xanax or Valium. Nevertheless, Tony, Mike and Jimmy wanted me to go to the airport and start picking up the coke. I was a little wary about that and told them, "Give me awhile to think about this."

This whole business now seemed quite insane.

I needed to take it easy. I stayed at my parents' house, although I could have gone to one of my apartments, to my sister's and John's house or anyone of the people I sold to or bought from. Instead, I just wanted to go home for awhile and be left alone.

THE INTERVENTION

My father eventually found out what I was into through his police friends. This whole time, the undercover narcotic task force watched everything these cocaine dealers did, but they couldn't get inside; and they could not make any arrests. On the other hand, while they watched, they saw me come into the picture, and they saw me with these big time cocaine dealers because Jimmy started to bring me with him to meet Tony and Mike and Hassuan, all the main guys who ran and distributed all the cocaine.

One night, my old friend, Erik, asked me if I wanted to come up to his house and party. I said, "Sure. I'll be right up. I got a case of Miller Genuine Draft I'll bring with me."

On my way out the front door with the cold case of beer I carried on my shoulder, my father told me, "You're not going anywhere tonight. We got to go to a party next door at the V.F.W."

"Why do I have to be there?" I asked.

He gave me an ultimatum, "Either you come over here, or don't come back to this house again."

So, not even thinking anything about it, I went next door to the V.F.W. We got there and proceeded to the back party room that was very well lit. Tables surrounded the dance floor with chairs all around each one of them. I noticed my cousin Joey from Bloomfield. Big John and my sister were there, and seemingly all of my parents' friends who watched me grow up. Every person in the room cared about me. I'd already popped a couple of Xanax and smoked a half a joint down in the basement before I walked out the door, so I had a little buzz. My father even arranged for a D.J. to play music all night. We all started to drink, talk and listen to the music. Strangely, I went up one time to get a drink, and then my father got all the drinks after that. I told him, "I'll get the drinks, Dad. Sit down and relax."

His eyes looked pissed off, but he managed to keep a friendly attitude as he looked at the devilish drug dealer he saw inside of me and said, "No. I'll get the drinks, son. What are you having?"

"Captain and coke," I said.

He got me drink after drink after drink until I noticed he went to see Pat Sr., the cop, and Pat took something out of his shirt pocket and handed it to my father before he got my next drink. I watched my father open a capsule and dump the powdery substance into my drink. But, when he came back to our table and set my drink down, I'd purposely spilled it all over the table and acted as if it was an accident and said, "Oops. I'm sorry. Did I spill any on you, Dad?"

After he looked over at Pat, he told me, "I'll get you another drink."

They were really persistent about this, and I knew they were trying to slip something in my drink because I saw for the second time, Pat giving my father another capsule, in which my dad put in my drink. I watched every move they made. When my dad got back to our table this time, he said, "Try not to spill this one, son."

I said, "Dad, I'm a drug addict. How can you drug a drug addict? I seen you put something in my drink."

So, I chugged the drink in two gulps with whatever they put in it and slammed the glass on the table and said, "Okay. Lets go! How long before this shit kicks in? You know, you just put something in my drink, and I already took four Xanax tonight. I hope whatever you put in my drink doesn't cause a lethal effect." I said, with raised brows and a mean smile.

He acted as if he didn't know what I was talking about, shaking his head in agony; nevertheless, when I told him I took Xanax, he then looked worried.

He went to talk to Pat. I watched with a happy, but cold blatant stare not blinking once.

My father came back and asked if I wanted another drink. He tried to played things coolly.

This time when he got back with drinks, the questions started, "What do you got yourself into, son? Do you understand the severity and the consequences of what you're doing?"

"What the hell are you talking about?" I replied. "What am I doing?"

It was early in the night, and my father was in no hurry, so he changed the subject.

The music played, but nobody danced. Everybody seemed very complacent. My cousin Joey sat right across the table from me, and Big John and my sister sat at the next table over. All stayed as close as they could because they all knew what was going on and wanted to hear. In fact, I was the one who first danced with my mom's friend. The D.J. played some country song, and I always wanted to learn how to do the two-step dance. So, Marianne showed me how to two step, and we danced wildly all over the dance floor as everybody else watched. She had my heart beating so fast from dancing quickly around the dance floor that I had to sit down as the sweat dripped from my head.

Her drunken husband said jokingly, "Look what you did to the kid, Marianne. You practically killed him."

Whatever they put in my drink was kicking in, and I loved it. I never felt so good in my life. I even went over to ask Pat the cop in a cocky way, "Hey man, where did you get this stuff? Can you get me some more?"

He answered in a moratorium tone of voice, "What are you talking about?"

I talked, danced and yelled out of control. "I feel good!"

It was like no other drug I'd ever tried.

Eventually, everyone left except Joey, John, my sister, my mom and a few people who stuck around and watched in awe. At this point I'd gone amuck. I cruelly made rude remarks to my parents. Remarks I haven't and won't talk about ever again. I later apologized with all respect, for they were my parents.

It was about three in the morning. After hours of my father and Pat Sr. questioning me, Big John told me again, "Shark, shut up and get the fuck out of here while you still can."

So, I went over to the house, grabbed my little porcelain bong and when I came back outside, I noticed Pat Sr. hiding in the dark behind a great big pine tree. I fired up the bong, smoked it and put it in the bed of John's Chevy pickup truck. I walked around the building watching Pat Sr. pull the bong out of John's truck and smelled it to see what I smoked.

Now, my eyes were a fiery devilish red color as they always got when I smoked weed until I put eye drops in, but I purposely didn't put any eye drops in because I wanted them to see the devil inside. I went straight back into the bar. Joey left and went over to my parents' house. The few people who were left went up to the front bar. And, I followed. There was only Pat, my dad, John, a woman bartender, Harry who was just a drunk, who curiously watched from across the bar, Pat's wife and another cop I recognized. I now knew this was an intervention. So, I continued to play the game and truthfully answered almost any question they asked, except questions about drug dealers. Something held me back from talking about dealers because I was one of them. And, a dealer never talked to anyone about his business, especially to cops. Meanwhile, Big John sat behind me and was still telling me to keep my mouth shut and get out.

As I sat there with devilishly red eyes, Pat, the cop, used a tape recorder and taped everything; however, I was so fucked up he kept starting, stopping and rewinding the tape because my words weren't in the proper order he needed them to be in. I rambled drunkenly. He tried to pull a confession out of me as he started and stopped the tape recorder. He would take certain words out of the recording by erasing them. Finally, he managed to put together a confession. I felt an icy chilliness because I knew that wasn't justifiably legal. But, this was my family, and they cared.

My father sternly asked, "Who's giving you this shit?"

I thought it to be funny as I laughed with no reply at all. I figured out that they put Thiopental Sodium (Truth Serum) in my drink.

At this point, the bartender watered down my drinks, and she gave me another watered down drink, and I threw it at her and said, "Get the fuck out of here or put some alcohol in my drinks."

My father apologized for my actions and politely asked her to leave saying, "I'll lock up. You get out of here."

The questions continued, "Who does this? Where do they keep that? Give us some names?"

I answered to Pat, "Who the hell do you think you are, Dirty Harry? Go fuck off! I ain't saying anything."

"My son ain't going to jail. You're working for the 'Cali cartel' selling this shit. One way or another you're going to tell some names to Pat," Dad said protectively.

"There's been a war on drugs for some time now, and you can help us out. Maybe you can get paid, make a little money and they'll put you in the witness protection program," Pat said.

I told my father and Pat, "Get these fucking women out of here. Women like to talk, and I ain't saying anything until they're gone."

Pat told his wife, "Go home. I'll walk up."

They lived right up the street, but his wife didn't want to leave because this interested her. She probably never saw anything like this before. The bartender left, Pat's wife left and Harry left. I disrespectfully told Harry, "What the fuck are you looking at. Get the hell out of here. Oh! By the way, I fucked your daughter."

Everyone left, and the doors got locked. My father and Pat could do anything they wanted to do in this place. They practically owned the V.F.W. Now, it was Pat, my father and another cop my dad knew, along with Big

John. When Pat mentioned the war on drugs, I started to think about how fucked up my friends and I were getting on this cocaine. I told Pat that his son was a drunk, but he never got into hard drugs, although he drinks way too much. Also, I told him I wanted to screw his one daughter in sign language because I knew Pat Sr. knew sign language, and what I said wasn't that hard to sign; moreover, I told him his other two daughters were cokeheads. Pat's face raged with anger, but he still did his job, and that job was me: someone he watched grow up from the age of six and was a good friend of his son's.

Pat showed a merciless stare at me and said, "I need some names now!" He put his revolver on the bar. I laughed.

"What are you going to do, shoot me?"

"Only if I have to."

"I'm dead anyway if I tell you anything," I said with a faltered voice, as if disaster was headed my way.

After Pat mentioned the war on drugs again, I got patriotic and decided to tell everything. I thought I'd try to help my country and community. Plus, I thought this may be a way out, and I could get away from the cocaine business and the people involved in it.

I looked at them thoughtfully, shook my head and said, "Okay. Get your tape recorder ready."

It was five in the morning, and I asked about the witness protection program and the money they offered me. Suddenly, furious anger arose in me at these cocaine dealers I dealt with. Pat urged me on to get angrier and madder at these guys. Pat knew this was something big. After a whole night of questioning, it only took me five or ten minutes to tell them want they wanted to hear. All the cops knew these guys sold a lot of coke, but they needed an inside man. They were never able to make an arrest on any one of these guys. All they could do was sit back and watch. But now, they had me on the inside.

That night I gave them all the information I knew; I even mentioned Tony's and Mike's fathers. Pat knew who their fathers were because he was a cop back then also. My father even knew one of them indirectly because Mike's dad played numbers through my father's people.

I told them how the cocaine was brought in, and where it got shipped to and how many kilos. I told who lived where, and places that stored money and cocaine. I gave up all the main guys and the way in which they worked their businesses. I even gave up John, but nothing happened to him because he was going to help with the whole plan. The twenty-five thousand dollars Pat offered was a lot of money to me at twenty-three years old; in addition, I would get away from the cocaine that was destroying my life.

Pat told me exactly what was going to happen, and how I should handle it.

He told me, "You have to volunteer to go to jail for a weekend because you sold cocaine too. The Attorney Generals, or 'AG's', are going to want to arrest you, but if you voluntarily tell them, you will go to jail and do the work we want you to do. They will accept a weekend in the Allegheny County Jail."

Instead of me going to jail, I paid John $2,500 out of the $25,000 I got to do the time for me. I've never been in jail before but for a night and never intended to go to jail; therefore, John agreeably went and spent a weekend in jail for me. To Big John, a weekend in jail was nothing; plus, he made $2,500 in two days.

Pat told me, "Your lucky because the Attorney General's office cannot supply you with money to buy the cocaine until they get sufficient and substantial evidence. This way you'll make more money if you play it smart because you're giving them the proof they need." He continued, "Just remember we will be watching. You need to stay in the apartment you're in now. We'll use it as a safe house, and it will constantly be watched." I thought to myself, "Pat Sr. never mention microphones or cameras." I grew paranoid.

He told me, "You just keep on dealing, but only with John. You get the cocaine, and you give it to John."

John did it for the money; he wasn't into the rush of a cocaine high. So, I just continued dealing normally like that night never happened; I made sure to forget about that night. It seemed like I was now legally allowed to sell cocaine under proper supervision.

"It will be awhile before they even find out it was you. They'll send a close friend of yours to make sure they know where you're at, and what you do," said Pat.

"Donny," I quickly said.

"Who's Donny?"

I told him where Donny lived, where he could be found and who he hung out with, in addition to the cars he drove and where he worked. "Donny's the guy they sent to the dealers who dealt under the main guys, and he checked up on them and found out who they sold to and how much cocaine they used themselves; I ain't worried about that punk ass mother fucker. It's the big dealers I'm concerned about. They are going to kill me. I've already seen the unmarked guns they have."

"Don't worry about that right now; you have to act like you don't know what happened because they are going to act like they don't know it was you who set them up."

As fucked up as I was that night, forgetting wasn't very hard to do. My father and his police friends requisitioned me to do a job. And, I did it. And, I got paid.

"We'll let you know if you are in harm in any way; however, you have to be brave about this. Play it like a game because that's what it is: a game."

I wasn't scared because I had Big John, the cops and my father's crew on my side. With these people, I felt I was untouchable. I could have gone to Europe and stayed with family if I'd needed to. I had family in Liverpool, England. I took the twenty-five thousand dollars, but refused the witness protection program. They gave the money to my father, and he put it in an account that I couldn't touch until I turned twenty-five.

Now the cops watched me, the drug dealers watched me and the insurance company watched me. I still collected workers' compensation, and my attorney was a friend with Tony and Jimmy. So, one of my father's friends, who was an enormously big man who worked in the same building as my attorney worked in, went and talked to Tom, my attorney. Tom was wary of me, and I was wary of him because of the situation we were in together. He could have easily set me up. But, I thought about what my father's guy probably said to him; consequently, it must have been serious because Tom was definitely afraid of me even though he knew Tony and Jimmy. I saw the way his face looked when we'd go to the court hearings. He always looked pale. He was very jittery and every time I shook hands with him, he had sweaty palms.

Since the police didn't have any evidence, they couldn't arrest anyone. The business would have mercerized. Everything would have become profitable. They needed proof and evidence to prosecute them, and that's what I supplied them with: 'evidence.' They called me a mercenary, a person who'll do anything for money no matter how dangerous a situation nor the certain places and circumstances I'd overt myself to. But, I liked it. It's a rush! Although it was more excitement than money in the long run, the mixtures of the two were of a fundamental matter for me. So, I did what I was told, and I kept John supplied with cocaine. Every time Jimmy and I met, the undercover agents followed him. As they watched Jimmy, they saw whom he went to, and he went to the same exact people that I told Pat Sr. about; therefore, the police made a case because of the information I gave them.

BUSTED

Jimmy was the first one who got busted, but he kept his mouth shut and didn't say a word. On one of Jimmy's frequent trips to the airport to pick up the cocaine, the cops were at the cargo luggage pick-up with dogs and cop cars without lights flashing waiting for him. They told him that the crate fell off the conveyer belt and broke open, and they found eleven Kilos of cocaine in the crate. In reality, the cops broke it open because they knew the information I'd given them about the address on the crate, and where it was coming from. That's when Jimmy went away for a year. They offered him five to ten years in the Federal State Pen, or one year in a jailed boot camp outside of Harrisburg, Pennsylvania. He took the one year in the boot camp, and this boot camp was worse than the Marine Corps boot camp.

Cookie was the next who got caught; however, he never did go to jail or even to a court hearing, nor did he talk. They found him with a Kilo of coke that was in a brown paper bag. However, Cookie's family was connected, and he told the cops he'd just found a brown paper bag on the side of the road and was bringing it to the police station. He didn't even get any probation and probably never even saw a judge. That's the way Cookie picked up his usual weekly batch of coke. He uniquely told his dealer to put it in a brown paper bag and leave it in his cousin Frank's yard. Cookie'd just go pick it up and leave the money in a big envelope, if not paid in advanced it would be owed. None of us cared at all about money because we knew it was gotten faster than we spent it, and we all held wads of cash in our pockets.

Frank was a drummer, another guy played bass and Frank's older brother played guitar and sung and we all played music at Frank's house occasionally. Cookie's uncle, Frank's father, usually carried things like Rolex watches or very expensive jewelry, and they lived in a very big house, and he always dressed exquisitely in nice suits, along with the expensive new cars that sat in the long driveway or in the four garages. There were Corvettes, Cadillacs and Mercedes along with other nice trucks and vans. Frank was a good friend with Mike, but Frank never sold any drugs; on the other hand, he allotted Mike and Cookie to use his backyard for pick ups. I saw Mike one night in Tuggies, and I asked him, "What happened to Jimmy and Cookie. What's going on here, man? I'm lyin' low for awhile."

"Nobody knows anything," he replied very fast with a pissed off look about him, like he knew or assumed I was involved somehow, but he couldn't say a word; he didn't have proof.

If people wanted to get me, they couldn't act as if they were pissed at me. It was really hard for them to do, but for me, it made it quite easy to see who was on my side, and who was on their side. I was more lawfully connected than they were, and had a lot more experienced old-timer muscle and wisdom on my side. But, it was time for me to take precautions. I'd become estranged from society. There were few people I trusted.

PARANOID

I immediately got in touch with one of my uncles, Barry, and he took me to get my gun permit at the Sheriff's Office in downtown Pittsburgh, and then I went to buy some guns after we stopped at Primanti Bros. down by the river in the strip district and got a couple of sandwiches. The gun store was lined wall-to-wall with shotguns and rifles, along with some automatic assault rifles. Handguns were locked in glass cases with other gun and knife weaponry. I got a 9mm automatic handgun that held 16 rounds to a clip with one in the chamber and three extra clips. Next, I got a .357 magnum. It was a SP-101 Ruger revolver, which held only five deadly bullets, but it was easily concealed with a snubbed nose and hammerless features that was perfect to carry. Nonetheless, it was extremely powerful, and my favorite gun to carry. Then, I bought a Remington shot gun, with a very short barrel and held eight 12 gauge rounds. It was a shiny silver nickel-plated gun like the ones the Coast Guard uses. It was also impermeable to salt water. I also bought, a .38 caliber derringer that only had two tiny barrels and could be carried in a small pocket or a sock. My 380 Colt Mustang II was so accurate I could hit targets 50 yards away almost dead center, and it was small like the derringer, fit in the back pocket of my jeans and held eight rounds in a clip. I carried three other small clips. The Colt .44 caliber revolver was extremely large and hard to carry, but I found it to be nice to keep in the house with the shotgun. Finally, one of the last guns I bought was an automatic .45 caliber "Para-ordinance" with ten in a clip and one in the chamber, and I carried four other clips when I carried this gun. That gave me fifty-one shots with the 45mm. And, the 9mm gave me forty-eight shots with the extra clips.

I never carried only one gun; instead, I carried three or four. Usually, I carried one on my side, another in a shoulder holster, one on my leg, and sometimes either the .38 Derringer or the Colt 380 in my pocket. All the bullets I had in the guns were hollow points. A hollow point has a very small pin in the center of the bullet, which causes the exit wound to be massively large.

One day, totally out of the blue, a friend of mine, Greg, and I were at this gun store, and I saw the nicest assault rifle you could get. It was a Colt 223. Thirty rounds per clip, and I bought three extra clips that gave me one hundred and twenty-one rounds with the one in the chamber. The bullets for this gun were extremely deadly because that type of bullet just didn't hit a person; it spreads out when it hits a body and does not exit. It travels around inside a person's body and rips throughout causing terrible damage to the organs inside a person that leads to death.

I got the right machines to make my own bullets because ammunition was very expensive. So, Greg and I reloaded the shells we'd previously shot. I even slept with a gun under my pillow, and my shotgun laid on the floor right next to my bed within arm's reach.

I kept an arsenal of weapons locked up in a gun safe with enough ammo to fight a small war. I knew these guys, and they didn't fuck around. Frankie's father Frank Sr., who owned Amato's bar, had died suspiciously of a heart attack right after Jimmy got busted. Nobody ever saw him again. He was only in his forties and supposedly took a massive heart attack. Maybe Mike Sr. and Tony Sr. thought he informed the police because he knew dirty cops in Swissvale, and he owned the bar that the cocaine got shipped to. This knowledge enforced my paranoia.

Meanwhile, I took a year off from dealing when Jimmy was in the boot camp. As I kept a room in my parent's downstairs game room most of the time and smoked some pot and sat back in my recliner watching television or played my guitar. I never talked about "that" night to anybody. If I tried to talk about it with my dad, he'd only laughed and acted like he didn't know what I was talking about.

Time passed, and Jimmy was about to be released, so I started to wonder what my cocaine friends were going to do, and what they'd planned.

When Jimmy got out of the boot camp, I suddenly got back into dealing, but only with Jimmy and John. That was it, nobody else. My anxiety and paranoid levels skyrocketed. I was probably the first person Jimmy came to see, and he brought a Kilo of cocaine with him. He asked me, "Shark, can you help break this down into ounces for me? I don't what to touch any of the bags."

I suspiciously said, "Sure, I'll help you."

He's never asked that before of me. He had a digital scale to weigh the coke on, and sandwich bags to put the cocaine in. So, I broke down all the coke into ounces and asked, "Can I do a couple of lines, man."

He said, "Go ahead. Help yourself. Those four ounces are yours."

I was very wary because he acted as if he knew I talked, but he didn't say anything because he already had a plan concocted. Pat, the cop, told me this would happen. But, Jimmy and the guys could only assume it was me who talked. They didn't have any proof it was me as of yet, and they probably never would.

All along Jimmy tried to tell the cops he bought the coke from me. Jimmy wanted me to cut the Kilo up; thus, my fingerprints were on every single bag; nevertheless, the cops already knew whom he got it from, and they watched from an old abandon wooden house that sat atop a hill across the street from my apartment. So, I coolly sat back and played this game.

We were out one night at a local bar. Donny, Silky and I drank our drinks, and a lady approached me. She started to talk to me, and I really didn't pay her any attention. But then, she started to hit on me, and Donny and Silky urged me on saying, "Shark, you should go get some of that."

So, I politely talked to her and asked, "What's your name?"

"Nannette," she said.

I busted out laughing and said, "No, No, Nannette. Ha! Ha! Ha! Dominic told me all about you."

My dad's friend, Dominic, once told me while we were at Wheeling Downs Race Track to watch out for no no Nannette. Dominic was the guy who took pounds of weed off me behind the V.F.W. in his Winnebago.

He told me, "Just keep no no Nanette on your mind. I dated her, and she's bad news."

This was an attempt on my life, and I just laughed. They sent a woman to try and get me somewhere, but I knew she was with Mike Sr. because Dominic told me.

Tony's and Mike's dads were continually in contact with Tony and Mike and advisably told them what they should do and how it should be done. As for me, I already knew what to do.

I decided to disappear too for a while. I didn't hang out at Tuggies anymore and rarely saw anybody. John and I got together once a week. Jimmy and I met once a week also. I went out once in awhile to see what was going on, and I tried to get some information, but nobody ever said anything to me or nobody knew anything.

Eventually, I started to go out regularly, and I had to act as if I didn't say anything about the guys who got busted. Then, Donny started to hang around me all the time. He was their connection to me, and he was my connection to

ANTHONY T. ALIBERTI

them. Donny hung around me constantly, and sometimes a couple of us played tennis, basketball or racquetball. None of us had real jobs, so we did whatever we wanted to. Silky was another guy who hung around me also. The dealers had put money on my head, so anybody with some balls tried to contact me; however, there were only a few who found me, and only a few who had the balls to try something.

Silky was a little tough Italian dude; however, he never had the money to get involved with dealing. But, he definitely knew the right people like Donny, Fagnucci, Mike and Cookie.

Pat Jr. came along sometimes when he was in Pittsburgh, and he didn't have a clue as to the game I played with these cocaine dealers. He did know I was in with the guys, but that's all he knew. He didn't need to know anything, and I told him nothing even though he was on my side if needed. And, I did need him at times because he moved down south, and when I went to Hilton Head to get away after the busts went down, Pat always let me stay with him. It wasn't questionable. Plus, he was a really good friend who I trusted, but he drank too much, so I didn't like to tell him too many specifics. He talked when he drank.

Most of my medications came from the doctor and were legal. The pain medication not only took me out of pain, without a doubt, I caught a really nice buzz, but the cops couldn't say anything to me about the narcotics. The prescriptions were legal. But, the pain pills made me braver and bolder to do what I had to do; thus, the euphoria effect from the pain pills, especially if I took four or five of them, made me stronger, and I worked more willing and fully against the dealers. I also got prescribed anti-anxiety medication, which calmed me down. This way I never looked nervous. Since Jimmy got out of jail, some eighteen-months passed, and Donny and I got real tight. Every day we were in touch, and sometimes Cookie or Silky or Mike or all of them; furthermore, not only Donny, but most of the guys started to come out and played tennis all the time while we smoked weed right on the tennis courts. We figured, if other people were there or walked by and smelled the pot, fuck it. We didn't care, and we went on doing what we were doing. Jimmy kept me supplied with cocaine still, and while I was in with my friends, the undercover agents watched. Everything and everybody got watched, and I knew it, but nobody else knew. I had to act as if nothing ever happened.

Now, I sat back, played this role and waited. I waited for them to try and kill me; however, since I knew I had to wait, I just merely watched and listened to Donny talk along with other people I knew who were involved.

Gino, Jay's older brother, heard things and gave me information about the coke dealers. I would let him know what I heard from the narcotics officers I knew since Gino still sold me marijuana. Gino played cards with Mike Jr., and that's how he heard things, but Gino never said a word about me.

This was a bad time. Sometimes, I wished for a quick death. I still did crystal meth and other drugs besides cocaine. The crystal meth kept me very alert. If I'd lose concentration for a second, I could get killed. I stayed in my apartment that constantly got watched. I still had money coming in from workers' compensation, some pot deals with Gino and the narcotics I got from Charlie Brown in Ohio, so it wasn't a big deal money-wise to keep an apartment.

Again, Tom and I went to court to settle my compensation case I had reopened, and we settled for $40,000 this time; however, every time I went to a court hearing with him, I got nervously paranoid. I used to go to court hearings packed with two or three guns on me dressed in a well-tailored suit. This was workers' compensation court, and they didn't have metal detectors, so I was able to carry weapons. I remember thinking every time I came out of court they would get me; indeed, I thought that was the only time they could get me alone, at the court hearings through Tom, a mutual connection between the dealers and me.

Another close friend of mine, Brian, threw a big party at his parents' house one Friday night. His father brought marijuana for everybody to smoke along with the weed we brought to smoke, and we had a keg of beer tapped and sitting on the back deck of the house. The regular crowd was there and then some, and most people snorted coke.

At this particular party, all the main cocaine dealers were there along with many other people. This was strange to see all the main guys in the same place at the same time. That was rare. I stealthily heard a couple of guys, who were a little too drunk, talk about beating the shit out of someone in the garage that was detached from the house and had a loft up above. I knew right then it was me they were talking about. Therefore, I looked for a way out, and I noticed a bunch of guys in the back of a pickup truck who were on their way to go somewhere else. I hurriedly jumped in the back of the pickup and got out of there. I told them to take me up by my house, and I walked the rest of the way home. I just disappeared without telling anyone good-bye. This shit was getting crazy.

Tony Gets Busted in L.A.

Shortly after I settled my work comp case again, Tony Jr. got busted in Los Angeles and didn't come back for five years. Tony went out there to send a shipment of cocaine back to Pittsburgh, and I imagine the D.E.A. from Pittsburgh got in contact with the D.E.A. out in California to let them know what was coming to Pittsburgh, how it came here and even the address on the crate.

When I heard about this, I knew they were going to come at me, but I did not know how they were coming. I knew Donny was involved, but he was just a 'keep an eye on him guy,' and he did keep a close eye on me. Donny either called me everyday or just showed up at my apartment unannounced and uninvited. He probably let Jimmy and Mike Jr. know what I did. So, I just played along, and I knew the cops watched, but how could they stop anyone from hurting or killing me? That was my responsibility while they watched. I'd take care of me.

I remember one time Donny, Silky and I were in Donny's little red Dodge Neon, and we'd just come out of a bar after drinking all night and were going back to my apartment to snort and smoke some coke, and I kept thinking that Silky was going to shoot me in the back of the head. I sat in the passenger seat, and Silky was right behind me while Donny drove. Silky was a short tough Italian guy and a very quiet person. However, they didn't try anything.

It wasn't the people I knew who scared me. It was the people I didn't know, the unfamiliar faces. Naturally, the cocaine and crank I was doing made me even more paranoid, but the arsenal of weapons I kept calmingly settled me down a little bit. I knew they had to get me in a trust position, so I never trusted anyone, except Jay.

Once, as I walked into a bar in Regent Square, I saw this much stouter and more dandified man follow me into the bar. I was with a friend, Brian, who really didn't have a clue to what was going on, but he told me that the man was Mike Sr. As soon as I heard that, my mind easily adjusted to an avenue of escape. So, I grabbed Brian and told him I needed to go somewhere, and we left. My driver's license was suspended at this time, so I had to rely on other people to drive. Wherever I went, I always planned a way out, just in case. Sometimes, it was better to be paranoid than dead.

Jimmy came over as he usually did, for our weekly deals, only this time he gave me a quarter-pound of 'cut up' cocaine, and I asked him, "What's this shit?"

He replied, "This is what I got this time. Try to get rid of it."

Before he left, he grabbed my head and kissed both of my cheeks. I betrayed Jimmy, and now this was Jimmy's time for revenge. I thought to myself, the time is here. Jimmy's strange mannerisms were seemingly from mafia movies. I knew Jimmy, and this wasn't the Jimmy I knew. Jimmy never gave me cut up cocaine, and this shit was really cut to the max. Plus, he never talked to me in that finality tone, and he was always straight up with me. But, not this particular time. Jimmy knew he would never see me again; however, I knew that was the last time I would ever see Jimmy.

THE ATTEMPTED HIT

One early afternoon, I was at The Plaza Bar drinking a few beers and a woman approached a guy who sat at the end of the practically half full bar. I saw her ask a question, and then the guy pointed towards me. Gradually, she walked towards me, and I turned my head, as if I didn't notice her coming. When she approached me, I wondered what the hell was going on. She asked nervously while she smoked her cigarette, "I have two tickets for tonight's penguin game, and my husband I can't make it. Do you want them?"

I paused, took a drag off of my cigarette, looked at her and said, "How much do you want for them?"

"Nothing. You can have them. We have season tickets, but we'll be out of town tonight; in fact, we're leaving right now and won't be back until tomorrow night. Do you want the tickets?"

"Well, let me at least give you a little money for them. You're giving me these tickets for free?" I asked curiously because when I looked at the tickets they were very expensive seats that sat right behind the Penguin's bench. She handed them to me without hesitation.

"Yes. Take them," she said and walked quickly out the front door.

I found this really to be strange. A woman came right to me, as if she was told to, and just gave me these tickets. Why me? The bar was half full with the afternoon drinkers, and she didn't ask any of them; in fact, she didn't even sit down to have a drink.

As I sat and finished my beer, I thought less about the woman and wondered whom I was going to bring with me. I was going to see if my old girlfriend Missy wanted to go, but before I called her, in fact, before I even finished my beer, Donny paged me. So, I called him and told him, "Some lady just gave me two Penguin tickets for tonight."

"Take me with you?" he asked. "I'll buy the beer and some pot. Cookie got the bomb bud."

I told Donny I was at The Plaza and didn't have a ride. So, he came and picked me up in about an hour. When Donny got to The Plaza, we drank a couple beers, bought a couple six packs, went down to my apartment, snorted some coke, smoked some weed and drank some more beers. I'd bought some crystal meth, or crank as it's called on the street, the week before and had some left, so I asked Donny, "Did you ever try crank before?"

"What is it?" he asked.

"It's just like coke, but it lasts longer. It's stronger, and you don't have to snort lines all day long to keep your buzz going."

"I'm game. I'll try it out," he replied, not knowing how this drug would affect him, and I played it down because I knew how it was going to affect him. I laid out two little lines, snorted mine and when Donny snorted his line, he said, "Fuck! That hurt. What the fuck was that?"

"Oh, I forgot to tell you it burns a little bit, but wait until you feel it kick in."

Shortly after we did the crank, I'd noticed Donny started to quickly talk nonstop and paced throughout my apartment. That's how crank affects a person who's not used to doing it. Donny did not even realize how much he said, nor what he was telling me about. So, we kept drinking beers, and I kept feeding him lines of cocaine. I was on the crank too, but I was used to it, whereas Donny couldn't shut up. I even told him to shut up, but he told me, "I feel too good. What was that stuff you gave me? Man, that shit's wicked. I'm flyin'! Let's get out of here and do something."

I told him, "Chill out. We got awhile yet."

Suddenly, he bolted out to his little red car and grabbed a gun. As soon as I saw it, I knew this was Cookie's unmarked ,25-caliber handgun because I saw it before; however, why did Donny have it?

I took the gun off Donny immediately and asked, "What are you doing with Cookie's gun?"

I took the clip out to see if it was loaded, and it was. I never showed fear; nevertheless, I was scared, but in an excited way. I wasn't dealing with everyday petty crooks and thieves; instead, I was dealing with organized drug dealers who knew how to play the game. I tried to further take the gun apart to see if I could take out the firing pin, the spring, barrel or any other unnoticeable part so the gun couldn't be fired. But, Donny grabbed it back off of me, put the clip back in and as he wiped the gun off said, "I'm wiping my fingerprints off of this in case it kills anybody." He used the kitchen towel to wipe off the gun.

"I'm just holding onto it for Cookie. I'll go put it back in my trunk."

Donny foolishly put himself in a bad situation for the coke dealers who wanted me; however, I had Donny right where I wanted him, and he talked up a storm all day long. He mentioned things to me that seemingly sounded not quite right. He described the lady at The Plaza who gave me the Penguin tickets, but I'd never told him what she looked like.

The day progressed, and we continued to snort cocaine on top of the crank we were doing. Donny was fidgeting around and very jumpy. He would make phone calls quietly, but I heard him talk, and when he got off the phone, I'd go pick up the phone like I was going to call someone and hit the redial button to see whom he called. However, the phone just rang and rang, and I'd never get an answer. They probably used some kind of code, similar to the codes we used when we dealt drugs over the phone.

I never asked whom he called because I didn't want to look suspicious. But, I knew whom he talked to, and whom he called throughout the day. Just because I knew I had connections, I still wasn't totally shielded from anyone.

We proceeded to the Penguin game, and Donny still didn't shut up for a second. He talked enough that I really didn't have to say a word, but I did. I figured now would be a good time to question him, so I nonchalantly asked question after question, and he kept on singing like a little bird. He told me everything that would happen; in fact, at one point he said while he puffed on a joint, "You're just like Henry Hill from the movie *Goodfellas*. You know that Shark?"

"Oh yeah." That's all I said because we'd just went and saw the movie a week or two ago. I didn't need to say anything else because Donny talked and talked. The crank probably saved my life that night.

At the Penguin game, Donny paid for parking, and we walked into the Civic Arena. As we walked toward our seats, I noticed two big strange guys in dark brown trench coats with brimmed hats on following us. When I told Donny to look at them, he paused, and without even looking back said, "What do you expect with what you did Shark? I'm surprised it's only two guys and not an army."

At that moment without any conscious reasoning process, everything came together in my mind. My .357 magnum was tucked close and firmly in the front of my waistline, and my 380 automatic was strapped to my leg, but I would never pull a gun on somebody unless they pulled one first. That was something my uncle Barry once said. He told me, "Don't ever pull your weapon first, and if you do, shoot, shoot to kill, so there's only one story: yours."

Donny bought beer after beer at the game, and when the game was over, he asked, "Do you want to go to The Attic, Shark?" The Attic was a college bar we hung out at in Oakland, and he said, "I'll buy dinner and all the drinks. There's a good band tonight, and we'll shoot some pool, or we can throw darts."

I knew Donny all too well. He spent more money that night than he ever did when we went out partying because the money wasn't his. He was my set-up man. However, Donny didn't know that I knew that he was my set-up man. Even at the Penguin game he went to make phone calls. Now, we were at this bar in Oakland, and I didn't have a driver's license, so the doorman didn't let me in until Donny went into the bar and told the bartender what was going on, and then the doorman stepped aside, and I walked right into a bar full of college kids.

We were in the nightclub for about fifteen minutes when Donny asked if I wanted some food or drinks. I was too nervous to eat, but I did continue to drink, and the alcohol churned in my stomach as an array of horrified thoughts raced through my mind. Donny went and made another phone call while I racked up the pool balls at the pool table and picked out a cue stick. When Donny came back, we played two games of pool and then I looked up, and I couldn't believe what I saw. About ten guys walked in at the same time and scattered in pairs, with the two biggest guys at the doorway. These guys were older and did not look like college students. This was it. The hit I've waited for. I recognized Hassuan's older brother and Tony's little brother; however, I didn't know the rest of the guys and didn't want to.

I thought quickly. Then, I made a phone call to Big John and told him what was going on. John told me, "Do whatever you have to do to get the hell out of there now!"

I told him, "If I don't call you back in an hour, it was Donny who set me up."

"Get the fuck out of there!" Big John said again.

With all the fear that encircled me, I still thought of an escape plan. I told Donny my brother-in-law just paged me, and I needed to get back to my apartment to meet him. He needs an ounce of coke for the Pagans. Donny went over and whispered something into Tony's little brother's ear. And when he returned, he said, "If we got to go, we got to go now. Let me take a piss first."

I looked behind me as I stood at the bar and saw Hassuan's brother sitting on a stool, and he looked right at me and fiercely mumbled, "Yeah, now what are you going to do?"

131

He said it in such a low toned voice I barely heard him; I ignored him and left with Donny. All the guys who came into the nightclub didn't know if I called the police or backup guys on my side, so they let me walk out, figuring they would get me after the drug deal I'd told Donny about with my brother-in-law.

As we walked out of the building, my hand never left my .357 magnum. Paranoid thoughts raced through my head, and I knew they'd planned something else. They figured they didn't know whom I called, so they just let me walk right out. I didn't feel safe until we got to Donny's car, and I was ready to pull my gun on him and ask, "What the fuck you doing you mother fucker. You tried to set me up." But, I didn't say anything because Donny was still rambling on at the mouth. I thought I'd hear what's next.

Crystal meth or crank stays in your system for days, and it keeps you talking as Donny still talked. He said, "Man that was close, huh Shark?"

"Yes, it was, but now I got to get to my apartment to meet my brother-in-law."

In reality, John never planned to come to my house; therefore, the whole ride back I tried to think of something to tell Donny why John wasn't there. With the alertness I had, I thought of many different excuses to tell him, but at that point I was just happy to get the hell out of that bar. Donny told me to roll up a joint, and I did. Then, we smoked it on the ride back to my place. The night grew later and later.

GATOR

When we got to my apartment, I made the excuse that it took us too long to get here, and John left already. I kept a pissed off look on my face and acted like I just lost out on four hundred dollars. I should have stayed put, although I figured let's get this over with. We went down the street to Tuggies. We were there for five minutes, and a fierce looking man called 'Gator' came into the bar. His face was strained and urgent. There wasn't a soul in the place except for Donny, Gator, Ducky the bartender and me. I couldn't wait for the totality of this all.

Gator sat catty-corner to me at the bar while Donny hovered over us and still wouldn't shut up. Ducky made the drinks. He was on their side; however, Ducky knew whom I was connected with, so I didn't expect any trouble from him. On the other hand, Gator was the one I needed to look out for. He was Mike's cousin and showed me a wad of hundred dollar bills while he tried to befriend me and asked, "Do you got any coke on you Shark? I'll buy it, and we'll all do it after Ducky locks the doors. We'll go down to the basement and do it."

Now this was the bar down the street from my place. I knew we always did the coke upstairs because there wasn't anything in the basement; on the other hand, there was another bar, a card table and a dartboard upstairs. But, the upstairs was always shut off from the public.

I needed to think quickly again; how the hell was I going to get out of this one? When I walked around the bar to play Ozzy Ozbourne's song, "Flying High Again," on the jukebox, Ducky grabbed me from under my armpits, pushed me up against the wall and frisked me for a gun, but the hammerless snubbed nose .357 magnum was so small he didn't detect it. As he frisked me, Ducky asked with respect because he knew whom I was connected with, "I'm allowed to fuck with you ain't I?"

"You're allowed to fuck with me anytime, Duck," I gently said to him as I stared directly into his eyes.

When I got back to the bar, Gator grabbed my hand, similar to an arm

133

ANTHONY T. ALIBERTI

wrestling hand position, with our elbows on the bar. There we sat, hands
locked tight, and Gator asked scornfully, "Why did you rat out Jimmy, man?"

"What the fuck are you talking about?" I replied, as I squeezed his hand so
hard and tight he let go.

Donny said, "I'll be right back."

I remembered Cookie's gun was in his trunk still. I got Donny so fucked
up on crystal meth he'd slipped up all day long. He gave me clues as to what
was going on when he was actually supposed to keep his mouth shut. At one
time Gator even asked Donny, "Why don't you shut the fuck up man?"

I could tell that Gator was straight, sober and meant serious business, and
after I asked him what he was talking about, Gator ignored me and changed
the subject as if he didn't even say anything, nor did he say anything else
about Jimmy. I acted as if I was really trashed because Donny and I had been
drinking all day; however, the crank kept me very aware, and I knew Gator
planned on killing me. Donny tried to hand Gator the gun without me seeing
it, but I was sharp to everything that happened, for I needed a way out of there.

I saw the gun switch hands but acted like I didn't. I wasn't afraid when
Donny had the gun, but when Gator got it, I was scared. So, I called up Jay.
He lived right up the street from Tuggies, and he didn't know anything and
wasn't involved with anything; on the other hand, Jay's brothers, Mickey and
Gino, were widely known not to be fucked with, and Ducky the bartender
knew that.

Jay's phone rang four times before he picked it up, and those four rings
seemed like an eternity; nevertheless, when he did pick up the phone, I told
him, "Jay. I need you to come down to Tuggies right now please?"

"For what? It's after midnight," Jay said briskly.

"I need you to come here right away," I said.

He said, "I'll be right down."

Five minutes later Jay arrived, and I took him on the other side of the bar
away from Gator and Donny. All the while, I played it coolly until Jay got
there, but I was extremely nervous, fearful and shook on the inside. Ducky
knew with Jay there nothing could happen. I quietly told Jay, "You have to
come down to my apartment with me right now, so just shake your head and
say okay."

Jay and I have known each other our whole entire lives, and he could tell
something was wrong from the serious tone of my voice and the startled look
in my eyes. Jay agreed to do what I told him and shook his head for all to see.

I walked back over to Donny and Gator, didn't say a word to or looked at

Gator, although I told Donny, "I got to go get Jay some blow, and I'll bring an eight-ball back with me."

When Jay and I got to my apartment, I told him everything that happened, and I mean everything. I never told a single soul about this; however, I knew I could trust Jay, and I had to tell him. While I was telling him I grabbed my .45 cal., which was locked, cocked and in my shoulder holster, and I put my shotgun in my acoustic guitar case. Jay was astonished to see all the guns and to hear the story I told him about being an informant.

All the time over the last year or two, while Jimmy was in jail and when he got out of jail, there was a rumor going around town that somebody turned all the major cocaine dealers in. As far as Jay knew, I was one of the cocaine dealers.

"That was you? How come you didn't tell me?"

"I couldn't tell anybody. You're the first person I told in two years. We got to get out of here. Can we go up to your house?"

"Yeah. I guess. If we have to."

"If we don't, they're going to come here. I already seen the gun, and it's an unmarked gun."

"What's that mean?" Jay unknowingly asked.

I told him, "They can kill someone, and the gun can't be traced back to anybody."

"Lets go," he said.

I grabbed my guitar case, with the shotgun inside, and we walked right by Tuggies and up to Jay's house. As we walked by Tuggies, the lights were out and it looked closed, but Donny's car was still out in front parked. I kept my hand inside my coat and on my .45 automatic. The night I've waited for, all this time, was here now.

The first thing I did at Jay's was to make sure every door and window was locked, and I even had Jay double check all the locks. Jay's girlfriend at the time was a bartender at Tuggies, and she heard about 'the guy' who turned all the coke dealers in. When she found out it was me, she couldn't believe it either because I was considered to be a main man in the cocaine business around town. Plus, I supplied the bar she worked in with coke.

Shortly after we got to Jay's house, I heard Donny's mouth as he still rambled on, and then I heard Gator's voice. He told Donny to shut up, and Gator asked Donny, "What the hell are you on man?"

They came to Jay's house to get me. Donny blabbered something. I heard them out front, so I opened the door, pointed my shotgun at them, and before

I could say anything, Gator shot twice at me with the little .25 caliber automatic he had. It sounded like a cap gun, but it could still be deadly. Then, I fired my shotgun into the ground in front of them. A warning shot, and I hoped somebody would have heard the shots and called the police, but it was about three o'clock in the morning. I didn't get hit when he shot at me; however, after I fired back, I got down on the floor, shut the door and locked it. Jay yelled downstairs, "Shark, what the fuck was that?"

"They just shot at me, man. Stay up there."

One of the small .25 cal. bullets lodged in the thick wooden door and I didn't see the second bullet anywhere. I wanted them to try to break in the door before I shot point blank at them because I knew the laws, and if I would have shot at them outside, I might have gone to jail for murder. Moreover, I needed to shoot to kill. That's why I needed them to try and break in. If they tried to break the door down, I could justifiably shoot them and get away with it because it would have been self-defense: justifiable homicide. Plus, I really never wanted to kill anybody.

Donny still talked and talked, and Gator asked again, "What the fuck are you on?"

"I don't know. Shark gave me a little line of something today at his house, and I've been flying high all day," Donny said rapidly, and he continued to talk until Gator told him to shut up again.

They tried to get in the back door and all the windows. I needed them to break the door open so I could shoot them.

I tried to call Pat Sr., but he was at work downtown. He lived right up the street from Jay's, and I figured he was my best bet. His wife answered the phone, and I told her what happened because she was at the V.F.W. that night I turned on everybody, and she watched me grow up. With my shotgun in hand, I called my father at work. It was after three in the morning, and I knew he would be at work because he always started early. I furiously blamed him for all this.

After all the time my father denied that night at the V.F.W. ever happened, he didn't deny it now, although he never admit either.

I told him, "Dad! The shit's goin' down! What the fuck you going to do now? I got two guys with guns outside; they already shot at me and they tried to get me at a bar earlier!"

He was speechless as he paused and asked, "Are you alright? Where are you?"

"No, I'm not all right. I got people tryin' to kill me. What the fuck! I'm at Jay's house."

"Where's Jay live?"

"Forest Hills, Avenue 'A'. What are you going to do now? You did this to me; now you get me out of it."

"Just settle down and stay on the phone with me," he ordered.

My father called the police on another phone he had, and then said to me, "The police are on the way, but don't hang up. Stay on the phone with me."

I was frantically scared and bitterly pissed off at my father as I yelled in fury at him, "Why did you do this, Dad? Why? I don't see any police cars. What the fuck, Dad; what the fuck's going on?"

I told my father what kind of car Donny was in and gave a detailed description. I told him, "It's a little red Dodge Neon." I cursed and screamed at him while he remained calm, but his voice sounded worrisome. I heard Donny and Gator at the back door, and Gator talked about how to hook up a device to the phone lines outside the house, so I told my dad, "Wait, Dad. Shut up for a second." And, he did.

With my shotgun pointed at the back door, I saw their shadows and told my father, "They hooked something up to the phone line. They're listening to us."

We both stayed silent on the phone. Jay called me from upstairs, and I went up to see what he wanted. He asked, "What's going on man?"

"I'm waiting for the cops to come."

"They're coming here?"

"Not in the house, but they're going to drive by," I said with paranoid hysteria.

I continued to look out the window with my father still on the phone, and I asked him, "Where's your police friends now, Dad?"

I stayed by the window and waited, and then I heard two or three revving engines that sped down the street and in the back alley behind Jay's house. As I looked out the window, I calmly told my father, "Okay. There they are now."

137

ON THE RUN

I waited until daybreak and had my mom drive down to Jay's and get me. I knew I was safe for now with the police drive by and the morning sunrise. She drove down, picked me up and brought me back to her house. My father, still at work, called and made sure everything was all right. We decided I was to go to my grandmother's house in Stanton Heights. So, I took my mother's Cadillac and went to my grandmother's house; I needed to get out of the area. When I got there, I called my uncle, Barry, who lived in Bethel Park, and he came to get me within the hour. My grandmother is 100% English. Before we left her house, she told me, "If it's that bad, you can always go to Liverpool, England, and stay with my family."

When we got to my aunt's and uncle's house, I needed to calm down, so I sat around for awhile, but I couldn't seem to get calmed. I had some Valium back at the apartment, and I needed to get back there to get them. I asked my aunt and uncle if they needed any money because I kept all the money from the last coke deal with Jimmy. I wasn't worried about paying him his money, so I kept my usual profits; in addition, the money that I normally gave to Jimmy went into my pocket.

Barry said, "I don't want any money. You're family, I will take your guns, though."

"I ain't giving you my guns. Fuck that," I said, but he convinced me to give them to him.

He saw the state of mind I was in, and he was a very smart man who had his own family connections on the other side of town. To put me at ease he said, "I have a gun. Don't worry about it. You're on the other side of town, and nobody even knows you're here."

I gave up the guns, but I held onto the 380 Colt Mustang II that was strapped to my leg and two clips that held eight rounds apiece in my coat pocket. He didn't see that gun or the clips, and I didn't tell him I had it. I felt safer with a gun.

That night we went back to my apartment in Barry's four-wheel drive pickup truck. When we got to my apartment, we saw Tony Jr. who sat outside in a little dark blue car across the street. He was alone and probably waiting for me to show up. Tony was smart and knew I would have to go back to my apartment at sometime. But, what he didn't know was whom I was with, so all Tony could do was sit and watch. Barry stood outside the door with his hand on his gun, which was in his jacket pocket, and I kept my Colt 380 in the back pocket of my jeans. We were ready for anything. I went in my place to get the valuables out of my apartment, the little bit of pills and weed that I had left and my clothes and personal products also. I told Barry I saw Tony, and Barry looked at him and asked me, "Is that him over there?"

"Yeah. That's him."

We left my place and drove around the block, and sure enough it was Tony. We just drove right by, and Barry looked down from his truck into the car in wonder of whom this guy was.

REVENGE ON DONNY

Meanwhile, Donny went back to work in Cleveland. Donny's job went from four to six month intervals. At times, I'd head up to Cleveland with friends, and we partied at the Flats, an area of streets that surrounded a huge square-shaped boat dock by Lake Erie, which were filled with bars, nightclubs, strip-joints and people. All the bars, clubs and restaurants specifically sat around a water inlet and ferryboats took people from one side to the other.

Charlie Brown, my old cocaine and narcotic connection, lived in East Liverpool, Ohio, so I called him up and arranged a get together, which usually meant I was coming up to get some pills, and we set a day and time. Early one Sunday morning, I drove my uncle's Camaro up to Charlie's house, picked him up and we went to a local diner, got some coffee, breakfast and talked. I asked him, "I need you to do me a favor if you can. Some guy back in Pittsburgh set me up to be killed, and I want him hurt."

"Yeah, what did he want to kill you for?" he shockingly asked.

"Well, it's kind of personal, and it's a long story, but there could be some money in it for you, and if you can get a couple guys together, head up to Cleveland and find him."

Charlie cut in and asked, "What do you want me to do? And, how much money do I get?"

I showed him a picture of Donny and told him, "This is him. His name is Donny. He hangs out at The Club Zone in the Flats on Friday nights, like clockwork."

"Are you sure, every Friday night? How bad do you want him fucked up? And, you still haven't mentioned any money, Shark."

"He's usually goes there right after work, on Fridays. You'll have to find him. I got twenty-five hundred for you, and you pay your people out of that. What do you say?"

Charlie was a stocky, broad-shouldered guy and knew a lot of people. He demandingly asked, "I want something up front."

140

"How about a grand? Maybe when you find him, try slipping one or two of those Thorazines you got into his drink, or do whatever you got to do, but get him out of the bar, take him somewhere and beat the shit out of him and leave him lay. I figured you know the area pretty well, and you don't live too far away from Cleveland. Plus, he doesn't know you."

Charlie asked, "Just beat the shit out of him?"

"Well, I want proof. I know your word is good, but bring a camera. I want to see him fucked up before you get the rest of the money, and make sure you tell him Shark says hi."

So, I gave him one thousand dollars, grabbed a bag of pain pills and Valium and went back to Pittsburgh. When I got back to my aunt and uncle's, I laid low and waited. With the Valium I got from Charlie, I finally got a couple of good nights of rest.

Two weeks later, Charlie called me on my cell phone and told me, "Come on up. I got a picture for you."

"I'll stop up tonight, if that's cool with you."

As soon as my aunt got home with the car, I gave her a hundred dollar bill, hopped in the car and went up to Charlie's. He showed me a picture of a beaten man, Donny. I felt that I couldn't just sit back and do nothing, but because of this retaliatory act, my mind eased.

Moreover, one day, shortly after Donny got home to his high-rise apartment, which sat on the eleventh floor, an eighteen-wheeler semi truck filled with gasoline 'accidentally' crashed into the very same high-rise building Donny lived in. If someone had lit a match, the whole building would have blown up. I betrayed Jimmy; and Donny betrayed me. I got my scare, and Donny got his scare, for he was home in his Cleveland apartment when the gasoline truck hit the high-rise apartment building. Donny knew what he did to me, and by having him beat up was my revenge; however, I knew nothing about a gasoline truck. On the contrary, my father often traveled to Chicago and Cleveland on business, and he knew people who lived in both cities. Although I probably wasn't told for my own protection, I assumed my father somehow set up the gasoline truck hit on the building that Donny lived in because my dad knew from the intervention at the V.F.W. when I told him that it would be Donny who sets me up. But, my father waited until the coke dealers came at me first. I was in Bethel Park with my aunt and uncle while this happened, so nobody could connect me to the truck that hit the building; undoubtedly, I found out about it on the streets, from Gino and Mickey.

HIDDEN OUT

I stayed in Bethel Park for a good two weeks, went on a shopping spree with the free $7,000 that I never paid Jimmy with, and gave my aunt a couple hundred. Barry and I hung together for those two weeks, and one Wednesday night, we went out to a guy's house where they got two young, beautiful girls they'd hired to put on a wildly exotic sex show, and my uncle Barry said to the girls, "He's the special one tonight," as he pointed at me.

That meant I got the blowjob after the girls got each other off with their sex toys in front of all us guys.

Another day, as I was on my way to Century Three Mall to spend some more money, I'd called Mickey and told him everything that happened. It took me about a half of an hour to tell him everything, and who was involved. He needed to know because he was in with some of these people, and I wanted him to hear my story before he heard it from someone else. Jay, Mickey and Gino were like family to me.

Next, I had to go see Gino in person because he and I never talked on the telephone; hence, he was the man with the most influence. I told him everything. I got into detailed information, and I even let Gino know that the cops asked about him, but their main concern was the cocaine dealers.

"What did they ask about me?" Gino asked.

"As soon as Pat Sr. and my father mentioned your last name, I told them they're like my family, so go fuck off or arrest me."

Gino asked, "Why would you turn people in? You know better than that, Shark."

I replied respectfully, "Gino, you know I would never do anything like that to you guys. You and your brothers and sisters have been like family to me, and I only gave up the coke dealers. You know me; I wouldn't do anything that jeopardizes my marijuana and pill connections. The cocaine destroyed my life and the lives of my good friends; plus, I got paid $25,000. I couldn't pass it up."

He replied, "Twenty-five g's ain't much to do something like that, Shark.

You could have made more than that on the streets."

After that, I heard things had calmed down around my area of town, so I left Bethel Park and headed home to my parents' house. I stayed there for two nights, and then I went out to my sister's and Big John's house for a week and stayed out in Herminie. I went from the south, to the east, and then further out east, although I could have gone back to Bethel Park or even out to Moon township to stay with my other uncle. I managed to get away; however, they still looked for me. Something like this just doesn't go away over night. I was practically on the run or hiding out for the next couple of years.

PEOPLE KEPT AFTER ME

As I hung out with Big John and drank in the bars where he drank, I felt invincible. I knew of many family members who'd take me in if needed; however, as John was fearfully and fiercely known, I'd thought I'd stick around him for awhile. After all, he was involved with most of the schemes that went down, and I always knew I could count on him.

We partied and drank in a local bar, Potters, out in Herminie one night, and my old friend Silky had a girlfriend who was in the bar that night. One of the guys she was with bugged me during the night. I told him to quit bugging me and to leave me alone, and then he came up to me and asked me if I wanted to go outside. I was half passed out with my head on the bar from drinking and popping pills all day, and this guy kept egging me on. So, I said, "John, this guy's fucking with me."

John stood up, tall, scary and mean looking, and the guy looked like a dog with his tail tucked under his ass. John approached him and loudly said, "Are you fucking with my brother-in-law! You better not be. Who the hell are you? If you got a gun, I'm going to kill you."

John simply grabbed the guy by his collarbone, patted him down for a gun and quietly said to him, "If I ever catch you in here again, you're done for. Who sent you to him?"

The guy said, "I'm here with Silky's girlfriend, and I wasn't going to do anything."

John replied, "Don't fucking lie to me," and he asked me, "Who's Silky?"

"Nobody to worry about," I said with a shake of my head.

Eventually, I moved back in with my parents, and my sister and her family had to move there too until they found another place because their landlord sold the house they lived in. We still lived right next door to the V.F.W., and as enough time went by, I got a little less worried. I even went over to the V.F.W. drinking, playing pool and throwing some darts. I knew in that place I was protected. That was my father's place.

PAY BACK

One night over at the V.F.W., Jimmy's friend, Schretti, the boxer who beat me up before over a little bit of money he schemed from me, came in with an entourage of about six guys. That night in the bar, there were my friends, who weren't in the coke business, Big John and a couple of unknown drunks. Schretti played like he was good friends with me, but we actually hated each other, and I played like I was good friends with him because I planned something in my mind. Schretti was a boxer, and Big John was a boxer too, so I figured it was pay back time. I introduced Schretti to John, and when John put his hand out to shake hands with Schretti, Schretti was amazed at the size of John's hand and got a terrifying look in his eyes. Schretti left and went back to his friends.

Meanwhile, I told John that he ripped me off and beat the fuck out of me once before. I also told John they probably came here to fuck me up. As I set down two hundred dollar bills in front of John, I didn't say but one word: "Hospital."

John told me, "Get him in the back room away from his friends, and I'll come in the back doors to get him."

So, I nicely asked Schretti if he wanted to shoot a game of pool in the back. We went into the back room. What Schretti didn't know was there was another door to get into the back room. John went out the front door as Schretti's friends watched him leave while I unlocked the back door to the back room, where we shot pool. Suddenly, John ran in and grabbed Schretti, dragged him outside, I followed and calmly said, "Now you got a fair boxing match, Schretti. What can you do, man, huh? Don't ever fuck with me!"

John tossed him around like a rag doll and beat the shit out of him. We left him lay there, and we walked home right next door. He couldn't complain to the police; in fact, he couldn't even stand up as John and I watched from over the newly varnish coated wooden fence that separated my parent's house from the V.F.W. Schretti's friends had come out after they didn't see him in the bar. They helped him up and put him in the brand new black Lincoln Town Car they drove.

Now, we had our own little war going on. The dealers I used to deal with, Tony, Mike, Jimmy and Hassuan kept sending people after me; nevertheless, John fucked up anyone they sent. Another time in the V.F.W., it was pretty much the same scenario except the attempted assassins were two big, fat bikers. John and I sat on one side of the bar, my friends sat down at the corner and the two bikers sat right across from John and me. These guys were never in this place before and were not welcomed. It was late, and my father's friend Bombo, a broad, heavy, six foot plus man, bartended that night. John was drunk and looked to pick a fight. The guy loved to fight. John started to torment the two bikers saying, "What do you guys want in here. You're kind don't come in this bar."

Words were exchanged, and I told John who the one guy was. His name was Ray, and he was considered one of the toughest guys around.

"Not anymore," John said with a sardonic smile. Big John always laughed before he started to fight because he knew nobody could take him.

He said after finishing his beer, "Ha, Ha, ready Shark? You'll never see nothing like this again."

I knew Ray from a girl named Heather I used to date; only now, she was with this big biker. She set me up, and that's why the bikers came to the bar, but Heather didn't know anything about John.

One thing led to another, and they were going outside to fight like men. When John followed Ray to go outside, Ray turned around and hit John in the forehead with a half full bottle of beer. It really didn't faze John that much, and another biker hit John a second time on the side of his head, but John didn't budge, so the one biker pulled a knife out, and John said, "I don't fight with weapons. Pussies do. Are you a man or are you a pussy?"

Bombo the bartender came out from around the bar, and after I chugged my beer, I smashed my empty beer bottle over the head of the guy with the knife from behind, and Bombo got the knife off of him, and we both made sure that guy didn't move. I've never seen such fury in John's eyes. He grabbed Ray, a three hundred pound man, threw him against the wall and got him on the ground with his knees on Ray's arms and threw lefts and rights nonstop to the face, and blood squirted out of Ray's nose and the gouge in his eye. I never saw someone get beat up so badly in my life.

One of my friends must have called the police because they showed up, and Bombo still watched the other biker with me so I knew he didn't call anyone. Even though John's left eye was red and runny from getting hit with the beer bottles, it took six cops to get John off of the biker although I still wonder to this day if the cops let John beat the fuck out of him, sort of like a message from my dad, because they sure did take their time getting John off of him.

I went out a couple of nights after that, and I talked to Heather at Tuggies. She told me her boyfriend was in the hospital, and he couldn't even open his eyes. That was probably the biggest guy they could throw at me and down he went. The drug dealers got the message that if they tried to touch me, they would get hurt. John was my bodyguard, and he was big.

My family moved out east to a wealthier community, about twenty minutes away from where we originally lived, pretty much right after the attempts on my life; otherwise, the people may have eventually gotten to me because they knew where I lived, or they could have done something to the house or our vehicles. We thought about moving soon after Gator and Donny tried to get me that one horrifying night. But, we waited to move to save our integrity. Twenty-some years my family lived in the same town, and we knew all the same people. The V.F.W. was my father's main hangout. Now, we still knew all the same people in the same town; we just lived in a different house and in a different town.

I still had friends on my side that I always took care of, like this guy Matt. We were really close friends from back when we worked on the road. Plus, I always gave him free coke when we went out bar hopping together. He knew old man Mike Sr. Matt was also a friend with Jay, Mickey and Gino's family, for he went to high school with Mickey, and they grew up together. I walked in a bar one evening, and Matt and Mike Sr. were there; however, Mike Sr. didn't know me, but I knew him and kindly introduced myself. The only words that came out of his mouth were, "You're the Baker's son," and then his eyes turned to a look of death because this was the very first time we met.

I said, "Who?"

Old man Mike remained silent as if he didn't know what to say or how to react. Then, I just walked away because I was a cocky little motherfucker, and I didn't care who the fuck this guy was. However, that same night Mike Sr. went to Tuggies with Matt, and Jay just happened to be in Tuggies too. This would have been the third time I ran into Mike Sr., and it wasn't a coincidence. When I got to Tuggies, I parked my car nearly right next to the entrance, got out and headed towards the front door. I saw Jay, Matt and Mike Sr. inside through the window with the neon lighted beer signs and an open sign that was next to the door. As I was about to walk in the front door, Matt saw me walk by the window, so he ran outside and told me, "Get the fuck out of here. Mike Sr.'s looking to fuck you up and he's packing," he said while Mike Sr. talked to Jay with his back turned from the window, so he didn't see me.

Although Mike Jr. never got arrested, his father was still pissed off because I fucked up all the cocaine dealers' money in-take. So, my life was still in peril; nevertheless, I smoked my grass, popped my pills, took some acid and drank a lot of alcohol, and eventually it seemed as if I could go anywhere I wanted to. I never saw old man Mike again nor did anybody else ever try anything on me ever again, although I still thought that they may try, so I kept a very low profile, just in case.

BACK TO THE FLORIDA KEYS

It was now 1994, and I was twenty-four years old. Jay and I took another trip down the east coast and saw Pat Jr., Jay's brother Dante Cat and finally Joe down in the Florida Keys. I bought a new black Chevy Impala with a 454 engine in it with my settlement money, and we drove that down the coast. We enjoyed the regular water sports we normally did in the Keys. It truly was beautiful there, and at night, there were so many stars in the sky, which appeared just as golden glitter on a black piece of paper. The temperature in the Keys stayed at a nice, balmy 85 degrees year round.

I kept running out of pills when we went down the coast, so I kept going to see my doctors in Ft. Lauderdale and in Hilton Head, and I got refills on my medicines. I never worked legitimately that much because of my back problems. A couple of odd jobs here and there were available to me under-the-table, and I took them if they paid well. My back doctor told me to take it easy, but I took it a little too easy like regularly going down south with or without Jay. Now, I sent money down to Pat by Western Union, and he picked up my prescription pills for me at Hilton Head pharmacy and sent them back to Pittsburgh in a large brown bubble-wrapped business envelope. I always sent extra money down for Pat to have, since he went through the risky trouble I put him in, and he picked up my pills for me every month. It looked good to keep up appearances with the different doctors in different states, so I usually saw the doctors when I got to the towns.

Pharmaceuticals
and Doctors

At this time, I was off the cocaine, crank or any other kind of speed, but I got intensely hooked on pills, especially pain pills. I knew a good friend, Harry, in Pittsburgh, the guy I went to the Pirates game with on the school bus with our fathers when we were younger. Harry was in with a guy who robbed a little local drug store, which sat off the main road and hardly had any security. Harry's friend stole very big boxes of the pain pills, Vicodin-ES. The pills were in the pharmaceutical bottles and sealed tightly; in addition, the boxes were still taped. I got Harry to sell the Vicodins to me very cheaply because he didn't know how much they were worth on the street; nevertheless, he made quick money when he sold me the bottles, which were sealed, whereas I broke the seal and sold them individually at a higher profit. They came in bottles of a hundred, and I bought the bottles for three hundred dollars apiece; meanwhile, I sold each one of them for six or seven dollars apiece doubling my money and taking my Vicodins free, unless somebody wanted the whole bottle, and then I sold the sealed bottle for five hundred dollars, and I made a quick two hundred. I'd buy one or two bottles at a time, and they sold like they were seemingly legal. Everybody around town liked to take Vicodins, yet I swiftly got the opportunity to help unseal the boxes, buy all the sealed bottles of pain pills off this guy and distribute them in a matter of weeks.

Monthly, I went through a series of painful injections in my back from a pain clinic doctor. Sometimes I received eight injections in one office visit, and he usually prescribed me thirty to forty Vicodins too, so I always kept an updated prescription bottle with my name on it, which came from a legitimate doctor. Hence, if I ever got caught with the pills, I legally was allotted them. I really was in an extreme amount of pain, and not one doctor wanted to operate on me because of my age. Doctors rarely saw someone as young as I have such problems with his back. The pain I suffered from was unbelievably severe from six years of heavy labor and numerous car wrecks. Therefore, I took pain pills and Valium, as well as the injections of mar-cane, sera-pin, zylocaine and cortisone that these pain clinic doctors gave.

Another friend of mine, Gary, and I played the guitar together, and we took the Valium he got from his sister who worked in a doctor's office. She stole all the sample packets and gave them to Gary, who sold mostly all of them to me. I bought the Valium off of him and gave him some back graciously because he always sold them to me cheaply. We jammed back at the house while we smoked weed for the better sounds and better guitar playing, sometimes we did lines of coke from a big pile I'd throw down. I would courteously give some of my drugs away to the good and close friends I hung out with.

I kept a savings account that I hardly touched; instead, I made my money on the street and at the bars by the narcotics and weed I sold. And, I still keenly used the scotch tape on the ten- or twenty-dollar bill scheme with the poker machines. No bartender cared, and the owners could never catch on, as long as I went from bar to bar.

THE ATTEMPTS ENDED

I worried less and less about the cocaine dealers because Hassuan had gotten busted with ten kilos and received ten to twenty years in the Federal State Penitentiary. So, the only cocaine dealer left that hadn't gotten busted was Mike Jr.; nevertheless, the guys who got out of jail probably went right back into the coke dealings because that's all they knew, and it was easy money, but I wasn't involved at that point, although I had caused them a great deal of time, money and hassle.

I lived with a woman and her two fraternal twins. Her name was Cheryl. We lived in a house under HUDD, section eight, and they paid the rent, for Cheryl was a single mother with two kids and section eight didn't know about me living in the house. It was a very nice house and had a little front yard with a really big backyard where I grew a garden of vegetables: everything from tomatoes, to cucumber, to eggplant, garlic to sunflowers and pumpkins, in addition, to the hidden and scattered marijuana plants I grew up on the hill behind the garden. I must have had about seven or eight plants that grew taller than I stood and as wide as a Christmas tree. Out of the eight plants I grew, two of them made it through to the harvest season because the deer and other little varmints got to the rest of them. I hunted down the ground hog and killed it with my 380. I actually shot at a deer I saw chewing on one of the plants with my 380 automatic. It sounded like a cap gun and scared the deer away, but none of the neighbors thought anything about it.

When I harvested the plants, I hung them upside down from the basement ceiling, and I got approximately two pounds of primo backyard marijuana after I cut it all up with scissors and weighed it on my triple-beam scale that I kept in the basement hidden. I used the seeds of the crystallized weed, which made my plants crystallized. I immediately contacted Gino, for he knew the right connections to get rid of the weed I wanted to sell in an instant. I profited thousands and gave Gino his share of the money.

Cheryl's brother in-law, Frank, was a cokehead and knew the dealers I helped put in jail; in fact, he got his coke off of those particular dealers. One day, Frank asked as a favor, "Shark, can you drive my mother's car to Philadelphia? You'll be following me in my truck."

I was shaky about it because I knew that he knew the dealers I informed on; nonetheless, I said, "Sure. I love long drives. Long drives let me think deeply without interruption while I gazed at the country. And, it reminds me of my days working heavy construction on the road. Driving was my favorite part of the job."

He'd gotten some blow right before we left, but we didn't start doing the coke until we dropped his mother and her car off at his sister's house. His sister made spaghetti, meatballs and sausages for dinner, for she knew we were coming. She even made homemade Italian bread. After we ate dinner, we booked a room at Ceaser's Palace in Atlantic City. It was a hundred dollar a night room, and Frank offered to pay; on the other hand, he snorted up a lot of coke with me and didn't ask for any money, so I gave him a fifty for my half of the room. On the way there, we smoked Cuban cigars, and he talked about Jimmy and Tony and those guys, and how they just sold cocaine for a living and never held a real job. He said he didn't like the way they worked like that, as he was a businessman, older and had a more sophisticated manner about him.

When we got to Atlantic City, we checked into our room, snorted some more lines and went down and gambled. We both had a lot of money and gambled expensively while we drank the free alcohol the casinos offered. It seemed like a tight night, for the casino was hardly filled with anyone, although it was a weeknight, and we weren't winning that much money until we sat next to each other and played the dollar slots. We just about had enough gambling for the night, and then Frank's machine hit big; meanwhile, the two machines I played hit all sevens in a row on both machines at the same time; granted, the sevens didn't come up in the correct sequence to hit the big jackpot, but Frank and I still won thousands. All three slot machines that sat precisely right next to each other hit exactly at the same time, and the noise that came out of these machines was a loud clanking noise of dropping money and lights flashed from the top of the slots; thus, two security guards came rushing over as Frank and I yelled loudly and gave high-fives to each other in a joyous motion with great big smiles on our faces. Soon after that, we decided to keep our winnings of thousands and got out of the casino before we lost it all back. Frank was seemingly not a threat to me, and I found him to be a trustworthy man, although I constantly looked over my shoulder and wondered if anything would ever happen to me.

Every year the V.F.W. next door to the house where my parents used to live would have a really big picnic, with lots of food, beer, and horseshoe games and outside gambling like chuck-a-luck, dice and also games for the children like egg-tosses and potato sack races. I've gone to these picnics since I was a very young kid and hung out with my friends, my dad and his policemen friends and his normal crew of guys he hung with. I had a little bit of money and didn't really see the need to work, so going to this picnic was relaxing and lots of laughs, but my money was running out. I didn't have a steady income. I even took Jay and Mickey sometimes, who enjoyed it as much as I did. After all, at the picnic they served free food and beer. However, a fee of ten dollars was asked upon entering the back parking lot, where the picnic went on, but I just said a quick hello with a nod of my head and walked right into the back parking lot. I never paid for anything at the V.F.W. Everybody at the V.F.W. knew me and always told me that my money was no good here.

Jay and his brother Mickey rented out an older brick house with three floors and three entrances, a two car detached garage and when they needed another roommate, Jay immediately thought of me and asked me to move in with them. And, I did. I'd broken up with my old girlfriend and needed a place to stay, and Jay didn't live with his old girlfriend either. Mickey went from girl to girl after his separation from his wife, so the living arrangements were perfect.

Mickey and I grew marijuana in the dark upstairs attic, which looked to be as a hidden room with only one window that we covered totally up with a huge thick black blanket, so we could control the amounts of lightness and darkness the plants needed to grow well. A growing machine allowed us to start the plants early, for the weather wasn't warm enough to grow them outside. The machine had florescent lights, which turned on and off by themselves on a timer. We started the plants inside the attic in January, so when March or April came, they were already big in size and ready to go outside in the backyard.

PSOAS (THE BAND)

Jay was still involved with music, and he got offered a job with the band "Psoas" as the drummer. Psoas was a locally famous band and desperately tried to make it in the music business. This band released two CD's that were professionally recorded. Woody Harelson's brother Bret donated $7,000 to the band so they could make another CD. Bret came to Pittsburgh once and heard them play and liked what he heard. Afterwards, he talked to the band and got to know them over drinks and herb. That's when he offered them the money.

Psoas had a bunch of people who regularly followed them around and listened to them play. They played their own style of music with originally written songs. Psoas usually went out on extremely long and rough tours, and it was time for the band to go on another long tour again, and they needed a bus driver, rodee, someone to deal with public relations and a soundman. Jay told them about me, how I traveled in the past, knew the country, loved music and played in a band with him in the past; furthermore, I worked a soundboard very well and knew how to connect the PA's speakers and monitors; in addition, I knew the music business, and I knew how to sell the band's merchandise.

I did the public relations while we traveled from city to city, and I sold thousands of dollars worth of the band's CD's, t-shirts, hats and bumper stickers. The band really liked me, and the way in which I worked. Indeed, they never saw anyone like me before; in fact, at first I scared them a little bit because I had that unshaved bearded face, and I had a will to live life on the wild side, but they needed me, and Jay assured them I was cool.

Sex, drugs and rock-n-roll was the life I lived for the next year, and I faithfully got involved in all three. The tour started in Elkins, West Virginia. That was the first gig, and then we went on to Charleston, where Psoas was very well known, and all of their fans showed up there in this old, low-down, raggedy, small bar.

We drank for free at every bar we played in, and most of the people smoked weed also. I brought a lot of drugs with me, as I normally did, and the band jammed for crazed audiences. I also found drugs in the different cities we traveled to. Sex naturally came along with the lifestyle.

We traveled in a very old, run-down Winnebago that was probably built in the '70s, and we towed behind us this old wrecked up maroon van; in addition, we kept the equipment in this van. The Winnebago was so old when I floored the gas pedal, it only went 55 miles per hour, sixty if I was lucky. I was the biggest pill popper in the Winnebago. Everybody else just smoked weed, except the one girl singer, Michelle. She had deep blue eyes and jet-black hair and talked in such a cool manner, slowly and used words from the '60s. She was into heroin and occasionally popped a pill or two.

One time, everybody was asleep except us. As I drove, she came up to the front and started to talk to me. She told me it was that time of the month for her, and she felt like shit. I thought to myself, "Why is she telling me this?"

So, I asked her, "Want a Xanax?"

"What's a Xanax?" She asked in curiosity.

"Here's one. Take it, it'll make you feel better. I know a lady back home who uses them every month."

Michelle took the Xanax and talked to me for about fifteen or twenty minutes until the pill kicked in and hit her strongly. Then, she went to the back top bunk bed and fell quickly asleep and didn't awake until we got to Boulder, Colorado. Michelle must have slept for ten hours, and when she awoke, she came right to me and said, "Antonio, thanks, man. I feel so much better."

They all called me Antonio. I don't know why and didn't ask because I was just having too much fun, and it sounded good to me. As we drove across the country, we smoked joint after joint. Everybody brought his or her own marijuana, so there was an overwhelming amount of weed in the Winnebago.

We didn't shower for days and hardly ate. We stayed in the Winnebago most of the tour and showered only when we stopped at the travel parks that had shower facilities. The majority of the people in the band were vegetarians and liked to eat organic foods and pita bread with humus. Although one time when we stopped at a rest stop for trailers and R.V.'s, I saw a little old restaurant that sat across the street, so I disappeared into this restaurant and ate the biggest, greasiest hamburger they made. Nobody in the band knew were I went except Jay because he knew the ways in which I thought, and I saw him walk into the restaurant, and he came right over and sat across from me in the booth and ordered the same thing.

He asked, "Why didn't you get me before you came here?"

All the members of the band always slept in late; on the contrary, I was up early because I was elated from the sights of the country. I normally drove until I got tired. Then, someone else would take over, so we kept up with the tour's agenda, which the band's manager had put together. I helped anyway I could even though they didn't pay me. They didn't even pay Jay, and he was the drummer. We really didn't need money. We enjoyed the excitement of the music business. We traveled around the country and played music for people in bars and got excessively high on drugs and a few of us had sexual experiences with one another.

One time we pulled into this raggedy, small bar in Kansas City. There weren't that many people in this bar, but the show still went on or else the band wouldn't get paid. While we unloaded the old red stick shift van that was packed tightly with the equipment, this older black man who looked to be homeless tried to steal some of our stuff, but I chased him away with a baseball bat we kept in the RV. While I chased him, my bottle of pills fell out of my pocket and spilled all over the ground. I was incensed. During the whole gig, this same guy just wouldn't go away. I talked to the bar owner, and he told me, "I'm sorry about this. We've been having trouble with this guy for awhile now."

Also, I brought my Colt 380 caliber gun just in case we ran into any problems. The owner even looked out the back door occasionally and told us, "That guy's always around here causing trouble."

We were obviously in a very bad neighborhood.

Since we didn't have to be in Denver, Colorado, for another two days, we hung out in Kansas City for a little while to get food and some other supplies we needed, and I found a doctor there who I conned into prescribing me pain pills. I showed him my legal prescription bottle I kept with me, and my driver's license and told him, "I'm from Pittsburgh, PA, and I'm traveling with a band I work for, and last night I chased a guy who tried to steal our stuff and lost all my medication."

Actually, I only lost a couple of pills because I picked most of them up after I dropped them, but I told the doctor, "I still have to go onto Colorado to work, and I don't have enough medicine to last me until I get back home."

The doctor asked, "How are you paying for this?"

I pulled out a wad of cash and said, "I only have cash. Do you take cash?"

"Yes. I'll take care of you. How long before you'll be back home?"

"I got another month on the road," I told him, and he got his prescription pad out and wrote me a prescription for ninety more pain pills. He probably helped me because I paid by cash, I was quickly leaving town, but his fee was phenomenal. I always made sure my Xanax was safe because I now went into seizures and convulsions if I didn't take them, for I had grown quite dependent. I then went to a grocery store that had a pharmacy inside and got the prescription filled. After that, we headed to Denver.

Shortly after that we stopped at a rest stop because we all slept in the Winnebago, as we regularly did, and needed to go to the bathrooms to clean up a little bit. When I was in the bathroom, I noticed a truck driver and since I was way more experienced about traveling on the road, and we were in the middle of the country unbeknown to me, I asked the truck driver if he knew a quicker way to get to Denver other than route 70, and he told me about a new highway that just opened that took us from where we were to Denver. The people in the band disagreed with me; however, I didn't care what they thought. I made a living traveling around the whole country, and I knew what I was doing and where I was going.

After we arrived in Denver many hours before the band expected us to get there because I took this new road, we sat patiently and waited for show time. While we waited, I went out and explored Denver. I found a pretty large tattoo parlor where I got a tattoo of a little small brightly colored green marijuana leaf on my chest. We played at a rough downtown bar in Denver that normally hired punk rock groups, and we didn't really fit in because we weren't a punk band. Downtown Denver wasn't a bemused placed to be. We hated this area and hurriedly got out of there and went to the next gig in Boulder, Colorado.

As soon as we pulled into a shopping center in Boulder, it was just getting dark, not a cloud in the sky and the moon and stars were shining so brightly Jay, Michelle and I looked at it for at least a half of an hour as we smoked a joint with our heads tilted back glimpsing at the moon, the stars and the largest snow-covered mountain crest I'd ever seen in my life.

One of the girls that played percussion and sang in the band knew somebody from Pittsburgh who now resided in Boulder, and we stayed at this house. There wasn't enough room in the house for all of us to sleep, so Jay, Michelle and I stayed in the Winnebago. While the three of us sat inside the Winnebago, we smoked some weed, talked and laughed tremendously. Then, Michelle went up on the top bunk of the beds in the back. Jay and Michelle seemed like they wanted each other sexually, although neither was making anything really happen. So, Jay and I sat down on the big bottom bed that was red cushioned and could easily hold five people, and we looked at each other slyly as we talked quietly. I motioned for Jay to stand up and talk to Michelle who was directly above us. He nervously stood up and said a few words. I heard them talk as I sat right beneath them, and I said, "Come on back down here, Michelle. You don't have to be afraid."

She came back down, sat right in-between us on the big red cushioned bed, and we continued to talk until Jay and her started to get involved with some foreplay as they sat right next to me. So, I got up and moved to the next bed on the side of the RV. As I watched them, Jay worked his way down to her pussy, played with it and ate her out enough that she took off all of her clothes. Then, Jay got on top of her and started to fuck her. Michelle looked over at me as Jay was on top of her, and she tilted her head back, then opened her mouth, looked right into my eyes and motioned for me to come over and stick my dick in her mouth. And, I did. She seemingly loved it as I sensitively started touching her very softly on her tits. I could tell from experience that she wanted both of us at the same time. As Jay fucked her, I continually played with her hardened nipples, she sucked my cock and only took it out of her mouth to say four words in an exotic way, "Fuck me harder, Jay!"

When Jay got off, Michelle seemingly loved it, and she squirmed around to me and told me, "Stick it in, Antonio. Come on fuck me. It feels so good," she moaned.

I stuck it in her grasping wet pussy and enjoyed the sloppy seconds as Jay watched. I fucked her so hard until we both groaned and moaned delightfully in pleasure as we came together. And then, we all fell asleep sexually satisfied on the big bed under the top bunk in the back of the Winnebago.

I was the first one to awake the next morning as usual, and I went into the house and politely asked if I could take a shower. After I took a shower, the guy who lived there and the bass player in the band, Paco, asked me if I wanted to go hike up a mountain, and I said, "Yeah, that sounds cool."

Everybody else slept in late. The three of us took the red van with the equipment still in it. I was the only one who knew how to drive a stick shift, so I drove up to the bottom of the mountain called The Flat Irons. The guy who lived in Boulder was originally from Pittsburgh and told us an easy way to remember the name of the mountain. He said, "Iron City beer comes from Pittsburgh right? So, just think about drinking a flat Iron City beer. You got a flat iron."

When I got out of the van, I saw a snow-covered field that was slightly sloped upward, which led us to the mountain, and said, "I might not make it the whole way up there, but let's do it." We began the hike from the parking lot, in order to get to the bottom of the mountain, we had to cross the snow-covered field.

The guy who lived there knew the mountain because he hiked up it several different times, and he went first as he led Paco and me. It was the longest I'd ever walked up such a hill, around bends, strictly following the snowy trail while we looked at the snow-covered trees and many other sets of rock formations; one was about as high as a football field straight up. I am certain that all the pot, cocaine and cigarettes I smoked in the past took my breath away and without a doubt stopped me in my tracks several times, and we took our pulse rate with a little digital pulse monitor; hence, Paco's heart rate was normal, and so was the other guy's, but when he took my pulse it was extremely high. So, we rested for a minute and every which way we looked we saw mountains, trees, ice and snow and other hikers. As we gradually got to the top of the Flat Irons mountain, it was absolutely beautiful. I looked down and unbelievably saw what appeared to be a sea of clouds underneath a bright blue sunshiny sky. We were actually above the clouds at an elevation of about eight or nine thousand feet.

I naturally took a bunch of pain pills, a couple of Xanax and smoked a big joint all by myself before we hiked up this mountain, and I was deeply out of breath when we got to the top. So, we sat down and just looked at the marvelous sight in front of us for about an hour. We saw differently sized and shaped white clouds along with the other visible snow-covered crests and peaks of all the mountains that surrounded us. I brought a joint to smoke when we got to the top, but I needed to catch my breath first, and then I lit up the joint, and we smoked it on the top of the mountain as we gazed around at the sights.

When we got back down from the mountain, Jay was mad because I didn't wake him up to go with us, but he was asleep, and I didn't want to wake him up because only three people could fit in the little red van with the equipment in it. Paco always packed the van up with the music equipment like it was a puzzle.

Paco and I got back with the rest of the band, and we all went out together all over the town of Boulder, Colorado, and circulated, promoted and attentively told the people of the town and the tourists that there was a great show tonight at the theater. A very good and well-known band from Pittsburgh, who played originally composed songs, was in town, and they were going to play live in concert. We handed out flyers with the time, day and place we were to play. We also put the flyers on business windows.

I was very good at the public relations part of the business mainly because I took pills that gave me a friendly effect of bravery that allowed me to talk to anyone in a nicely-toned manner. But, the show that night didn't go that well. Not too many people showed up, but I got it all on videotape anyway. This performance was in one of biggest venues in Boulder, so I set up a tripod with Jay's high tech camcorder on it about half way back from the stage, and even though there wasn't a big turnout, I got some great sounds and very well-taped images of the band. That was the biggest venue on the tour.

We put this show behind us and headed up to the "Top of the Square," a place that was distinctively cut out of the mountain into a square, and sat three-quarters of the way up the mountain. There were about four or five bars up there, but we only played in one of them. The Top of the Square sat at a high elevation of about eleven or twelve thousand feet. I swear I must have driven uphill and around curves and bends that were also straight up for over an hour. It seemed like we drove into a big giant wall of mountains. Everywhere we looked, to the right, to the left, behind, in front of us and beyond the hilltop we drove up, were differently sized and oddly shaped mountains all around us. We even saw some mountain goats upon the hilltops, yet we were still far from the Top of the Square. When we arrived at the Top of the Square, we still were only about half way up the mountain.

The gig at the Top of the Square went very well. Specifically, this was the place to party. Every bar was packed. There was a really big turn out at the bar we played; furthermore, I advantageously drank beer after beer for free, and I always smoked joints in between sets. The band usually played three sets per gig. There were other places and towns we played in Colorado that I have no memory of, but I know I was somewhere and high as ever.

Then, our tour agenda took us up to Wyoming to play two gigs: one being in a very small coffee shop, and the other was a gig at a pretty big nightclub. The coffee shop gigs were lame and boring, but the nightclub gigs jammed with a packed house and rowdy audiences. All loved Psoas, and even if the people who lived in these towns never heard the band play before, they still liked the style, the sounds of the music and the looks of the band. Since there were three girls and three guys included in the band, the band attracted both men and women.

Laramie, Wyoming, was really a nice place with nice people, and it gave us a chance to chill out for awhile. The view up there was immaculately gorgeous. The snow covered mountains, and the snowy plains glared as the sun shined and glistened over vast white colored flat lands. Everything was totally covered with snow, and the vehicles we drove weren't made for that kind of snowy weather.

After those gigs, the bass player, Paco, needed to go to the airport back in Denver to pick up his girlfriend who flew in to see him for a few days, so I drove the whole way back down to Denver's airport in the morning when I woke up while everybody else slept in the back except Paco. He sat up front with me and kept me company. When we finally arrived at the airport, I pulled up very cautiously because I didn't know if I could make it into the pick up area. I smoked weed the whole drive down, and I wasn't sure if the Winnebago would make it under the under pass. I didn't know the height of the Winnebago, so I got out and looked and saw I could make it under, and Paco got out, looked and directed me slowly up to the under pass and assured me that the Winnebago would make it under too, but it was very close. So, I drove under and made it; however, I didn't see the airport signs that hung from the underpass and read, "U.S. Air, Continental, TWA and American Airlines." When I drove underneath the underpass, the top of the Winnebago smashed right into the Continental Air sign, which hung lower from the ceiling. Pieces of glass flew everywhere as I saw it come down in front of the window of the Winnebago; in addition to the glass, the noise from the crash was so loud startling everybody awake.

Anyway, the Denver police came, and the officer demanded me to get in the front seat of his car. I went back and sat in his police car while the airport workers cleaned up the mess of glass, metal and plastic. I sat in this police car with my very small 380 caliber automatic gun in one pocket and a big bag of marijuana in the other pocket as I gave the officer my driver's license and other information. First of all, it's illegal to carry a weapon in the State of Colorado. And second of all, I had enough marijuana in my pocket for the cop to take me to jail right there and then. While this may be true, the officer didn't even notice anything suspicious. Then, the officer exited his squad car for a second to talk with an airport worker, and while they talked I swiped a Denver police cap from the front seat of the squad car. The officer returned and told me, "It was only an accident, but I have to give you a citation for reckless driving."

When I was done with the officer, I got back in the Winnebago and told someone else to drive, and Jay took over the wheel. I wasn't even a little shook up over the incident because I've been in so many accidents that this was just another one, so I took a couple of Xanax and the rest of my pain pills on the way to the next gig in Steamboat Springs, Colorado.

When we got there, I needed to hit an emergency room because I'd taken all of my pain pills and felt the withdrawal symptoms of the narcotics hitting me. We stopped at a hospital somewhere in the proximity of Steamboat Springs, Colorado. Thus, I conned another emergency doctor to give me more pain pills after he gave me a shot of Demerol with the same excuse I used with the Kansas City doctor. I told him, "I'm out of medication because we've been on the road for so long, and our last gig was up here, and then I'm going home."

He really didn't want to prescribe me anything and didn't see the need to, but he called my doctor back in Pittsburgh to confirm the prescription I showed him was legal. After he talked with my doctor, he gave me just enough pain pills to last me until I got back home. I'd left the emergency room in Steamboat Springs and enjoyed the town we were in.

Jay and I treated these towns we traveled to as tourists, for music was just second nature to us. As far as I was concerned I was seeing and touring the country, as I did when I worked heavy construction. Only this job wasn't like a real job. I did this for the fun of it. After all, working this job allowed me to get drunk, stoned and completely fucked-up and then go to work!

On our way up to the gig we needed to play that night, we drove up this extremely long hill as we passed large green elevation signs with white numbers and letters that read 5,000 feet, 7,000 feet and 14,000 feet. As soon as we stopped, that's when it hit me that I was also out of weed. So, somehow I needed to get a large enough quantity of weed to last me until I got home. I got little bits of weed off the people in Steamboat Springs, but I couldn't find anyone to sell me a large quantity of weed. I was panicked.

I called Jay's brother, Mickey, and he sent me a little bit of weed that weighed slightly under an ounce through the overnight mail systems, and I sent Mickey two front row seat tickets to The Who concert I was going to miss in Pittsburgh. I just went to the post office, mailed the tickets and picked up the weed. It needed to be somewhat under an ounce because if I got caught with an ounce or anything over an ounce, the law states that's distribution, and the fine and penalty were much greater. The weed was put in dark emptied out caster oil bottles, so nobody would smell it. Also, I called my mother to have her Western Union me more money.

The band was scheduled to play for one night, Friday night. The place jammed. But, the outcome of people who came to see and hear Psoas play ensured the owner of the bar that people would come back the next night. The bar was really long and not so wide; however, it was one of the biggest bars in town. They had about four or five pool tables, poker machines and four or five dartboards. This bar was overwhelmingly packed with people, and it had one of the longest bars I'd ever seen. I even met some people who smoked pipes filled with marijuana right in the bar with me. I walked outside, and there were people getting high out there and nicely asked me to join them in smoking a joint. Everybody I met in Steamboat Springs was friendly, loved live bands, shared their drugs and nobody griped about anything.

There were even people who stood outside and waited for a chance that maybe somebody would let them in. That Friday night, the bar made so much money they asked the band to come back the next night, Saturday, and the owner even offered them more money to come back another night. The owner of the bar appreciatively paid for us to stay in a motel down the street, and that gave us all a chance to shower and get cleaned up a bit. I thought I'd shave my beard off now, and I did. After I finally shaved, everybody in the band except Jay said, "Oh! There he is." That was the first time the band saw me without a beard.

One night, we all went up to the hot springs. Mostly, everybody there was naked and in the hot springs, so we also got naked and went in the springs. The water in the springs was so hot the steam came off of the water like the water from the springs was on fire. While we were in the springs, Michelle, Jay and I smoked a joint over in a desolated corner of the one spring. I already popped some pills before we left the motel and made the first move on Michelle. I gently rubbed her upper thighs and worked my way to her pussy as she blissfully grinned and raised her arms in a stretching motion as she spread her legs open. The three of us lustfully engaged in a threesome again right in the fiery hot water of the hot springs.

Jay, Michelle and I stayed in one room, and the other four people in the band stayed in the other room. There were two beds in our room; nevertheless, we used one bed for a while, and then I went back to my bed. Michelle switched beds and got laid-out hard that night by both Jay and me. This twenty-one year old girl loved the love and sex we gave her. Then, she slept most of the next day while Jay and I went out to get cappuccinos and a few souvenirs for our family members.

Saturday night, the place got packed again. Everybody bought all the t-shirts, CD's and bumper stickers. I actually sold out of everything I had to sell. I turned people away when they came by to buy a t-shirt or anything else I sold with the bands name on it. Some women even invited me to go to some parties after the gig. I was ready and willing to go to some parties, but I couldn't go because this was the last gig, and everybody else wanted to get home. In the bar on that last night, I talked with an older hippie looking guy with white hair and a very long white beard. He must have been going on sixty. He told me that all the big bands today came through Steamboat Springs before they became famous, like ZZtop, The Grateful Dead and even The Eagles. After they were done playing, the leader of the Psoas introduced everyone in the band and lastly, he wished a special thanks to me. As a result, everybody in the bar yelled Antonio at the same time so loudly that I got the biggest smile on my face and couldn't help but to laugh. That was the greatest feeling and the greatest moment of my life.

BACK TO PITTSBURGH

About the time we left, there was so much snow that the bulldozers had pilled it up along the sides of the road. The heavy white snow was pilled so high it actually covered the top of the stop signs. But, that didn't stop us. Everybody in the band wanted to get back to Pittsburgh.

As soon as we got home, I needed to see my doctors and other dealers on the streets to get my drugs. I was slowly running out of money because of the doctor bills and the drugs I constantly bought. But, it was good to be back in Pittsburgh.

We played a gig at the Star Lake Amphitheater and opened up for the Pittsburgh band Rusted Root who opened up for the famous notoriously known guitar player Carlos Santana. We now traveled in an old silver painted stick shift school bus with a bad clutch, for the Winnebago was dead after that tour. The new school bus was all torn apart in the inside and reconverted with long bench like seats along the sides, and two very wide and large bunk beds for sleeping in the back. While I drove to the Amphitheater, a line of cars was lined up waiting to get into the place; however, we got a V.I.P. parking pass since we were playing there that night and were allowed to drive right past all the cars.

But, as I drove recklessly fast past the cars I accidentally hit one of the cars, actually I sideswiped it. I did stop, and one of the other people on the bus who traveled with us to this show was a paramedic and told the guy who drove that car to come find the big silver school bus after the show. And, he did, so another guy who was with us, Claude, a friend of mine who was an auto mechanic came with me to see and fix the damaged car I'd hit. As soon as we got to the vehicle and looked at it, Claude told me the damaged car was quite easy to fix, and he fixed it in a matter of minutes. The guy was satisfied with the way his car got fixed and didn't pursue any further trouble, such as to exchange insurance information.

The girls that played in the band Psoas knew the girls that played in the band Rusted Root and that's how Psoas got to play that gig at the Star Lake

166

Amphitheater. When I met Carlos, I tried not to show the thoughts and feelings I felt. I just said, "Hi, how are you. I'm a guitar player too, and I've liked your music since I was very young."

Carlos spoke with an accent and said, "Thank you. You're band sounded pretty good out there. I heard you guys from back here. I like that new sound you Pittsburgh bands have."

"It was an honor to meet you, man," I said. Carlos left, but I talked much more with his brother, who looked just like Carlos and hung out under a huge awning where they kept the food and alcohol. They had big green plastic tubs filled with ice and just about any kind of beer you can think of, including the imports. The foods consisted of shrimp cocktails, sandwiches, and chicken, different types of pastas and salads and humus with pita bread for the vegetarians. The food sat on three long tables, which were placed in a rectangular shape with one side open. Trailers and very big tour buses were parked in the back. Anyway, I drank a couple of beers with Carlos's brother, bullshitted a little bit, and then I went back out to the front of the stage to see the show. Once I had gotten some pills and booze in me, I could talk or hang out with almost anybody.

We then played some gigs up state in New York. The first gig was in Oneonta, New York. It was a one-night gig, and the place wasn't all that lively. The bar sat on a dark corner and there weren't that many people; indeed, this bar was probably one of the smallest bars the band ever played in. Then, we went to Cornell College, where the young college girls raved and ramped around the college campus, and the guys wanted to see the girls in the band, and all were really attracted to the band because one of the local radio stations played Psoas's songs all the time. These were the times when I loved the public relations part of the job. I got to meet and talk to so many different girls that I felt like I was in heaven. Gig after gig and place after place, the music allured the women in.

Then, we went onto Ithaca, New York, where we played one gig, and then I ran into a major problem. I'd ran out of Xanax, and if I didn't take them, I could have fatally gone into seizures, so I found the closest medical center, and they gave me problems because I was from out of town, and Xanax was a controlled substance. I called my doctors back in Pittsburgh, and they needed to fax my whole medical history up to this medial center in order for the doctors up there to prescribe me another prescription. It was some kind of New York law or something. Any other place in the United States I could have conned the doctors. I always smoothly and coolly talked my way into getting the prescriptions off of any doctor. Everything and anything I said didn't work in this place. They absolutely would not fill my prescription unless my doctor back home in Pittsburgh sent all of my medical records, or they weren't giving me anything, so I stayed put and waited anxiously until my medical records got faxed to the doctors. Then, I got my prescriptions. This made the band angrily peeved at me because they needed to be in Buffalo that night for a gig, and I held them up.

On the way to Buffalo, we got a flat tire out in the middle of nowhere, and we didn't have a spare. A nice older hippie like gentleman who walked with a cane stopped and kindly offered his assistance, and we took it. Dual tires were on the back axle, so we were able to drive to this guy's house, and we left the bus at this guy's house, and this man and his wife actually were so nice they drove us to the gig. Three of us fit in the old red van that held the equipment and drove it to the gig while the rest of the band went in the guy's truck; thus, we made it to the gig on time and told the couple to stick around; drinks were on us.

After the up state New York gigs and a few more local gigs, it was time for the band to take a break, and they concentrated on making another CD.

And, that was it for me except for a couple of local gigs I helped them out with at The Graffiti and two bars in Oakland.

At The Graffiti everything was done professionally. The Graffiti was a really big nightclub with three floors and two bars. Other up-rising bands from different states like the band Clam-Bake, which originated out of Boston, they came to Pittsburgh and were booked to play at The Graffiti. It was a profit-making establishment. Before the show started, we all were downstairs in the greenroom, which was filled with marijuana smoke; in addition, all along the walls were tables set up with food and drinks. We smoked some pot and ate the food spread they laid out, and then it was show time.

I worked the door and collected the money that night because in a place like this, the band's producer worked the soundboard. So, I collected the money and my buddy Claude stamped hands as people rushed into see Psoas. When I got the first thousand, it went straight to the owner of the club. We both sat in his office and counted the money twice, and then I went back to work and drink. Any money that came in after that, the band kept as profit. I had two friends with me that night: Claude and Nico, the guy who got dishonorably discharged from the Army. One helped me watch the door and stamp hands, and Nico had brought some acid with him and gave me a hit. He and I started drinking beers that were put on the bar tab. We probably drank a case of Heineken between the two of us. I had my usual set up of t-shirts and CD's I sold, but all over the counter were empty bottles of Heinekens. I was tripped out pretty good when the producer came down from the soundboard and lighting controls that were on the second floor and faced the stage, and he asked me to come up and help him. I did, and I got Nico to collect the money at the door, and when the gig was over, he handed me two hundred dollars. He stole four hundred out of the twelve hundred dollars that came. At this point I didn't care because I worked hard traveling, loading and unloading the equipment; I sold the bands t-shirts and CD's, and they never paid me a dime. I cared more about working in the music business, in spite of the money.

The other club in Oakland Psoas played got overwhelmingly packed with people. I worked the door and took the money in. Eventually, I turned people away, for the place was packed. There were young kids that tried to get in free, but I stopped them. I wanted the money. One guy didn't have the money; instead, he gave me a little bag of good weed, so I let him go in. Another guy told me he'd go in and get money from his friend and bring it back, but I knew he wouldn't come back, so I went in and grabbed him, made him pay or leave.

He was a few dollars short, so I let him go back in and watch the band.

Eventually, I stopped working with the Psoas altogether. Money was very low for me, and I never got paid when I worked for the band, so I needed a way to make more money. I wasn't dealing drugs, and I didn't have too many different schemes going on because I wasn't in direct contact with people anymore, for I was basically still hidden and only trusted a few people. But, I needed a way to make more money.

OUT OF THE BAND
AND BACK TO LIFE

Mickey and I hung out at the strip bars around town, and one time, we brought Jay with us. He met a twenty-year-old brown haired stripper with a really nice figure and just the right size tits. Her name was Kim, and she started to live at our house because Jay and Kim hit it off right away. This girl knew she looked good and liked to show her body. One night, Kim went into Mickey's bedroom, lifted up her shirt and showed Mickey her tits. Then, she wanted to fuck him, but Mickey just let her blow him. She teased me also behind Jay's back; nevertheless, we told Jay, and we all decided to keep her around for awhile for fun.

Kim came down to my room one night while nobody else was home, and all she had on was only a long t-shirt; no panties and no bra. First, Kim and I sat on the silky tan leather couch, and we both looked and talked to each other in a flirtatious way. Kim spread her legs as she was laid back on the couch and let me get a glimpse of her pussy. Secondly, she played with my bulging cock with her foot, so I started to play with her pussy with my foot. Finally, we moved to the bed and kissed passionately. Then, I went down and ate her out until she quivered and told me to fuck her; so then I fucked her roughly. I only fucked her twice in the short time she lived with us.

Kim stayed with us for about two months and always came home with wads of cash. I was usually home while she worked. Kim kept her money right on the floor of Jay's bedroom, and I counted it once. There was over one thousand dollars. I uncaringly took three hundred and put it in my pocket. I did this continuously while Kim lived with us. Kim was young, and that was a lot of money for a young girl to keep track of, so I took advantage.

She was a stripper, and she put on sex shows. That's why she always brought home cash. One night, we got Kim to bring a couple of girls over to the house; thus, we got a discounted fee. Three girls, not Kim, came over with all kinds of differently shaped and sized sex toys, and they put a sex show on in front of us. Kim watched with Mickey, Jay and me. After their show, we all got blowjobs right there in the living room. The three of us chipped in and gave them a nice tip. But, my money situation had gotten so low that I did odd jobs, which didn't pay that much.

Meeting the Undercover Drug Agents

At the V.F.W. picnic that year, my father brought me up to the chief of police who was also an undercover narcotics agent. My father knew the police chiefs of four different boroughs. This chief of police knew I needed a job, and he showed me his separate 'drug task force badge' and asked me, "Do you want to work for these guys? They need someone like you right now, and they'll pay you to work for them."

The house I lived in was in the perfect place to arrange drug deals with people who lived in the neighborhood, and I lived with Jay and Mickey, so it appeared that I was a cool person, and nobody would have imagined I'd do something like becoming an informant. So I told him, "I'll think about it and come up to the station to see you if I'm interested." After about a week of pondering the notion in my head, I boldly decided to go and check this whole scene out. I went to the police station and saw the chief. I knew the guy most of my life. He put me in contact with another officer on the task force who I knew from my cocaine dealing days. I met with him at a local Dunkin' Doughnuts shop. He was in plain clothes, drove an unmarked car and took me to get interviewed by the head of the drug task force at a fire hall on the top floor in a pretty well hidden back room where four other agents waited for us to arrive.

I didn't like this particular officer that took me there because I knew he was a dirty cop from my old street days. He snorted lines of coke, and he took blowjobs from women who wanted to get out of trouble. So, as soon as I got the other agents alone without this one cop there, I told them I thought he was dirty, and I would not work with him. The other agents said okay, and they told me that I was an extraordinary and unique confidential informant because nobody ever dared put down as many dealers and as much cocaine as I'd done back when I did Jimmy, Tony, Mike and Hassuan. We'd discussed some names, and how much I was going to get paid for this work. The money didn't sound like much compared to the first time I did this; however, these dealers were not as big and didn't deal with as much weight, but the excitement of it all caught my interest.

GETTING PAID
TO BUY COCAINE

These agents wanted to start with a friend of mine who I grew up with, P.J. I told them I wasn't going to help put P.J. in jail. An agent who worked under Pat Sr. assured me that P.J. would not go to jail. They had other plans for him. We also discussed a couple of big time dealers they wanted me to help them get. A guy named Mark, who bought the cocaine in kilos and sold it as ounces. I told them I knew him and would be happy to help if the money was right. We then discussed a guy named Spoon. Spoon's the guy who supplied P.J. If P.J. didn't put him down after he got busted, I was to go in after Spoon and another guy named Al, who was a pretty large dealer and a lot older than I was.

The plan was that I needed to start buying off of these dealers and then introduce an undercover narcotics agent to the dealers to get me out of the picture, or else I'd have to go to court and testify, and nobody wanted that, especially me. So, I really needed to gain the dealers trust in order for this to work because the Attorney General's undercover agents had policies and procedures to go by.

The buy paid me. Every time Jocko or I bought any amount of cocaine from any one dealer, I got paid two hundred and fifty dollars. I didn't even have to be there. That didn't seem like much at first, but after a period of time, it added up. I even got forty dollars to make a recorded telephone call while I sat in the undercover agent's office. I called up the dealers at first with a microphone taped to the earpiece of the telephone that had a wire on it that led down to a tape recorder that an agent worked. He told me exactly when to dial, what to say, what information to get and when I should hang up the phone. If I could get the undercover agent introduced to the dealers, that put me out of the picture and out of the risk of being made as an informant, and the dealer would then be selling cocaine to a plain clothed cop. This way the dealers could only assumingly think I set them up, but they had no proof. If I got made, the word would have gotten out on the streets that I was an informant, and then I wouldn't be able to make any more money.

The first guy, P.J., was extremely easy because I knew him my whole life, and he'd never thought that I worked for the task force. Even though I hadn't seen him in a long time, he was still my friend. One night, I went back into Tuggies, a place I feared to go, but that's were P.J. worked as a bartender and a cook. I'd grabbed P.J., and Jay, and we all went outside and smoked a joint. If he knew I smoked weed, he trusted me more. That was the best way I befriended somebody. I hung out with them without the agents around and on the days I didn't make a buy for the cops. The task force didn't really care about marijuana. They wanted the hard drugs. The cocaine, heroin or crack was what they looked for. Every time I bought coke from somebody I needed to be wired. The wire was taped with duct tape under my shirt to my chest and was very uncomfortable because there was a little box that went around my waist, slightly down the front of my jeans and was connected to the wire and microphone. We normally met at their office or at an undisclosed place where they took my guns, searched me for drugs or money, so they knew they were getting the drugs from the right person and paying the exact price, and then they followed me to the place were we made the buy. They would give me the amount of money I needed to buy the coke with. At the buy, I would always get the seller to say things twice to make sure it definitely got recorded.

"What's up P.J.," I'd ask. "What do you got for me?"

"A half-ounce," P.J. said.

I'd ask again in astonishment as if I didn't hear him, "What do you got?"

P.J. said louder, "A half-ounce."

"How much do you want for it?"

"Seven hundred and fifty dollars."

I'd say surprisingly, "How much?"

"Seven hundred and fifty dollars," he repeated.

"Seven fifty, man you can't do me any better than that so I make some money."

"No. I'm not even making that much off of you," he replied.

I knew he made some pretty good money off me because the cocaine was cut up. I needed to play the roll of a cocaine buyer, and I was really good at it because I've done it most of my life. So, I knew how to act, what to say and when to say it.

The undercovers heard the whole deal go down; moreover, they got it on tape. I gave P.J. the money that the undercover cops gave to me to buy the coke with, and P.J. gave me the half-ounce of cocaine that I in turn gave to the undercover task force agents back at the undisclosed meeting place. They would make me sign a paper from the Attorney General's office saying that everything done and or discussed was strictly confidential, and my signature proved I'd gotten paid. Then, they gave me my two hundred and fifty dollars. I actually got paid to buy cocaine for the police, and I unbelievably continued to do so tax-free.

It worked the same way the next time only I brought one of the undercover agents with me, and I introduced P.J. to him as my brother-in-law. I still wore a wire just in case we separated; however, P.J. didn't have the coke on him and had to go get it. He told us to wait in the parking lot, but he was a small time dealer, and I knew him very well, so I told the agent to follow him as we were in his royal blue Trans-am. Jocko, the agent, didn't want to. I assured him everything would be fine because P.J. told me where he went to get the stuff. He mentioned he went to an apartment complex called Seville Square the other undercovers were listening on the wiretap I had on, and they got there before we did. Because of this, the undercovers knew where P.J. got the cocaine.

After three or four buys that I made with the wiretap and with Jocko, the agent, I assured P.J. that my brother in-law was cool, and P.J. trustingly sold him the cocaine. Now, I was safely out of the picture, but every time they made a buy off of P.J., they called me up and told me to come get my money. I didn't have to do anything except go sign a paper and collect my money. Just because I made the introduction to the undercover agent, I got paid whenever he bought anything else.

They used a unique way to bust P.J. The one undercover agent, who worked under Pat Sr. in Chalfant, patrolled the streets in his police uniform and squad car one night. Jocko set up a deal with P.J., so the agents watched him get the cocaine, the agent in the marked squad car pulled him over for a traffic violation, going through a stop sign, knowing P.J. had the cocaine on him, searched his car, found the cocaine and arrested him. The funny thing about it was that they said P.J. went through a stop sign, but he really didn't. Jocko wasn't even around to buy the coke because he knew P.J. was going to be arrested. The plan they'd concocted worked perfectly.

They kept their word. P.J. didn't go to jail; instead, they tried to get him to turn on Spoon, and he talked. P.J. told them what they needed to know. That was who I was supposed to go after next, but they weren't going to pay me when they got someone to do it for free. I could have made money on

Spoon, but they used P.J. because they didn't have to pay him. That's the difference between a snitch and a confidential informant. P.J. worked off the charges against him by turning Spoon in. He snitched on him, whereas I got paid to go into a dealer's house and buy cocaine.

I got to be close business friends with Jocko as we worked together, and I trusted his judgment. He told me, "We need you to get in close with Al and Mark. These guys are big time dealers. We tested you with P.J. Now it's time to get the bigger guys."

The agent who worked underneath Pat Sr. brought me downtown to meet Mike Fischer, the Attorney General. I asked, "Why do I have to meet him?"

"You have to talk to the D.A., and Mike Fischer wants to talk to you," he told me.

When I got downtown and met Mike Fischer, he said to me in a grateful way, "Thank you for your help. You're doing a great service for your community."

As I shook his hand I said, "No problem. Whatever I can do to help, and it's very nice to meet you, sir."

Then, I needed to answer a series of questions from another lawman or an attorney of some sort. He asked very politely, "Nobody coerced you into doing this, did they?"

"No sir. I just don't like drugs."

"How did you find out about these guys who sell cocaine?"

"The one guy asked me if I wanted to buy some, and I went and told a couple police officers I know, and they sent me to the task force. The other guys I just know from word on the street. Plus, I'm not afraid of drug dealers."

"That's all the questions I have for you. Will you be willing to testify if need be?" he asked.

"We worked something out where I'd rather introduce the agent to the dealer than testify, but if I have to, I will," I bravely told him. We shook hands, and he thanked me.

The agent who took me there and I left and stopped for lunch at a deli downtown; however, this agent started to have a beef with me because of the way I talked. I could talk in a ruthless manner and didn't give a shit who anyone was, including the cops. I wasn't kissing anyone's ass, and this guy didn't like the way I came off. So, one day I went to Pat Sr., the undercover agent's chief of police, and Pat paged the agent and told him to come up to his house. When the agent got there, he tried to tell Pat I was a cocky motherfucker, and I was; nevertheless, Pat Sr. told the agent, "Leave him alone. Let him do what he wants, and you better make sure nothing happens to him."

I laid tire right in front of both of them when I pulled away.

Over the screeching squeals of the tires, I heard the agent say to Pat, "Look. You see what I mean?"

Pat just said, "Use him and pay him. You know what he's like. He's not afraid of anyone."

After all that little hassle, it was time to work and go get Al. I met with the task force agents again, and they told me to go get in with Al, and I did. At first, I befriended him. Then, I set up the deals.

Befriending Al was not that easy. We played tennis together and just hung out and bullshitted, maybe smoked some weed. I appeared to be cool. No cop was going to smoke marijuana; plus, I'd gotten that little tattoo of a marijuana leaf on my chest that I got in Denver when I traveled with Psoas, and I always made sure it was visible to the drug dealers. People hardly ever took me to be an informant because of the way I acted, and the drugs they knew I did. I knew how to act on the streets. I knew the sayings, and I could even do drugs if I wanted, and I normally did.

Money Earned Legally
and Excitably

It was almost eight or nine months after we did P.J. That's how long it took me to get Al to sell me coke. I probably could have asked him sooner, but I didn't want to appear too anxious. So, I asked Al if he would sell me some coke because I could make money off of a couple sales. I let Al know about my brother-in-law who sold coke to the Pagans motorcycle gang for me in the past. He didn't know, but I fabricated the whole story that I told him.

He said, "Sure, why not. When do you want it?"

I put him off by saying, "How much money do I need to get for an ounce?"

"You can have it for fourteen hundred," he replied.

"No way. I'll give you twelve-fifty.

"Let me get the cash together, and I'll call you tomorrow."

I called Jocko and asked if they were ready, and they said, "Yeah, we've been watching you."

This time the wiretap was in the form of a pager, and all I really needed to do was wear it on the side of my pants. It didn't suspiciously look odd. At first with Al, we bought an ounce, and everything got recorded perfectly. That was enough to bust him right there and then, on the other hand, they wanted to show he was trafficking the coke on a weekly basis to a number of different people. So, I needed to make a buy every week, and then get Jocko introduced somehow. This was different because Al was an older, more experienced man and knew the business better. That's why I really took my time and gained his trust. I continued to buy from him. Only now, I bought two ounces at a time with the money that Jocko photocopied and then gave to me to give to Al. They recorded all that was said and marked him as a cocaine supplier. I literally just kept on buying off of him with the task force's money, and I collected my two hundred and fifty dollars every week until I got Jocko introduced and in on the deals.

I told Al, "My brother-in-law from Irwin can get rid of some weight because he already supplies the town, but this coke is way better than the junk he gets. Jocko would probably buy an ounce a week on top of the ounce I'm buying, but he wants to see the shit first before he gives me that much money. He really doesn't want to give the money to me without the product."

Al asked, "Is this guy cool?"

I assured Al he was very cool by telling him, "He's my brother in-law. He told me he doesn't like to give that much money out to anyone. That's a lot of money, Al, and he trusts me, but he doesn't know what I'm going to do with all his money. I showed him my coke, and he loved it. They don't get this kind of quality out where he lives."

So, I asked Al if I could bring him down one day to meet him, and Al agreed, although Al wanted to check him out first.

Jocko played Al coolly that day like Al didn't mean that much to him, and he made it seem like he could go elsewhere for cocaine; on the other hand, he made it look like Al's coke was better than anything he'd ever gotten, and the next day Al said to me, "Okay. You bring your brother in-law and the money for two ounces, and I'll hook you guys up."

I told Al, "You can make a lot of money from him. He's big time and can get rid of ounces of coke in a heartbeat out in Irwin."

"You got to be here with him," Al said.

I replied, "Of course. I want to get my coke too. Al you know me. This is my brother in-law. Can't you take care of him? With the garbage cocaine they get out there, we can all make big money."

Jocko, with his long hair and his street smarts from being in the business so long, acted really suave and played it perfectly. He majored in criminal psychology and knew when to talk and when to listen. So, Jocko and I went to Al's place, which was furnished comfortably with expensive furniture. Al had nice leather couches with rich looking mirrors that hung above, and he had a pool table and dartboard in the furnished basement with a fireplace, a big screen TV, and a stocked bar. The back-up task force agents were right down the street just in case something went wrong. I didn't need to wear a wiretap because Jocko was present at the scene, but back-up agents were right down the street. One thing I didn't like about Jocko was that he always kept his hand on his gun. But, he never showed his paranoia. I knew him; therefore, I saw his paranoia. They take my guns off of me and put me in a dangerous position, but they needed to protect themselves with their guns. He was used to being in dangerous positions and probably got a gun pulled on him before.

When Al offered us a line of coke, we always refused and used the same excuse. If we start, we won't quit, and Al respected that because coke dealers who got high on their supply risked their business and jeopardized everyone else's. After about a month of bringing Jocko to Al's, Al trusted him now, and I told Al, "I'm headed to Florida for a week or two man. I need a break."

I asked Al in a calm, but cool manner, "Would you take care of Jocko while I go to Florida?"

He obligingly said, "Yeah. He seems cool, and since he's your brother-in-law, I trust him, and I'll take care of him."

"Thanks man. I appreciate it. You can make some serious money off Jocko."

I really didn't go to Florida, but that was just an excuse to get me out of the picture. One thing was for sure, I never wanted to testify or go to court, and so I did whatever I needed to do to get Jocko in on the deals. He continually bought about twenty ounces of cocaine off of Al in the period of about two or three months, and I got paid every time Jocko made a buy. Jocko bought an ounce a week, and that was two hundred and fifty dollars in my pocket every week, but I couldn't leave the house for awhile because I was supposedly in Florida. I made close to $4,000 off of Al and loved every minute of it, especially the minutes I wasn't there and still got paid.

Al had a prior criminal record, so he was going away for a long time. When they busted Al, the agents barged right in his front door with a search and arrest warrant. I could never watch a bust go down, but I heard about them from Jocko. At the same time there were other agents who kept tabs on Mike Jr., and they watched him like a hawk and the people he dealt with. Internal Affairs even got involved because of the dirty cops.

They saw where Mike went, whom he dealt with and when the deals got done. Two of the undercover agents flew in their planes, which had the highest quality surveillance equipment. They could read a license plate number from many miles up and even recognize the people's faces with the high technological cameras they used.

I remember the one officer said, "My plane has a double engine and can fly at very high altitudes."

The other cop said, "My plane got a single engine, but I got the quality in surveillances. I fly out of Allegheny Airport. Where do you fly out of?"

"That's where I fly out too."

As I listened to the conversation about whose plane was better, I got the information I didn't expect to get. Now, I knew how they watched people from their planes. I immediately went and told Gino about this because I still dealt marijuana and narcotics with him, and he always gave me information about what Mike Jr. was up to; in addition, I even helped Gino with his landscaping business as a regular job, and I made extra cash or sometimes took my payments in pain pills or weed. Gino thought they used helicopters to watch people until I let him in on what I'd heard. I told him one day at work while we drove in his new red dump-truck that the undercover task force used planes like that one, as I pointed in the sky at a small plane that flew very low and was right in front of us.

The agent on the task force who paid me and who worked under Pat Sr. called me up one day and told me that Mike Jr. got busted. He told me this because I'd mentioned to him about Mike Sr. being after me for the busts that happened a long time ago. He said to me with integrity, "You might want to lay low and watch out for the old man. Okay. I'll see you later. Be careful."

It was a very short conversation, and he didn't tell me any details; however, I got more information on the streets. Mike Jr. got popped in a Harmarville motel trying to buy five kilos of cocaine from an Arab guy we went to school with. They were onto him from the night way back in the V.F.W. when I gave his name to Pat Sr. It took a long time to arrest Mike Jr. because his father knew dirty cops, and his father had other connections on the streets. So, I did lay low and watched my back cautiously. Mike Sr. already came at me once, so I knew he'd come again if he got the chance. All my guns were locked and loaded, and I was ready for action because of the effects of all the pain pills I took and the state of paranoia my mind was in. My doctors couldn't prescribe me enough pain pills for the habit of mine that grew so large; therefore, I needed to go on the streets to get more pills, and the guy I got the pills from knew Mark. It was Bird, the same guy I supplied cocaine to when I used to sell coke, only now he bought his blow off of Mark.

BIRD AND MARK

At first with Bird, I brought Jocko right to his house. We pulled up in Jocko's brightly blue colored Trans-Am, but Bird didn't have anything and wasn't at will to go get some caine. Also, Bird was keen and knew something didn't seem right that particular day. Although Bird and I had our disagreements in the past, he still accepted me into his house, and he sold me all kinds of narcotics like Morphine, prescription strength narcotic cough syrups called, Tussinex and Hicodin, regular pain pills, and sometimes, I even did heroin with him; however, I never got too deeply involved with heroin because I knew the consequences of being hooked on heroin; it was worse than being hooked on cocaine.

Bird liked to smoke crack most of the time, so I started to smoke crack again for the first time in a long long time. I couldn't believe it. I told myself I'd never smoke that shit again; nevertheless, one hit is all it took, and I went off on a crack smoking frenzy without the Attorney Generals drug task force knowing about it. Yet, I continued to work for them and with the money I got from the task force, I spent on narcotics or crack. It had been years since I'd smoked crack, but once I started: Look out! I went on a rampage, although it paid off in the end. Consequently, there always was an end, a bottom and a surrendering of one's physical body, mentality and spirituality.

Nevertheless, I got paid at this particular bottom, and the bottom ended after we did Mark. When I dealt with and set up Mark, I got wickedly hay wired, and the agents saw it in me; but they wanted Mark badly because he was the biggest dealer at the time, and I was the only one who knew how to get him. I was in. Lucky for me, Mark was more into pills than I was and took different kinds of pills also. Benzodiazepines were pills that slowed you down as would a sedative and made a person unaware, tired, and took away any paranoid feelings a person may have had, and Mark took them like they were M&M's. So, Mark remained calm when he dealt with me. I knew Mark from the past, for we worked together before. I wondered if he knew I informed on other dealers, although it appeared he didn't know. He knew I dealt with Bird, so he thought I was cool and took my money and business away from Bird and put the money in his pocket.

Since we knew each other in the past, Mark trusted me right of the bat and started to supply me with cocaine. I would give him some marijuana and pain pills without the undercovers knowing about it. We also hung out and played tennis and drank beers every once in awhile; however, I never put myself in a position where I would endanger my life. I used my wits and my street smarts. That's how I always gained the trust of the people I set up. I needed to have some drugs on me, do some drugs and let people who sold the drugs see me do these things. This way whomever I dealt with thought I was cool; nevertheless, I hated cocaine terribly and especially the dealers who sold the coke to kids and other people. It ruined people's lives. Yes, I took some pills and smoked pot, but I never sold it to people anymore. There wasn't any money in pills or weed that compared to the money that was involved in the cocaine business.

Mark called me on the phone one day and asked me if I knew a P.J. who got busted selling coke, and I simply denied it and said I didn't know a P.J., when actually I was the one who popped him. Nevertheless, Mark seemingly trusted me, and I told the undercover agents it was a good time if they wanted to start on Mark. He was always fucked up on narcotics, which impaired his judgment. So, they called me in to their office because we never really talked on the phone about the set ups we made.

At the office, we discussed the way things would be done. I could never set up a deal on my own without the agents knowing about it because they needed to get people together for back up; they needed to get the money and follow police procedures. The agents told me how I should set up the deals, and it usually started out with a wire tapped telephone call like all the other deals; however, now we were involved with a very big time cocaine dealer who bought and sold kilos of cocaine. In certain situations, the agents asked me my opinion about how we could do buys, how we could introduce Jocko, or when the introduction could be made, of course the undercovers had the final say. Then, through the phone call the deal would be made. A time, place, quantity and price would all normally be arranged in an encoded way of talk, but Mark was so fucked up on narcotics he didn't even realize what he said on the telephone. After that, we waited for the time that the deal would go down, and I would be properly instructed on how to go about doing the deal. Although I probably knew more than the undercovers knew about how to make a deal go down smoothly because of all the dealings and informing I've done in the past, I had to listen and do what they told me to do for our safety and for the policies they needed to follow.

The first deal with Mark went down in a McDonald's parking lot where there were a lot of people around, but I had a wire tap on me so the other agents could listen and record what was said. This time the wiretap was in the form of a cellular telephone, and I found it to be the best and easiest wire I'd ever took along to a drug deal. Even if I got searched for a wire, Mark would have never found one, and it didn't look like a wire to the drug dealers; it looked like a normal cell phone.

Jocko and I met Mark after the recorded phone conversation at the McDonald's parking lot, and Mark was uneasy because I brought another person with me. As we sat and waited for Mark to come, the leader of the task force noticed a mark unit, a squad car with lights and Murrysville police written on the side of it; thus, he radioed to the Murrysville police department to get the marked unit out of the area, so it wouldn't jeopardize the buy that would be made. Jocko, and the other two guys in the blue blazer also had hand held two-way radios, so they were able to communicate with each other; furthermore, they all heard the buy go down with Mark and me from the wire. If we pulled away they would know where to go. Then, Mark showed up. He pulled his car right next to Jocko's Trans Am, and he motioned for me to come into his car. We really didn't want the buy done like that. They wanted to make the deal right there in the parking lot; on the other hand, I had to go and get in Mark's car because when you're a buyer you do what the seller wants you to do, and Mark started to drive away after I got in.

"Whoa! Where you goin'? Stay here."

I knew the other agents were listening, and Jocko needed to stay put in the parking lot, so I told Mark, "Don't go too far man. I got this dude's money."

"Don't worry about it. We'll just take a little ride."

Since I knew the other agents heard us on the wiretap, I demanded very loudly to ensure the other agents had my back: "Just go across the street to Ferry's Pharmacy."

We drove over to the pharmacy while we made the deal, and I did just what I did to P.J. I made Mark repeat everything twice by asking, "I got this dude's cash. What do you got for me?"

"You said you wanted an ounce," he said slowly like he was all pilled up.

"An ounce of coke. Let me see it. How much is here?" I made him repeat. He said it louder, "An ounce."

"How much you want for this?" I needed a price recorded.

"I got to get at least twelve hundred for it," he slurred.

Just at that time, I saw the other two agents drive into the pharmacy in the big blue Chevy Blazer as we pulled out; however, Mark didn't have the slightest clue to what was going on or who was in the Blazer. They heard me on the wire telling Mark to go to the pharmacy, so they quickly followed us while Jocko sat and waited in the parking lot.

I said loudly in unbelief, "How much you want?"

He replied again, "Twelve hundred, man. It's not cut up either. That's pure coke."

"Man. You're killing me. I'm not going to make that much money on this," I said.

"Give me the money, and I'll take care of you next time."

"Alright. Get me back over there. He's probably wondering where we're at," I said coolly.

We drove back over to Jocko, and I hopped out of Mark's car and back into Jocko's.

As soon as I got in the car, I gave Jocko the cocaine, and he got on his radio and planned a meeting place with the other agents as we pulled out of the parking lot.

"Okay, it's done. Where we meeting at?" he asked another agent.

The other agent said, "How about behind the Hill's store up the road?"

"Ten-Four. We'll be right there."

When we all got behind the Hill's store, we listened to the recording, and everything went perfect. Then, Jocko and I went back to the office, where my car and guns were. I saw them weigh the cocaine on an electronic scale and test the purity of it with a little test-tube like container. And, it was very pure and bluish in color.

They made me sign the usual form from the Attorney General's office, and they paid me my money, gave me my guns back and I went on my way after we planned another meet to buy another ounce.

Jocko told me, "Just make sure you call me first before you do anything."

"Alright. I'll see you next week."

Jocko and I got to know each other really well. We even ran into each other every now and then because we lived in the same area. On the ride to one of the buys, he handed me his loaded .38 cal. revolver as we talked about and compared our guns. His gun was a very light six shooter that was made out of graphite. The density of this gun bewildered me; in fact, I've never seen a gun like this one, and I collected guns. Federal Agents were not allowed to carry anything larger than a .38 cal. He also explained some of the laws and procedures that federal agents needed to abide by.

During the times between buys, I got closer and closer to Mark and keenly won over his trust. Although he may have trusted me, I needed for him to trust Jocko. So, every time we were together I talked about how much Jocko liked the blow and how quickly he sold it. I never mentioned to Mark that I was going to introduce him to Jocko because I was just the middle man and supposedly made a couple hundred dollars off of Jocko, so Mark thought; otherwise, if I introduced them, I would be cut out of the deals and wouldn't be able to make any money. I let Mark know how much money I charged Jocko, hoping he would cut me out of the deals and make more money by selling the coke straight to Jocko.

I constantly needed to hang around with Mark, so we played tennis a lot, compared our guns and went to the shooting ranges. Although Mark packed guns, I never got nervous because I knew Mark, and he was all talk and no action. I knew he wouldn't pull out a gun on anybody unless his life was threatened.

A week went by, and it was time to get another ounce of blow from Mark. As I kept in close contact with Jocko and the other members of the Task Force, we all agreed to set up another buy. This seemed too easy. At first, the recorded phone call was made. Only now they had a judge's permission to tap Mark's telephone. This allowed the task force to hear all of his conversation, not just the ones they recorded when I called. They heard who else he regularly talked and dealt with, and those people were either his people he sold the coke to, or the person he bought the coke off of; however, they didn't know who was who, and all they really did was listened in. It was my job to find out whom he got his coke from. If I could find out, it would be less work and easier for the agents. My primary purpose here was to buy the cocaine for the drug task force, and I usually always took the cell phone wire tapped so they could hear and record the buy that went down. The next buy, I went right to Mark's house, and he questioned the second cell phone I had because he saw I had two phones on me.

I quickly replied, "The one phone is a work phone my boss gave me. I've been doing some landscaping with a good friend, and I also get weed off of him. This phone is so he can get in touch with me, or I can get in touch with him. Do you know anyone who would take a pound or two? I get it really cheap."

"I'll ask around. How much for a pound?"

"I'll give it to you for eleven hundred," I told him.

I really spoke the truth about that with Mark, but the undercover agents thought I played Mark with a spoken line of bullshit; on the other hand, I still dealt marijuana with Gino, but the task force didn't know that. If they did, they seemingly didn't care about marijuana that much. Anyway, I bought the cocaine off of Mark and gave it to the agents and collected my money from them. The validity of my work made them not care if I was into a little bit of marijuana or pills because I helped on very big cocaine busts that they may not have been able to do without me.

Every time I saw Mark, I still talked about my brother in-law Jocko, and how he dealt coke too. I alluringly told Mark, "You could sell it to him for a lot of money."

Mark replied, "I'll sell it to you, and you can sell it to him like always. I don't want to meet anybody I don't know that well."

"I just hate having to go to Lower Burrell and then here and back to Lower Burrell because I really ain't makin that much money. He's family, and I can't charge him that much. It's really just a bunch of riding around for me and not that much of a profit," I told Mark.

This went on for months and months until I went on my gut instinct, and one day Jocko came along with me to Mark's house while I made the buy, but he sat outside in his Trans Am that he drove up in the part green and brown dying grass that was lightly covered with gravel and patches of brown dirt, which made up Mark's driveway that led to the back door entrance to his house. Jocko stayed in his car and waited while I went into the house and made the buy. However, when I got inside and talked to Mark, he told me, "Sit down and chill out for a while."

"Jocko's outside in the car waiting for me."

"You brought him to my house?"

"Yeah," I said without hesitation and quite loudly, as if I was offended. "He's my brother in-law, man. Come on."

"Well, tell him to come in here. I don't want anyone sitting outside. What if the cops are watching me?"

"You're just too paranoid, man. The cops ain't watching you," I told him while I laughed inside; nevertheless, I kept an impassive face.

So, I went out to the driveway to get Jocko. I told him as I stood over the driver's side opened window of his car, "Let's go, man. You're in."

"What?"

"I got Mark to let you come in. Lets do it. Mark told me that he didn't want anyone sitting in his driveway in case the cops were watching."

Jocko cautiously got out of the car, and we both went into the house. The introduction was about to be made after a long period of investigation and cocaine buys. I introduced them by saying, "Mark, this is my brother-in-law Jocko. Jocko this is a good and long time friend of mine, Mark."

Mark and I sat on Mark's expensive, yet very soft, leather couches while Jocko stood with his hand on his hidden gun. Mark wanted to bullshit, but we needed to take care of the business. Two other agents sat close down the street in their Chevy Blazer with tinted windows and listened to us through the wiretap.

As Mark kept rambling on, I finally said, "Lets go, man, I got to be somewhere."

Mark asked Jocko, "You're not a cop are you?"

I quickly cut in and told Mark, "Come on, man. This is my brother-in-law. He ain't a cop."

Jocko didn't talk too much and just shook his head as he glanced over at me, and he said in a revolted tone, "What's going on here, Shark?"

Mark reached behind him into the couch cushions, and I knew the blow was stashed in there, but Jocko thought Mark had a gun behind him, and Jocko looked at me when Mark turned his head. I gave Jocko a look of calmness and coolly nodded my head, so he'd chill out. I thought he was about to pull his revolver out, but he remained tranquil. Mark pulled out a brown paper bag from behind him and pulled an ounce of coke out of the brown bag. I gave Jocko back his money so that he could give it to Mark, and he did; moreover, Mark handed him the ounce of cocaine. Now, what the Attorney General's Drug Task Force just did was illegal. So, when we all got back to the office, I told them in a humorous way like I really didn't care anyway because I'd made a lot of money working for these agents, and we all had gotten to know each other, "You know what you did was illegal?"

"What did we do that was illegal?" one bold officer said.

"A cop can't be in on a drug deal if there's a wire tap recording it. I can get you on this one," I replied.

Another nice officer said with a smile on his face, "The wire must have broke. We didn't hear a thing that went on inside."

The other agent backed up that story. I laughed and said, "Now, I think Jocko can buy straight from Mark, but you guys are the professionals. What do you think?"

"Great, then we can get you out of the picture, and you won't have to go to court and testify," one officer said.

So, I continued my relationship with Mark, and sometimes, I told Mark to take a little pinch out of Jocko's bag, and when Jocko and the other officers brought the cocaine back to their office, they weighed it on their electronic scale, and the coke weighed slightly under an ounce; it came up short. That's how I thought; there's always a way to get over on anything or anyone, even the cops.

I kept in contact with Mark, and the task force listened to his phone calls; nevertheless, I never spoke about anything when I wanted coke off Mark because I knew his phone was tapped and didn't say anything to him on the telephone about drugs nor did I ever tell Mark his phone was tapped.

I knew the severity of using cocaine, so I figured I would stop doing coke when Mark got busted. But at this point, it didn't seem like he was going to get popped for a while, so I went back to Bird's house and started to smoke crack with him and his wife. He knew other places to get the shit because Mark just dealt in quantity, and we couldn't really see him all the time for a little bit of blow to cook up into crack and smoke it.

BACK ON THE CRACK

So, Bird and I went to Braddock and bought already cooked crack off of little dealers, who were young black kids that waited on the corner for crack heads like us to come along and buy some rock (crack) off of them. They kept the rocks in tiny balloons made out of rubber. It was like an edible substance type of rubbery plastic that could be swallowed if needed. And, when the cops tried to get them, they actually ate the balloons to get rid of any evidence, and the cops never found anything on them when they searched these young crack dealers. But, in a day or two when the kids took a shit, out came the sealed balloons of crack ready to be washed off and sold. This way, they didn't lose the rocks or the money they got when they sold the crack.

I concocted a plan on how to rob the small time crack dealers in Braddock. I'd go down to the usual places on the usual corners in Braddock strapped with a couple of my guns. I brought the bigger holstered guns that would easily scare or intimidate these younger kids like the .44 or the .45 caliber revolvers, although sometimes I'd run into older and more experienced dealers. I would always use the same line when I got the dealers into my car as they normally did to sell the crack. Once I had them were I wanted them, and I'd never let more than one dealer at a time in the car, I asked for a hundred piece or a two hundred piece while I flashed some money in front of them, and they took the crack out and showed me it, and I asked, "Let me check it out. Is it real? I don't want to get ripped off."

They said, "Yeah, dude, it's real. That's a two hundred dollar piece you got in your hand. Where's the money?"

That's when I said very loudly with preemptive force, as I pulled out my 45 automatic, "Task Force, don't move motherfucker. You're under arrest!"

With my gun pointed at them, they opened the door as quickly as anyone could imagine, bolt out the door and shriek down the street. I saw them run like the wind in my rear view mirror as I drove away with the door still opened and the crack in my hand. When I got down the road a bit, I reached over and closed the door or sometimes I got the door to close itself, if I veered sharply enough. This scheme worked all the time, and I got a lot of free crack with the craziness of my addicted mind.

This Braddock scheme reminded me of the time when I was in Oakland, California, in 1992. Back when I worked heavy construction, we'd go on the hunt for crack. My buddy Rock and I searched the streets for crack; consequently, one time we definitely searched the wrong street because a bunch of black folk from teenagers to more experienced adult crack heads almost stole the rental car we rented. We were talking to these crack dealers when one older black man dressed in rags and a green army coat stuck his filthy dirty hand into my window and grabbed my shirt and demanded the keys to the car, so I put the car, which was still running, into neutral. Therefore, the keys wouldn't come out of the ignition when he tried to grab them. Rock told me to just run them over, but I talked my way out of it by tricking them into thinking I was going to get out of the car, and as soon as they got away from the car, Rock put it in drive, and I floored it out of there.

Nevertheless, of my mental state I still worked with the Attorney General's drug task force, but they noticed the morbid haywire state I'd changed in to. After all, they weren't stupid. The one agent who knew Pat Sr. and paid me all the time saw how I acted differently from the first time I started to work with them. It came along with the business; otherwise, they would never be able to arrest anyone. It took a drug dealer and a drug user to help put the big drug dealers away and get a majority of the drugs off of the streets. It was kind of like a sacrifice. I got hooked on coke again; meanwhile, the task force put the major dealers behind bars.

Plus, I was always on pain pills and Xanax, and those drugs counteracted with the little bit of cocaine I did, for the cocaine gave a speedy euphoric high while the pain pills and Xanax had a calming effect. I got off the coke more easily when I did the pills. I did pills the whole time I worked with the undercover agents, and they knew that, but they never let me know that they knew.

GOING DOWN SOUTH AGAIN

I continued to work with the task force. We were in contact every week; however, Mark never saw me again. The investigation still went on, and Jocko proceeded to buy even larger quantities of cocaine from Mark. I decided it was time for a road trip; however, Jay couldn't go because his band played and traveled all the time, so I went alone. But, before I'd left, I stopped in Braddock and got a big two hundred piece of crack to smoke on the drive down the east coast. The workers' compensation case had reopened just closed, and I had another $40,000 in the bank. I rented a car, went to Braddock, got the rock and then drove on down route 79. The crack lasted until I got over the Blue Ridge Mountains of the Carolinas, and then I made it to Hilton Head. When Pat saw me, he looked away and said, "What'd you do now, Shark?"

I rolled up a joint, and Pat got us a couple of beers. We sat around for a while and bullshitted. I told Pat everything that went on from the time at the V.F.W. picnic that particular year to what I had just done. I told Pat about the chief of police who approached me. Pat knew most of the police officers because of his father. Pat called me crazy and said, "Somebody's going to kill you one of these days."

I said, "I'm not afraid of them drug dealing assholes who think they own the world. Plus, it's exciting."

Pat was in the electrical union and always had work somewhere. So, when I asked him if he wanted to go to Miami with me, he said he couldn't take that much time off work. After we drank a couple of more beers and smoked one more joint, I took off again heading down route 95 to Florida. I made it through Georgia and at about three thirty in the morning I pulled into a hotel in Ormond Beach, just north of Daytona Beach. I stayed and hung out with the Tiki bar owner, and I could tell right away he was from up north by the way he dressed, talked, the gold around his wrist and neck and his slicked back black hair.

We started to talk money and investments, and he told me that his investment with the Tiki bar was through the hotel. He told me, "The alcohol is where the money comes in, and I made the Tiki bar out of some old wood and dried out palm leaves."

I mentioned that this seems like a pretty cool business; however, he only made big money when the seasons were in. In the wintertime he hardly did any work, sometimes boarding up the bar.

I didn't hang around Daytona Beach too long because I was going down to Miami. I booked a room for nine hundred and fifty dollars a week at a hotel with an ocean view, swimming pool, spa exercise room, beach chairs, umbrellas to sit under, and everyone at the hotel was at my beck and call. People even came out to the beach and took my drink order. As I hung around Miami, I checked out all the hot spots and the outside shopping malls, there just happened to be a car show at the convention center that week, so I went and looked around at some very nice and expensive looking cars.

Everybody in Miami spoke different languages and came from other countries like Germany, France and mostly all the islands in the Caribbean. I met people from Jamaica, Puerto Rico, and one part of town was all Cuban people. I went back to Mangos, but I still had the Keys to travel to, so I didn't hang out in too many different bars. I enjoyed the sunshine outside on the beach and the boardwalk with the many palm trees. Indeed, all the women were beautiful, topless and wore g-strings. They were practically naked.

It took me two and a half hours to get down to Key Cujo, where Joe lived. At Joe's, we took the two jet skis out on the crystal clear shallow waters of the Keys. Joe and I went from island to island and saw his friends. One of Joe's friend's houses was laid out right on the water, and we drove the jet skis right upon the grassy beach. The house looked bigger than it really was because he had a big outdoor sunroom, and that's where we hung out and drank some beers. I had my pills in me, but I needed to smoke a joint and fired one up. Then, Joe's friend grabbed his jet ski, and we all went out to some deeper waters where we all did different tricks with the jet skis.

While I was in the Keys with Joe, we got on a little seaplane, which ran by propeller only, and we went out to the tiny island in the Gulf of Mexico called Dry Turtogus. We took off early in the morning and the take off seemed shaky, but I'd never been on a seaplane before, so I didn't know what to expect. As the plane sped up, it lifted right off of the water. The view was beautiful, and we saw some of the islands, which made up the Florida Keys, from a bird's view. The water was colored differently in different parts because of the changes in shallowness and the depth of the water. When we got to the tiny island, we swam with sharks, sea turtles, a few stingrays and a bunch of other colorful fish that were differently shaped and sized. The water was extremely rough with tremendous waves that broke onto the shore, which made it very difficult to swim. We didn't wear life vests because we didn't bring them, not that the life vests would have helped. But, on the other side of the island the water was very calm, almost like glass. There, we snorkeled and checked out an old abandon fort that was partially still together. The fort was probably used back when the Cuban missile crisis occurred.

The seaplane arrived at the designated time for us to leave, and I quickly hopped in the front seat with the pilot, and we all wore headphones because the plane's engine was really noisy. During the flight on this little plane, we flew low enough that we actually saw the marine life in the water beneath us. Also, the plane was so small the wind would make the plane drop or rise several feet in an instant. We had had coolers full of beer and some sandwiches because we stayed on this island all day; however, everything was gone in this late afternoon. I kept my little waterproof container that fit around my neck with a string, and that's where I kept my pills and rolled up joints; indeed, I could go into the water with this container around my neck, and whatever was inside it would not get wet. It had been a long day of sunshine and snorkeling, and we would be very relieved once we got back at Joe's house.

After I got cleaned up at Joe's, I got ready to go back to Miami, but Joe didn't want to come. He had to work and didn't want to leave his wife. I only stayed with Joe for four days. On that fourth day, I left early in the morning and drove back to Miami, where I was going to stay and check out the nightlife. As I drove up the long road and bridges that connected the islands, I stopped to call home; I always kept in contact with my family. I asked my mom to wire me one thousand dollars to the Miami Western Union. Then, my father got on the phone and told me my friends were looking for me. By my friends, he meant the task force because they contacted him when they couldn't get in touch with me.

I called the task force agent who I dealt with when I arrived in Miami, and he asked me where I was, and what I was doing. He stated, "You're not allowed to just leave out of town while you're with us. You have to at least let us know. We thought maybe you were dead."

"I'm in Miami. Then, I'm going to go back to Hilton Head to see Pat Jr."

"Okay," he said. "We're going to bust Mark now, so why don't you stay down there awhile. There's a great restaurant down there called Joe's Stone Crab Inn, why don't you check it out."

"Yeah. I've been there. It's a real nice place with good food. When you busting Mark? And how?"

"Just get back up to Pat's house and call me from there."

They never really could tell me anything; plus, they were pissed. I knew they would be because I just picked up and left town without notifying anyone. Plus, they didn't like to tell me how the busts went down. But, I was very daring and asked a lot of questions.

Chance to Make Quick and Easy Money

When I got back to Miami, I booked in at a cheaper motel that only cost three hundred dollars a night. This time I stayed up and partied in the many crazy bars in Miami, if I could get in. Finally, I went into two different bars, but they didn't compare with Mangos, so I went back into Mangos. The place was packed, and girls were dancing on the bar to the music of the live Latino band that played. I met two guys: one was dressed all in white, and the other in black and white. They seemed cool, and we got to talk. As I listened to their accent, and sometimes they talked in Latin to each other, I asked, "Where are you guys from?"

"Cali."

"California, what are you doing here?"

"Cali, Columbia, not California."

They asked, "Where you from?"

"Pittsburgh. Do you know where I can get some blow?"

"How much you want?"

"An eight-ball," I said.

They looked at each other, grinned, laughed and spoke in Latin. Then, they told me, "We'll give you a kilo for sixteen hundred dollars."

I brought my .357 cal. revolver because I was really paranoid, so I said, "I only wanted a little bit for myself right now, but I'll go check it out for that price."

"Wait a couple minutes. Lets drink a beer, and then we'll go to our place."

I left Mangos with the two guys from Cali in their black Mercedes, and I tried to learn some Latin, and I did as I sat in the back seat on the way to their condominium. These two guys spoke both English and Latin, and they just looked like cocaine dealers. We went down some dimly lit roads lined with palm trees away from the bright neon lights from Miami's South Beach, and

197

finally pulled into a little town right on the water. Nice cars and houses were everywhere, and all the people had access to the ocean from the inlets that surrounded mostly all of the land we were on. The condo we went into was made of white brick in the front, but when I walked in and went upstairs, it was all glass, and I could see the white water breaking onto the shore.

One guy said, "Sit down and relax. You're okay here. We got beer, liquor and women coming over. If you want the kilo, that's no problem. If not, that isn't a problem either."

I paced back and forth as I looked out of the windows, checked out the bar and the high tech surround-sound system that was connected to a big screen TV, along with the stereo equipment they had. The speakers hung on the walls all around the room and even on the balcony, and I told them, "This place is beautiful. I could live here forever."

One of them ran upstairs, and the other walked around like he was waiting for someone. I asked him, "Why are you walking around so much."

"I'm waiting for the ladies to get here. Wait until you see them."

I wanted to take the kilo so badly because I could have made an extraordinary amount of money back in Pittsburgh. On the other hand, how the hell could I trust somebody who works for the Cali Cartel? I had my hand on my gun most of the time, yet I still felt safe. The one guy turned on some music and brought us a couple beers. The other guy got some coke and threw a bunch down on the round glass table, which was surrounded by a very large tan colored circular couch. We started to snort lines of coke and talk about the deal. I calmed down.

They offered a kilo for $1,600, and I could have made $19,400 if I sold it out right; however, if I broke it down into smaller bags and put cut on it, I could make $25,000 to $30,000. I didn't know what to think or do. First of all, if I took it, I could have gotten pulled over on the long drive home to Pittsburgh and got busted; secondly, I worried about these two Columbians, what they thought and what they had planned, or maybe they were just cool friendly drug dealers who enjoyed meeting new people.

I thought about the task force guys that I helped out back home, and I thought about the guys I set up with Jocko. So, I didn't take the kilo, but these guys were very cool. I explained my situation with the long ride home to Pittsburgh, and I didn't want to get busted. I started to think they could have been cops, but sitting on the table was probably an ounce of coke, which they also snorted. Then, four Latino chicks walked in elegantly dressed, and everybody was happy, laughing and having a good time. I tried to give these guys some money for the coke, but they didn't want it.

I talked, danced and drank with one of the ladies and eventually, we made our way out to the patio. This girl had long curly black hair, a very curvy figure and luscious lips. A bunch of big purple cushioned recliners that held two or three people sat on the patio. While the lights shined from the stars and moon, she had me dancing Latin style right on the patio overlooking the ocean. There were big-planted palm trees in all the corners; also, the sound of the ocean and the warm gusts of wind made everything seem so wonderful. On the patio were a hot tub, and a large swimming pool, which was lit up from underwater lights, lounge chairs and umbrella tables and chairs. After we danced all night on the patio, I slept with the girl after we had wild sex on one of the patio lounge chairs.

The next afternoon when we all got up, the sun shined and it was very hot. The girl I was with rode me back to my hotel in her big dark blue Lincoln Navigator. I said a short goodbye; nevertheless, I felt like I passed up the deal of a lifetime on the coke, but I had fun. I could have made at least twenty grand on the deal.

I walked along the boardwalk in Miami one night and ran into this older Jamaican guy who looked to be homeless.

I asked, "What's up?"

"Hey mun."

"I really need to smoke a joint. I'm all out of herb. Do you got any herb or can you get me some?"

"I have one rolled up, but I got no place to stay."

"You can come to my hotel room to shower and sleep if you want."

So, we went back to my room and burned a joint, and he also knew where to get some crack in the Cuban part of Miami. So, we walked over to the Cuban area, I bought some rocks, took them back to the hotel and we smoked them up. After we smoked all the coke, I laid and rested catching a little nap, for I was nervously paranoid about this Jamaican guy being in my room.

The next morning when the sun rose, I left with a little bit of weed the Jamaican gave me. I needed to get back up to Hilton Head Island because the agents back in Pittsburgh were awaiting my phone call from Pat's house. Plus, I told Pat I'd be back.

When I got up to Hilton Head, I stayed there for two weeks. Pat and I went out to this one local bar, which had about seven big screen television sets and half dozen pool tables. I always bet money when I played pool, and I always won because I conned the people I played against into thinking I didn't know how to play pool, then I'd run the table right off the break and take the money from the bets. But, sometimes I got into fights over hustling people. One time, I talked with a guy who knew Miami, and he knew the bar Mangos. We started to play some pool, and I let him win the first game. We played another game, but this time we bet fifty bucks, and I let him win that game also. The next game we played he wanted to bet one hundred dollars, and I let him win that game too. I said, "I have four hundred dollars left. I'll play a game for four hundred, and then I got to go."

The man agreed, we played the game and I ran the table on the break. The guy didn't even get a chance to shoot a ball.

"You hustled me. You little fuck."

"I just played a good game. I paid you when you won. Now pay me."

He tried to start a fight and pushed me; however, all the locals I knew surrounded him and I demanded my money. And, I got four hundred dollars. I learned at a very young age how to shoot pool. My father was a pool shark who always bet hundreds of dollars, and he usually won unless he didn't want to.

I'd become a local in Hilton Head. They knew me at the Tiki bar; they knew me at a bar/restaurant called Steamers and even at the sports bars. I had my personal physician and my surgeon prescribing me narcotics. When Pat got up to go to work, I'd go out fishing early in the morning. Then, I got together with some other friends I knew and played volleyball while we drank frozen drinks on the hot sandy beach. If I wasn't at the beach, I hung out with Pat's sister at the pool where they lived.

Eventually, Pat's sister, Marnie, and I became more than just close friends because she really didn't work either. Pat lived with another guy, Dave, and a girl, whom we called Jewels. Jewels fucked anybody, and her boyfriend stayed at the house mostly all the time, but when he wasn't there, and Marnie wasn't there, I fucked Jewels. But, Marnie was my main girl down in Hilton Head; I really liked her.

One day, I called the agent who paid me, and he said with an irritated voice, "You got to get back up here now."

"Okay. I'm on my way. I'll call you the minute I hit Pittsburgh."

MEXICAN

It was now September, and I needed to go home, so I packed up, saw my doctors one last time, got my prescriptions filled and headed north to Pittsburgh. I loved those long drives by myself, and on the way home I thought about what was happening with the task force. They owed me money and always promptly paid me on a weekly basis, but I'd been gone for two months. So, when I got home, I got a nice paycheck waiting for me from the undercovers. But, I wondered who they were going to want me to go after next. I knew of people; however, they were in charge, and I went after whoever they told me to go after.

September through December was the time the task force made the most busts, usually around election time because they wanted to look good for the Attorney Generals Office and other politicians. I arrived back in Pittsburgh in the middle of September and called the undercovers immediately. Jocko told me, "Mark's wife works in the mall, where our office is, and Mark must have gone to see her one day, and he saw me come out of the office, so I had to arrest him. But, he's not talking, and we need you to get Mexican."

Mexican was a pretty big supplier who took over the business when Jimmy, Tony, Mike and those guys got busted. He was a big tall guy with black curly hair and one eye crossed. Mexican strangely always kept every light in the house on. He lived in a newly renovated house on the inside, but looked to be very ugly and poor on the outside. I knew him a little bit from hanging around bars and seeing him with other dealers, but not enough to get in close with him. On the other hand, Mexican was very good friends with Mickey, who was my good friend, and Jay and Gino's brother. That was my way in. I got Mickey to get me close to Mexican.

I told Mickey, "I quit working with the task force and my brother-in-law needs coke for the Pagans out by Greensburg. I'll let you in on the deal, and you can make some money."

I hoped Mickey would buy my story, and he did. Mickey and I went to see Mexican a few times before any deals were made; nevertheless, I got in with

Mexican, at least as a friend. Then, I got Mickey to buy a half-ounce of blow for me off of Mexican without the task force knowing. I started to do the coke; indeed, I gave Mickey half of it, so I kept my word with Mickey because he was a really good friend, and I would never get him involved or in any trouble.

The next time Mickey and I dealt with Mexican, I handed Mexican the money, and he handed me the coke. I bought the coke straight from Mexican now; therefore, Mickey was out of the picture. Now, I talked to Jocko and told him I could set up a buy. I got Mickey safely out of the picture. Jocko asked me, "How did you get in with Mexican?"

"You know how sometimes you can't or don't tell me about certain procedures and other busts."

"Well, as an informant I'd rather not tell you my ways in and out. I do what I have to do, so the dealers trust me."

The Attorney Generals office opened up a new case on Mexican. But now, when I bought the coke, it went straight to the task force, and I got paid; thus, I didn't get to keep any of the coke for my own personal use or to sell for a little extra cash.

I ran into Erik, my old buddy from the working days one day at a local supermarket, and we got to talk. He was going down to Braddock to buy crack, and I told him, "I haven't smoked any rocks in a couple months."

He asked me to stop over his place later on that night. I wondered all day about what I should do because I knew once I started to smoke the crack, I wouldn't quit.

GOING HAYWIRE

I got to Erik's about 6:00 pm. He and his wife were all ready smoking the crack, and as soon as I walked in the door, Erik packed up the glass pipe with the white pearly looking rocks that smelled and tasted as sweet as candy. He handed the pipe and a lighter right to me. Erik and I used to snort ounces of coke together when I sold cocaine; indeed, we even cooked the powdered cocaine into the rock form of crack with a Pyrex glass test-tube. I stayed at his house all night long. We talked over our old working days, our old bar hopping days and our old crack smoking days while we smoked the rocks that we cooked. When I heard the birds chirping early in the morning, with the sun rising slowly I knew it was time to get out of there.

After that night, I thought to myself, I'm right back in the grips of the disease of addiction. The crack had got a hold of me. I even went back down to Braddock on my own and started to buy the rocks off the street corner that the little young black kids sold. And, I still saw a doctor who prescribed me pain pills and Xanax; also, I bought more pain pills off the street. All this, and I still went to Mexican's house to buy large quantities of cocaine for the task force. I was way out of control.

The task force agent who paid me saw I was getting out of control; however, my dad's friend, Pat Sr., had told this man to make sure nothing happened to me. Meanwhile, I was desperately running out of money. All this time, all the money from both of the worker's compensation claims I had gotten disappeared. I resorted to the lowest means to get the crack and sold a couple of my registered automatic handguns. I kept a collection of guns, so I thought nothing of it. I didn't think of the consequences of my actions. I put guns on the street that could kill anyone, including me. Since I only had to see the task force once a week, I usually spent the rest of the week smoking crack.

Nobody knew that I sold my guns for drugs, so I kept working with the agents. My mind was chemically altered, and I even went and talked to the chief of police of the township I lived in. I knew him, and he knew my father really well, and he also knew me very well. I asked, "Is there a warrant for my arrest?"

"No. Why; should there be?"

"No. I was just checking things out," I told him in a curious tone.

A few weeks later, I called and reported my guns stolen. The cops who came to my house looked wary because this sort of thing didn't really happen around the neighborhood I lived in. I knew both of the cops, and I still lived with Mickey and Jay. I had also stolen Mickey's gun and gold chains and sold them for crack too. So, I got Mickey involved with the police, and he hated that because he sold weed. The cops took fingerprints off of the medium sized brown gun safe I had, which I had broken the lock myself to make it look like a burglary, and they took prints off all the doors that surrounded it. Now, I made things worse. I just committed another crime. I filed a false police report.

One day, I started to walk into the undercovers' office and the sergeant of the police squad of the township I abided in was also walking in, to look for me; moreover, I never made it into the office door. It was about ten o'clock in the morning. I knew the sergeant, and he arrested me and took me into the task force office to tell the undercovers who knew nothing about what I had done. The sergeant took me away in handcuffs, and we went back to his station. At this station, my father and I knew the chief of police very well, and because I helped them take a lot of drugs off of the streets, they went easy on me.

The sergeant questioned me for an hour or so, and I kept trying to lie my way out of it. Suddenly, he told me, "Okay. I'm not going to sit here and be lied to all day."

So, I cut in and said, "Sir, I sold my guns for crack in Braddock and lied to you guys about it."

He put me in the holding cell until the chief got there. When the chief saw me and heard what happened, he said to me, "You hit the jackpot, didn't you?"

"I started to do the drugs."

The sergeant and I got in the squad car, and he took me down to the local magistrate in handcuffs. We talked on the way down, and he asked, "How much of that settlement money do you have left?"

It's gone. I think I got about twenty-five hundred in my pocket."

When we got to the magistrate, I knew his son and slept with his daughter, and he also knew me. He was furious at the situation. The task force agent who worked under Pat Sr. was there, and the sergeant who knew me and helped me out was there, and they both spoke to the judge.

When I stood in front of the judge's bench, he said to me in a raged tone, "You sold guns for drugs, and these officers are here on your behalf. This is a felony of the third degree! I don't know why, and I don't want to know. Your bail should normally be $25,000 straight, but these officers are making it twenty-five hundred at ten percent. If I see you in this court room again, that's it!"

This judge was pissed off. So, I got handcuffed, shackled and taken down to the Allegheny County Jail. When I got to the jail, I went through the usual search before I actually got into the holding cell. In the holding cell, out of nowhere the agent who paid me for the work I did with the Attorney General's drug task force showed up. He walked into the holding cell, stood right by the door and told me, "I'm going to bail you out. Just hang on until I can see what's going on. Say I'm you're uncle if anyone asks."

So, I sat restlessly in the cell for hours with the other people who got arrested that day. Finally, an officer working at the desk in the holding cell called my name out, and then he motioned for me to come to the desk as he held the phone in the air and said, "You got a phone call."

It was the agent, and he told me that a police officer wasn't allowed to bail anyone out of jail and asked, "Do you got two hundred and fifty dollars on you?"

"Yeah. Why?"

"You can bail yourself out of jail."

Luckily, I had more than two hundred and fifty dollars, and I paid my bail and got released after I sat in the cell all day long. The agent picked me up and wanted me to go into a rehab. I begged and pleaded with him that I would go first thing in the morning. I told him, "My car is still sitting up at the office. I didn't eat anything all day, and I just want to go home."

He nicely gave me a break, and we ended up going to Wendy's and getting something to eat. He paid for the food and also gave me the two hundred and fifty dollars back that I used to bail myself out of jail with. He directed me to say, if anyone asked, "You were making buys in Braddock and got caught up in using the cocaine. We pulled you out afterwards."

After that, he took me to my car and said, "You better go to the rehab tomorrow."

"First thing in the morning," I said.

After I spent a week in a rehab, I had to go do a buy bust on Mexican; instead of making a normal buy and turning the blow over to the agents, I used the cell phone tap, and as soon as I bought the cocaine I said, "This is really good shit."

That was the password, and the agents actually broke down the front door and stormed in with their guns pointed straight at us, and they were yelling for us to get down on the floor and let me see your hands. About ten agents were in the house and tore it apart as they looked for more cocaine and paraphernalia, and there were squad cars outside with the bright lights flashing. As for me, I needed to act like I didn't know what was going on, and the cops cuffed me and put me into a squad car. They took me away in one car and Mexican in another. However, I got brought back to the agent's office and was told, "Don't let anyone know you're around. Don't answer the phone, and don't talk to anyone for a week or two."

"I'm going out to my parents house for awhile. Nobody will know where I'm at."

Meanwhile, Mexican got taken to the local Magistrate first, and then down to the county jail. That's the last time I saw or ever heard from Mexican.

The people who worked in the rehab got me off the crack; nevertheless, I still continued to take pain pills and Xanax when I got out, which were prescribed from a doctor. I still continually got more pain pills and marijuana on the street and used those drugs instead of crack. Since Mickey got me involved with Mexican, I moved out of the house I lived in with Jay and Mickey. I moved back to my parents' house. My confidential informant days were over. I laid low and chilled out.

I hired the best defense attorney in Pittsburgh; thus, at the court hearing, two police officers who I knew were there, and I'm sure they talked to the judge before my case was called up because I saw them go into the judge's chamber. Finally, they called my case up and the D.A. prosecutor wanted me to do time for this action because there were guns involved. But, when the judge heard the case, he listened to my two attorneys and the D.A.'s attorney. The one attorney I had presented his case, but the D.A.'s attorney kept harping his mouth about the guns. He wanted the guns back from the street. Finally, my other attorney spoke loudly as he rushed up behind me, "Your Honor, those guns are gone. My client can't get those guns back."

The judge agreed and sentenced me to five years of probation, in which seemingly wasn't even a sentence because I only saw my probation officer one time, and he gave me a set of cards I was to fill out with information about employment and my address. So, I sent the cards in once a month for five years and went about my life.

I only hung out with my cousin Joey, Jay and other family members and the close friends that I knew I could trust. Every time I hung out with Joey, he always told me that his girlfriend's mother was young and hot and recently divorced. I wasn't involved with anybody at that particular time, and Joey just wanted to set me up with a woman.

DESI

One day after that, I was introduced to my cousin Joey's girlfriend and her mother, Desi who was a young petite redhead with a great figure and beautiful blue eyes with yellow that surrounded the black pupils. Joey's sister got married one Saturday, and I went to the wedding. Joey, his girlfriend and Desi walked up the street, as I stood on the corner in my black pinstriped suit with a gold and black shirt underneath and a black scarf around my neck and a cigarette in my mouth. Joey brought them right up to me on the corner. I took one last drag off of my cigarette then flicked it onto the street, I introduced myself to Desi, and I knew from that moment on I was going to be with this woman for the rest of my life.

At the family wedding reception, I first sat with my parents and other family members until I decided to go over to the table where Joe, his girlfriend and Desi sat. We all started to talk and drink rather heavily. I spoke tantalizing to Desi. She spoke in the same flirtatious way to me. We danced and hung out together throughout the rest of the reception. While we sat at the table and drank, she slyly put her hand on my upper thigh as I sat right next to her with my arm around the back of her chair. So, I moved closer to her and put my arm further around her. Finally, Joe, his girlfriend, Desi and I left and went to Desi's house in Shadyside.

Desi's house was a nice little redbrick family home; she had been recently divorced. At her house, we all sat around talking, laughing, playing around with Desi's computer, America Online and just having a good time. Joey, his girlfriend and I smoked some weed, and Joey and I popped a few pills. Desi didn't smoke weed. Suddenly, Desi and I were alone. Joey and his girlfriend left, and Desi unbuckled my suit pants and started to blow me. Soon after that, we were upstairs in her bedroom having the wildest sex ever. It continued through the next day and the night after, and eventually, I had begun to just stay at Desi's house.

Desi had two grown daughters who were in their twenties, and the one daughter sold pain pills, so I bought mostly every pill she had to sell. Her other daughter smoked weed, and I still always had the best weed and smoked it with her and my cousin. Joey was into heroin. I saw Joe snorting heroin one day and asked him, "Why do you do this shit, man?"

"It's just like taking a whole bunch of pain pills. Here, try it; you might like it."

When I tried heroin the first time in my life it made me throw up, and I honestly wasn't too thrilled with the feeling it gave me afterwards, but I snorted it a few more times later anyway; however, I never got hooked on it. I just liked my Xanax and pain pills. My cousin Joey ended up dying from a heroin overdose later in life.

Running Prescriptions

Desi's one daughter and her husband showed me a scheme on how to get any kind of pills from any pharmacy. They simply wrote their own prescriptions and took them to the pharmacy. After I hung around and watched them do this for awhile, Desi and I figured out how to print our own prescriptions out on a computer. I saw this was a very easily done process; I got special paper from Kinko's that looked like it came from a doctor's office. But, first I needed to get a doctor's DEA number, so I went and saw a doctor and got him to write me a prescription for some kind of narcotic. He had to use his DEA number because a doctor couldn't prescribe any kind of narcotics without a DEA number on the prescription. Then, I needed to learn how to write the prescription. It was easy to do, so I printed out the paper, cut it into little squares, wrote out the prescription that was usually for pain pills, wrote the doctor's DEA number on the square paper, forged the doctor's name and took the fake prescription to the pharmacy to get it filled.

Now, the tricky part came because pharmacists usually called in and verified most narcotic prescriptions. Nonetheless, two of us went into the pharmacy separately, and whoever handed the script into the pharmacist sat, watched and listened to hear if they called to verify the script; in addition, the other person would go up to the pharmacist and ask questions to keep the pharmacist occupied, but he or she was really listening to see if they called to verify the script also. We kept one person outside to watch for the cops. If the cops showed up, the person outside called the cell phone of the person who got the prescription filled. Mostly, all the time I wrote prescriptions for pain pills, they were only a class three narcotic. Pharmacists usually verified anything over a class three narcotic, but sometimes they verified class three prescriptions. It all depended on the pharmacist.

At first, I did this with Desi's son-in-law, Sean, but after I got used to running the prescription, I did it myself while Desi sat in the car and waited. We went out two or three times a week, always at nighttime while the doctors' offices were closed, and I brought in three to four hundred pain pills in one night, so I started to sell them to the few friends I had left for a nice little profit. One guy alone would take five hundred of them for six bucks apiece. And, I hooked Gino up because he was still into the narcotics. Moreover, I ran a couple prescriptions on my own while Desi was at work, and I took as many pills as I wanted to. It became addicting to just go to the pharmacy and do this. It was a rush!

I did this for years, and it just simply seemed much too hard to pass up. As the years went by, I drove up either route 30 or 22 or just went out of the area to a different township like Robinson Township. That's were I got arrested. We were driving around an area of town unbeknown to me in a location by GreenTree. That night, I went into every drug store I saw and about four of them were Eckerd's. One Eckerd called another, and they called the third Eckerd. At that Eckerd, the police waited to get me; thus, they had to catch me in the act, so they let me fill the prescription and then arrested me. The one cop cuffed me and took me out to his police car, and he asked, "Who else is you with?"

"Am I under arrest, officer?"

"Yes."

I didn't utter a mere word. I just got in back of his police car. I ran a prescription for ninety one-milligram Xanax at the CVS pharmacy around the corner from Desi's house before Desi and I left that night and went into the pharmacies. I had the Xanax on me when I was arrested and it was a legal prescription; nevertheless, the cops confiscated all of the Xanax. Granted, I carried a legal prescription for the Xanax, I knew the possession charge wouldn't hold up in a court of law. Desi took off in my car because she was scared to death. Also, Desi threw over three hundred pain pills I got that night out the window while she drove home. Meanwhile, I sat in the township jail until the cop who arrested me took me down to the Allegheny County Jail. I called Desi as soon as I could, so she could come bail me out of jail. And, she did.

When I got out of jail, we were driving home, and I asked her, " Where's the pain pills?"

"I threw them out the window."

"What!" I yelled.

"I threw them out the window."

"All of them?"

"I was afraid I'd get arrested! I didn't know what to do."

I lost all the pain pills and all the money I would have made when I sold them. Furthermore, I faced serious drug and forgery charges in Allegheny County, and I faced the same charges in Westmoreland County because I got busted in a Giant Eagle drug store in that county a couple months before this arrest. I used the same attorney in all my court hearings because he was the best criminal defense attorney in Pittsburgh.

ARRESTED AND SENTENCED TO RIP/ATS

My attorney, Desi and her brother came along with me to the Murrysville Magistrate in Westmoreland County, just in case I went to jail and needed bailed out. At the magistrate, I got a phone call from Desi's daughter, and she told me that her grandmother just passed away, so I put Desi on the phone because it was her mother. It was a shock to all of us.

The news was heartbreaking and terrible; thus, the magistrate let me leave on the condition that I would return in the morning, so we left and went to the hospital where the rest of Desi's family gathered. After a night of grieving with Desi, I went back to the magistrate's office first thing in the morning. I was now in Westmoreland County, and the courts, lawyers and judges offered me two to five years in the Federal State Penitentiary, or RIP/ATS: A federally funded program called Restrictive-Intermediate-Punishment/ Alternative Treatment Systems. The program was intended to rehabilitate people with the disease of addiction.

I wasn't stupid; I took the program. I went to the RIP/ATS program for over four months while I was on house arrest; everyday, Monday through Friday, eight hours a day. I managed to somehow get clean with the help of the counselors and other recovering drug addicts who had been clean for years and showed the newcomers *HOW* to get clean, a day at a time. We needed to be honest, open-minded and willing to get clean.

We made each other want to be clean. Plus, the probation officer was there mostly all the time, and he gave us all random urine screenings. I went to many twelve-step meetings, and I continued to go when I got out of the program. But, I had to do four months of house arrest, so I was home at my parents' house until Desi came to live with me. I did my four months, and I had Desi by my side and went to meetings. They let us out for work duty and meetings, so I was doing three, four to five months of meetings, going to RIP/

ATS, and got a job at a carwash down the street from where I lived. I was never home. On house arrest, but I was never home; nevertheless, I got clean from drugs in over the four to five months.

Desi and I both knew our love was forever. She stuck by me the whole entire time I got clean. It wasn't easily done, but it wasn't hard if I wanted to stay clean. I sometimes went to meetings all day long. I didn't work much, but I didn't use any drugs. I've spoke about recovering from drugs in the detoxes I'd went to myself. But, I still had charges pending in Allegheny County for running prescriptions.

At my next hearing, the possession charges were vindicated because I had a legal prescription for Xanax, and I didn't have any other drugs on me when I was caught in Robinson Township, so the prosecuting attorney could only charge me with attempt to acquire a controlled substance. The judge sentenced me to another five years probation to run consecutive with the five years probation I was already doing in Allegheny County for the gun charges I was arrested for a few years back.

My lawyer told the judge, "Your honor, I've known Anthony for a couple of years now, and if he had any pills on him, he would have taken them himself."

The prosecuting attorney wanted to charge me for selling narcotics. Then, I spoke for myself as my attorney requested and told the judge, "Your honor, I never would have done the things I did if I wasn't on drugs. I've been clean for awhile now, and I have a strong desire to stay clean. I go to twelve-step meetings and work a program of recovery."

The judge told me, "Keep doing what you're doing and stay out of trouble. I don't want to see you in here again."

CONTINUED CRAZINESS

An old friend of mine, Hirk, who was from the town where my parents lived and used to buy some pain pills every now and then, owned a construction company and decided to build a carwash and oil change center right up the street. Hirk hired me to work because he knew me. Desi and I got a place right across the street from my parent's house, and Hirk made me supervisor of the oil change center. I also always helped in the car wash and car detailing. I even helped to put the finishing touches on the place while he was still constructing it, and I was there working five days before the place even opened. Then, I found out that Hirk was dealing cocaine. He asked me if I was interested. And, I said yes.

In one year, from when we opened the oil change doors, I changed the oil in over six hundred cars a month. I built the oil change business up myself with the help of only a few guys if they were needed; however, Hirk bought all the supplies and the expensive equipment. Since he offered me cocaine, I thought I'd make more money, so I called up my old task force buddies, and they reactivated me as a confidential informant.

For a year and two months I worked there and got a nice paycheck. Plus, when I bought coke from Hirk for the task force, I earned an extra two-fifty a week from the task force. I made half-ounce cocaine buys from Hirk. Since Hirk was never around, I got to know his wife. She was one of the owners and was at work all day every day. I also worked every day, except for Sundays. I even saw other people who used drugs while they worked at the carwash.

Meanwhile, I stayed clean, went to meetings and went to more meetings. I talked to my sponsor every time I could, daily if needed. My sponsor advised me not to go ahead with the affair I got involved in. I got sexually involved with Hirk's wife, Linda. I didn't say anything to Linda about the cocaine, nor did I tell Hirk about fucking his wife.

Linda and I had momentous affairs, and we saw each other on a weekly basis. It was strictly sexual. So, for the whole year Linda and I met in a motel and had sex for hours; also, when we were at work we had sexual activity going on down in the oil-pit and in different rooms that were pretty much concealed from the public.

One day, I hurt my back really bad at work and had to take the weekend off. I told Linda to come up to my parents' house, and she did. But, Hirk had a private eye follow her, and Hirk showed up at my parents'. We tried to sit down and talk this all out; however, something like this didn't just get talked out. Hirk told me, "You can't work down there anymore. Just collect workers' comp."

After fifteen minutes of talk between the four of us, I said, "Why is she fucking me, Hirk?"

Hirk's face turned bright red, and he picked up the metal gold-plated fireplace shovel and smacked me in the face with it, but I didn't budge. I went after Hirk, grabbed him by his arms while he threw punches, which I blocked quite easily. Hirk kept throwing weak punches to my face, but I took every punch he threw. Finally, I picked him up by the neck literally off the family room green-carpeted floor. I got him down on the floor with his arms pinned, and I started to throw punches. But, I honestly didn't want to hurt the guy because I just had an affair with his wife, and I thought that hurt him enough.

Hirk didn't give in, and I could not get him to settle down, so I threw a couple of hard punches to his face and one hard punch to his already injured shoulder. Then, I ran out the door because of the uncontrollable fury I saw in Hirk's blood shot eyes. He quickly followed, for he was determined to physically harm me or as I thought at the time, kill me. He went into his little blue Chevy S-10 pickup truck and pulled out a .44-caliber revolver as I got into my car. I jumped in my car and peeled out of my parents' driveway screeching tire as I left. However, before I got away he shot at my car and hit it twice, but I didn't get hit. The bullets hit the passenger's side rear fender leaving two big round holes.

With zeal, the special drug task force arrested Hirk for the sales of cocaine, but I wasn't involved. Because of the affair I had with Linda, I lost Desi, my job and the place where I lived, and consequently, I got back on drugs and drank more heavily than I ever did.

Narcotics

The doctors put me back on narcotic pain medication again; consequently, my addiction grew worse. They gave me a highly addictive pain pill called Oxycontin. My life seemed in shambles and falling apart all around me.

I couldn't get Desi out of my head while I went through these court hearings and medical treatments. I felt more pain when the doctors stopped treating me, so I got some tests done on my own. I found out what really was wrong with my back because I paid the doctors and hospitals right out of my pocket. I didn't have to deal with attorneys, or the courts or the insurance companies anymore. But, different doctors prescribed me more pain pills, and I ate them like candy. I hadn't taken pain pills in such magnitude since I first met Desi and her daughters. All I thought about was if Desi was here, I probably wouldn't have started to drink and use narcotics.

One day, I called Desi up and asked her how she had been. She said she'd been fine, and then Desi got awfully quiet, and when she did talk she spoke in an insincere tone. How could I blame her? Therefore, I talked mostly, and she listened. Desi didn't ask how I was doing, but she sounded as if she really did care. I told her, "I'm sorry. I didn't mean to hurt you. I didn't plan on having an affair; it just happened. I'd be much better if we got back together. Will you give me one more chance, please? I feel like such a dick for cheating on you."

"Well, I'm glad you feel like a dick. That shows me at least you care about me. How do I know you won't find some other girl and cheat on me again?" Desi asked; however, she gave me another chance, and we slowly got back together.

My life slowed down drastically, and I didn't help the task force anymore; on the other hand, I concentrated on family life as I watched Desi's daughters bring three more little girls into the world.

I kept being treated by a psychiatrist, for I anxiously worried about my safety and the safety of Desi's grandkids. I was a mental mad-case. I always thought someone wanted revenge and would come after me, but as time went by, those paranoid thoughts drifted away. Sometimes, I wish the drug dealers or Hirk would come after me, but to this day, nobody has.

Today, I take medications because of the paranoia, the frightening thoughts, the night terrors and the physical seizures and convulsions I get if I don't take the medicines. I don't get a buzz nor do I get high from the medications I take anymore; instead, I take medicines to function normally in life, and it's hard for people and my family members to understand. In addition, I have to take medications to sleep or I will stay up all night long for days at a time. These medications are valid and do not pose a threat to my recovery.

I used to go to the same meetings regularly, and a couple of years ago I saw people coming into these meetings who I'd set up with the undercovers. I now pick meetings randomly. This way nobody knows my paranoid schedule. Nevertheless, the more I go to meetings the more people I set up keep showing up at these meetings.

My life has taken a dramatic change for the better. I even got reactivated as a confidential informant.

I go to school now; in addition, I work at the school I go to, and Desi shows me the way a family lives life. I am very much a part of her family as she is mine. But, every nightmare, every bad memory and every bad situation reminds me of what could still happen to me if I'm not careful. The fear still lies within me, and it probably will for the rest of my life. But, that fear, which is an extremely excitable fear, won't stop me from becoming reactivated as a confidential informant and making money by helping to take drugs off the streets; after all, I still know my undercover narcotic cop friends.